Cyprus
2006

KILLER ELITE

ALSO BY MICHAEL SMITH

Odd Man Out: The Story of the Singapore Traitor (with Peter Elphick)

New Cloak, Old Dagger: How Britain's Spies Came in from the Cold

Station X: The Codebreakers of Bletchley Park

Foley: The Spy Who Saved 10,000 Jews

The Emperor's Codes: Bletchley Park and the Breaking of Japan's Secret Ciphers

Action This Day: Bletchley Park from the Breaking of the Enigma Code to the Birth of the Modern Computer (ed. with Ralph Erskine)

The Spying Game: The Secret History of British Espionage

KILLER ELITE

THE INSIDE STORY OF AMERICA'S MOST
SECRET SPECIAL OPERATIONS TEAM

Michael Smith

WEIDENFELD & NICOLSON

Weidenfeld & Nicolson

The Orion Publishing Group Ltd
Orion House, 5 Upper Saint Martin's Lane, London WC2H 9EA

British Library Cataloguing-in-Publication Data
A catalogue record for this book is available from the British Library

ISBN-13: 978-0-29784-639-0 (cased)
ISBN-10: 0-297-84639-6 (cased)

ISBN-13: 978-0-29784-560-7 (trade paperback)
ISBN-10: 0-297-84560-8 (trade paperback)

Printed and bound in Great Britain by
Clays Ltd, St Ives plc

www.orionbooks.co.uk

The Orion Publishing Group policy is to use papers that are natural,
renewable and recyclable products and made from wood
grown in sustainable forests. The logging and manufacturing processes
are expected to conform to the environmental regulations of the
country of origin.

CONTENTS

INTRODUCTION

DURING THE 1970s, the British Army's special forces unit, the Special Air Service, and its marine equivalent, then known as the Special Boat Squadron, had exchange arrangements with their US counterparts, the US Army Special Forces and the US Navy SEALs. It was his time on attachment to the SAS that led Colonel Charlie Chargin' Beckwith, the founder of Delta, to model his new unit on the SAS. Similarly SEAL Team Six, the US Navy counter-terrorist force set up in the wake of Eagle Claw, the failed 1980 attempt to rescue the Americans held hostage in Tehran, drew inspiration from the SBS.

But there were a number of other US special operations units created in reaction to the Eagle Claw debacle. One of them was set up by another Special Forces colonel with his own experience of working with the SAS. Jerry King, who set up a special operations intelligence team for a second effort to rescue the hostages, had an SAS sergeant attached to him in the early 1960s while he was at Fort Bragg, North Carolina. The British soldier's skills made a lasting impression on King. But when he was asked to set up a permanent special operations intelligence unit to prepare the way for Delta or SEAL Team Six missions, he had no British model to work from.

The British had always employed an ad hoc system of setting up intelligence teams to work alongside the SAS on specific missions. I served on one in Oman in the 1970s, fighting Yemeni-backed insurgents. The teams did their job but were never likely to be as efficient as a dedicated special operations intelligence unit that combined all the various disciplines, signals intelligence, imagery intelligence and human intelligence, specifically matching the product to special operations requirements.

Jerry King's new unit, which was given the title the Intelligence Support Activity, was breaking new ground. It was highly successful but nevertheless suffered under an army top brass that was suspicious of all special operations units, regarding them as cowboys who could only get senior officers into trouble with the politicians. At times, the Activity had to fight quite literally for its life. It is a tribute to King and those who followed him that it not only survived but carried out a number of highly successful missions, often receiving no credit for what it did.

History is unlikely to be kind to Donald Rumsfeld over his decisions to ignore the military desire for more troops in Iraq, and the State Department concerns at the lack of preparation for Iraq's post-war reconstruction. But for America's special operations troops, whose use had been repeatedly stymied by the top brass, Rumsfeld's willingness to overrule the generals was a breath of fresh air. This was particularly true of the Activity, which had far fewer proponents than America's other special mission units.

The extent of the Activity's success in the war on terror was perhaps most vividly shown by the decision of the UK's Directorate of Special Forces to reverse the precedents of a shared history and follow the American lead. In April 2005, it set up its own human intelligence and signals intelligence special forces units, the Special Reconnaissance Regiment and 18th (UKSF) Signal Regiment, in a fitting tribute to the Activity's success.

I am grateful to all those who helped me in the writing of this book. Most cannot be named, for obvious reasons – the Pentagon told anyone who asked permission that they must not under any circumstances talk to me. But I am particularly grateful to Jerry King for explaining the circumstances in which the unit was originally set up and to Bill Cowan for his assistance in ensuring that the account of the Activity's operations in Lebanon during the 1970s stayed on track. Those others who helped me know who they are and know I am grateful. I thank those writers who have gone before me and whose work formed the basis for my research, of whom Jeffrey Richelson, Mark Bowden, Seymour Hersh and Steven Emerson are worthy of particular note. I must also thank Ian Drury and Barry Holmes at Orion, my agent Robert Kirby, my wife Hayley and my children.

1 DEBACLE AT DESERT ONE

SITTING IN THE forward operations centre in a filthy Egyptian Air Force hangar at the Wadi Qina air base, 300 miles south of Cairo, Colonel Jerry King was powerless to prevent the debacle at Desert One. As chief of staff to Major-General James 'Hammer' Vaught, the man in charge of the Delta Force attempt to rescue 53 American hostages held captive in Tehran, King could only listen with mounting anger to the frantic satellite radio messages coming out of Iran. Not that anyone out there at the Desert One staging post, 250 miles southeast of the Iranian capital in the Dasht-e-Kavir desert, could do any better. Even Chargin' Charlie Beckwith, the former Green Beret colonel who set up Delta and was leading Operation Eagle Claw on the ground, couldn't prevent what was by any measure 'a total goat-fuck' that left eight US servicemen dead.

The operation had been called off after three of the eight US Navy helicopters taking part in the mission developed technical problems that left the joint task force with too few to get both the hostages and the rescue team out. One was abandoned in the desert after an indicator light warned a rotor blade might snap, a second had to pull out of the mission when its gyroscope malfunctioned and the third was declared unserviceable after landing at Desert One. After some argument among the task force commanders over whether or not to go ahead, the mission was called off. It was then that a helicopter and one of the C130s collided, killing the eight US servicemen.

There was a whole bunch of reasons why they died and why the task force failed in its mission – the inter-service rivalry that meant every one of the four armed services wanted some involvement in the mission regardless of the fact that they had never worked together before, and all used different operating procedures; the decision to fly the helicopters off an aircraft carrier rather than in from a neighbouring country; the navy's poor maintenance of its helicopters; and the strange decision not to have air force pilots with experience of special ops fly all the aircraft, a move that would have at least ensured the mission got beyond Desert One.

But even if it had, there was another major problem that could have led to the mission failing at its most dangerous point, inside Tehran itself, and afterwards Jerry King, a straight-talking veteran of Army Special Forces operations along the Ho Chi Minh Trail, was not slow to make his views known. The CIA had fucked up big time. It had claimed, falsely as it later turned out, to have no one in Tehran who could help Delta prepare for what was always going to be a tricky task. King's disparaging view of the Agency's contribution was shared by virtually everyone else involved in Eagle Claw, not least the task force commander General Vaught. 'Intelligence from all sources was inadequate from the start and never became responsive,' he said. 'The CIA did not, would not or could not provide sufficient agents to go in country and get the information we needed.'[1]

WHATEVER THE REASONS for the failure of Eagle Claw, it certainly wasn't a lack of detailed planning. Preparations for the raid had begun six months earlier on 4 November 1979, the very day a mob of Iranian

Revolutionary Guards and militant students, supporters of Ayatollah Khomeini, forced their way into the US embassy in Tehran and seized the hostages. Jerry King, who was then chief of unconventional warfare for special operations in the Joint Chiefs of Staff operations directorate, was called in by Air Force General David C Jones, the Chairman of the Joint Chiefs of Staff, together with the Chief of Current Operations, Brigadier-General Johnson. 'We were told about the embassy seizure and I was ordered to develop some military options by the following morning,' King recalled. 'I was forbidden to inform or involve anyone else, including my immediate superior.'

Jones eventually backed down slightly to allow King to bring in two of his special operations colleagues so there were at least navy and air force representatives involved in his special planning cell, which was set up in the Pentagon's Eighth Corridor close to the River entrance. Those three men were to become the nucleus of the task force commanded by Jim Vaught, who was described by John T Carney, one of the US Air Force special operations officers brought in to set up the Desert One forward operating base, as 'a tall, lean, scraggly, quiet, gravely voiced but soft-spoken infantryman'.[2] The unit Vaught and King picked to execute the actual rescue mission was the newly formed Special Forces Operational Detachment – Delta, the counter-terrorist force that Beckwith had just recently set up, modelling it on the British Special Air Service (SAS), to provide the US with a counter-terrorist team. Delta was based at the Pope air force base – in what became known as 'the Stockade' – right next door to the Army Special Forces headquarters at Fort Bragg, Fayetteville, North Carolina. Beckwith and King were both veterans of special ops in Vietnam and had learned a lot about their trade serving alongside members of the SAS. 'I had an SAS sergeant assigned to me at Fort Bragg in the early sixties,' King recalled. It was part of the exchange mission that provided the inspiration for Delta. The sergeant and an SAS officer were sent to Fort Bragg while Charlie Beckwith and a Green Beret sergeant went to the SAS base at Bradbury Lines, Hereford, in England. For Jerry King, time spent with the highly experienced SAS sergeant was deeply rewarding. 'I was wet behind the ears,' King said. 'He taught me how to walk.'

Born in Canton, North Carolina, in 1937, Jerry King was an army brat, brought up at military bases in Germany, Korea and the Philippines. His stepfather was a career non-commissioned officer in the US Army. King enlisted into the army's airborne infantry and after swift promotion through the ranks was picked out as a potential officer. The rookie lieutenant's first posting was as a platoon commander in Germany. 'Facing the Fulda Gap and the possibility of a Soviet thrust, I began to realize that my survival was dramatically enhanced when I had more control over my unit's actions,' he said. 'The arrogance of the young but a belief reinforced over time.'

As a direct result of that conviction, Jerry King developed a hard-nosed attitude that would win him a great deal of respect, and quite a few enemies, in his chosen field of special operations. At 6 foot 2 inches and weighing in at just under 15 stone, King was a born winner. There might be others who were fitter, but very few could outlast him. Whether it was swimming underwater in preparation for covert approaches on targets or running marathons, he had the kind of mentality that meant he wouldn't give in. He joined the 77th Special Forces Group (Airborne) at Fort Bragg and was sent to Laos at the head of one of the White Star mobile training teams, which were training local forces to counter North Vietnam's use of the Ho Chi Minh Trail, the Viet Cong supply route that ran through Laos and Cambodia into South Vietnam. King subsequently led a Special Forces detachment in Vietnam and helped to set up the training programme for the Studies and Observations Group (SOG), the euphemistically named special operations command which, between January 1965 and March 1973, mounted several thousand highly successful cross-border reconnaissance missions into Laos, Cambodia and North Vietnam. At

28, King was deemed 'too old' for the gruelling missions but on a couple of occasions he managed to bypass the naysayers and went across the border anyway.[3]

He had known Charlie Beckwith when they were both young lieutenants and was not the Delta commander's greatest fan, but that didn't affect his judgement that Delta was 'the obvious choice for the entry force'. The first suggestion was that the raid to rescue the hostages should be mounted from eastern Turkey, which seemed a sensible option, allowing total flexibility in the type of aircraft used on the rescue mission and a safe base just across the border from Iran. But inexplicably General Jones ruled out the use of Turkey and two other friendly Middle East countries. 'What I considered a purely political and unreasonable decision by the Chairman forced us to look for an alternative launch platform,' King recalled. 'Carriers were the only feasible option available.'[4]

Eventually it was decided that the MC130 Combat Talon aircraft carrying the Delta personnel and a small security force of US Rangers would take off from Wadi Qina, making a brief stopover at the British air base on the island of Masirah, off Oman, while the helicopters that were to carry the Delta teams into a hide site close to Tehran and exfiltrate them, along with the hostages, would launch from the aircraft carrier USS *Nimitz* in the Gulf of Oman. That last decision created a whole raft of problems that would ultimately lead to the failure of the mission.

'The choice of a carrier as a launch platform virtually dictated the type of aircraft,' King said. They would be US Navy RH53 Sea Stallions, normally used for mine-clearing operations but big enough to carry the hostages and the Delta rescue team out of Iran to safety. It didn't take long for King to realise that the navy pilots who flew the aircraft were simply not good enough. 'I recommended we bring in air force pilots who flew the same helicopter with considerable long flight experience, including one who had participated in the Son Tay raid.' But the senior officer he had to ask for authorisation to replace the navy pilots was a US Marine general and the inter-service rivalry that would bedevil the Eagle Claw mission took over. 'Before I finished laying out a proposed solution,' King said, 'he picked up the phone and called Marine headquarters, claiming they had the right guys for the job at hand.'[5]

The plan was for all the aircraft to rendezvous at Desert One where the helicopters would be refuelled by EC130 tanker aircraft. The helicopters would then take the Delta extraction teams to a second staging post 50 miles south-east of Tehran where they would hide up for the day and wait for a team that had been infiltrated into Iran. It was to drive six pre-positioned trucks containing the Delta commandos to Tehran to snatch the hostages from the embassy compound and the Foreign Ministry, where three of the US diplomats were being held separately. Air cover would be provided by two AC130 Spectre gunships. The helicopters would meanwhile fly to Tehran and orbit above the city waiting for the signal to land and lift off the Delta rescue teams together with the hostages. They would then fly to an airstrip at Manzariyeh, thirty-five minutes due south of the Iranian capital where giant C141 Starlifter transport aircraft would be waiting to fly the hostages out of the country.[6]

Put like that it all sounded pretty easy, but Jerry King and his fellow planners had one major difficulty, the lack of any reliable intelligence. Charlie Beckwith complained that Wade Ishimoto, the Delta intelligence officer, was inundated with intelligence, most of which appeared to be of only limited reliability and had nothing to do with the hostages and their situation. 'Nearly every agency that sent us material used a different system,' said Beckwith. 'A report would come in stating that the source was "untested". The intelligence guys needed more than that. Was the source reliable on any basis? Another report might read: "An untested source received through an unofficial contact..." What does unofficial contact mean? Was the contact reliable or unreliable in the past? Some people in intelligence became highly indignant when we complained about the reports. An official came down to point out that well over 200 reports had been furnished to Delta. Wade Ishimoto explained, very nicely but firmly, that most of the information we received and laboriously read had nothing to do with the hostages. A report he pulled out listed fourteen items that had come from travellers who'd just returned from Iran. The fourteen items covered everything from the Turkish border area down to Baluchistan via Sistan in the south. Not one of these was even remotely related to the hostages.'[7]

There was plenty of imagery collected by the US Keyhole spy satellites and SR71 Blackbird spy planes. But what they needed could only be provided by human spies and Stansfield Turner, the CIA Director, had deliberately run down the Agency's men on the ground, the guys who provided human intelligence, what the spooks call Humint, in favour of technical means, the spy satellites that could photograph every detail of the embassy compound and intercept what the Iranian guards were saying to each other on their radio systems. Turner's view was clear: 'Not only do agents have biases and human fallibilities, there is always a risk that an agent is, after all, working for someone else. Rather than instinctively reaching for human, on-site spying, the United States will want to look to those impersonal technical systems, primarily satellite photography and intercepts.' If that claim had been made by the head of the National Security Agency, the US signals intercept operation, or the National Reconnaisance Office, which runs the spy satellites, it would have been understandable. Coming from the Director of the CIA, it was close to catastrophic.[8]

For Jerry King and the other special operations officers trying to plan the Eagle Claw mission, Turner's attitude seemed to go to the heart of their problems. 'We had zillions of shots of the embassy and they were magnified a hundred times,' one said. 'We could tell you about the tiles; we could tell you about the grass, and how many cars were parked there. Anything you wanted to know about the external aspects of that embassy we could tell you in infinite detail. We couldn't tell you shit about what was going on inside the building. That's where humans come in.'[9] The intelligence they needed had to come from human sources, said Carney, who flew in ahead of the mission to reconnoitre the Desert One staging post and lay out the landing lights. 'But Turner had decimated the agency's Humint ranks, and there was almost no human intelligence coming out of Iran.'[10]

The CIA was forced to rely more and more on technical means of collection and, as far as Jerry King was concerned, its few remaining operations officers were not good enough to make up the gap. 'As I later testified to Congress, the Agency had a bad habit of recruiting what I called the "garden party" set, occasionally valuable but the first to lose access in a coup or revolution,' he said. 'They lacked assets and general ability to work the alleyways and souks of the world.' The CIA's representatives in Tehran were among the hostages held in the embassy compound and the Agency claimed not to have 'a single contactable asset' inside the country.[11]

The rescue team desperately needed people on the ground inside Iran to produce the detailed intelligence they would require if they were to know where to find the hostages. They also needed someone to provide the trucks and equipment that were essential if they were going to get into Tehran undetected by the Iranian authorities. Jerry King decided that they had no choice but to put their own people in. 'The task force spent a long time screening the military for Farsi speakers,' he recalled. 'To further complicate the issue, Charlie Beckwith insisted that he have his own men. This in itself was understandable but no one in Delta acceptable to Charlie was trained in undercover operations.'[12]

The man they decided to send in was Dick Meadows, one of Delta's point men with King's planning team. Meadows was another old Vietnam Special Forces hand and a key player in the Son Tay raid, the legendary 1970 attempt to rescue US POWs from a prison camp near the North Vietnamese capital Hanoi. (When Meadows and the rest of the Son Tay team arrived they found that the POWs had been moved shortly before the mission. The intelligence was faulty but the mission had otherwise been executed perfectly and those involved became legends in the US special operations community.) Dick Meadows was the Special Forces sergeant sent with Beckwith on attachment to the SAS base at Hereford, and as a result had married the daughter of an SAS sergeant-major. He had been acting as a consultant, advising Beckwith on how Delta should be run. Meadows wasn't the ideal undercover operator. The Agency was concerned that he looked too much like a terrorist, asking King to try to get Meadows to wear a collar and tie rather than the turtleneck sweaters he favoured. They also complained that he didn't seem to be taking too much notice of their attempts to make him blend into the background. 'The Agency came back several times and said he's not catching on fast enough,' one member of the Delta team said.

But Meadows was a true pro with the confidence to carry off the flimsiest of covers, going into Tehran, on a fake passport provided by the CIA, as Richard H Keith, an Irish businessman working for a European car manufacturer. At the same time, the Agency said it had finally found an Iranian agent who could help Meadows buy the trucks and equipment he needed and brought Bob Plan, a former member of the wartime Office of Strategic Services, out of retirement to run him. Plan went in and out of Tehran virtually at will, providing confidence that there would be no problem getting other undercover agents into Iran. The trawl of the armed forces personnel files for anyone who spoke Farsi turned up a young USAF sergeant who had been born in Iran and he went in to act as a fixer for Meadows. (Other Farsi speakers the search turned up were added to Delta rescue team to try to minimise any problems on the ground.) But the best intelligence was gathered by two Special Forces sergeants based in Berlin, who spoke fluent German and could operate under cover as West German businessmen.

'They provided the best tactical info regarding the exterior of the embassy and guard locations, schedules, communication and weaponry,' King said.[13]

THE FOUR UNDERCOVER operators checked out the six Ford trucks and the two Mazda vans the Iranian agent had stored in a warehouse ready for the mission, drove the route to the US embassy the Delta rescue team would take, and sat for hours in a coffeehouse opposite the embassy compound checking out the efficiency of the guards. 'The skill, training, expertise and daring exhibited by this small group of military men was unique and of the highest order,' one former special operations intelligence officer said. 'Working quietly and carefully, and taking enormous personal risks in order to accomplish their missions, these men were able to obtain, and report on, the detailed intelligence necessary to properly plan for the execution of a rescue attempt in a hostile environment. They were able to establish the support mechanisms for the incoming rescue force. These included renting the buildings and facilities to be used as safe sites, arranging for the trucks and vehicles necessary for movement around the city, reconnoitring the landing and extraction sites, preparing reception parties and guides, and ultimately successfully exfiltrating all personnel when the inbound forces were forced to abort the mission.' That was in itself no mean feat. Meadows and his colleagues managed to get out only just ahead of the Iranian security forces who had recovered documents in the US helicopters left at Desert One that led them to the warehouse.[14]

'Not overly surprisingly, the CIA operative left Iran the day before the rescue operation was launched,' Jerry King recalled. 'I was deeply involved in coordinating these operations with the CIA. At the working level, cooperation with the CIA was not exactly enhanced when I accused the CIA liaison to the task force of using the CIA as a cover for his real job in the State Department. He was replaced not long after this conversation.'[15]

But the behaviour of the CIA was worse even than Jerry King and his fellow task force members believed. Shortly before the Delta rescue team set off, the Agency announced that a Pakistani chef from the US embassy, allowed to leave by the Iranian authorities, had fortuitously sat next to a CIA officer and told him precisely where all of the hostages, including the three thought to be in the Iranian Foreign Ministry, were being held. The Agency also passed on other important intelligence the chef had allegedly provided. 'Suddenly we were deluged with information,' one of the mission planners said. 'The lock turns this way, the window goes this way. The light switch is down the hall. It was a massive dump of intelligence.'

Jerry King was not alone among the task force members in smelling a rat. But it was only much later that the widespread belief that the Agency had been holding back on them would be confirmed. 'Eighteen years after the rescue attempt some of us learned that the CIA had received a covert communication that detailed some of the most important information we needed – the exact location of three hostages being held in the Iranian Ministry of Foreign Affairs,' said John Carney. 'The CIA claimed that it had stumbled only by providence on similarly detailed information on almost all the other hostages who were being held in the American embassy compound when a Pakistani cook who had been working in the embassy happened to be on the last leg of a flight from Tehran to Frankfurt and found himself seated next to a CIA officer. The CIA apparently fabricated the Pakistani cook story in order to protect its own source inside the embassy and gave up its information only after it was absolutely certain that the rescue mission could be launched.'[16] The Agency had someone in Tehran all along, a very good source supplying his bosses at CIA headquarters in Langley with top-grade intelligence. But it held back the wealth of vital intelligence he was providing until the very last minute because it feared that the existence of their agent and his sub-agents would leak out, putting its only source of information at risk.

Jerry King's judgement that the CIA had fucked up big time was backed up by the six-man Special Operations Review Group set up under former Chief of Naval Operations Admiral James L Holloway III to find out why the mission failed. The Holloway Commission, as it became known, was critical of 'certain elements of the intelligence community' for their failure to give sufficient assistance to the Eagle Claw mission in a timely enough manner.

'For an operation of the scope and complexity of the Iranian mission, a significant augmentation of existing intelligence capabilities was mandatory,' the commission said. 'This augmentation tended to evolve over time and in a somewhat piecemeal fashion. Certain elements of the intelligence community seemed slow in harnessing themselves initially for the tasks at hand. The group believes that intelligence community assets and resources could have been pulled together more quickly and effectively than was actually the case.'

Despite the commission's determination not to name names or attribute blame to anyone involved in the mission, it was clear that those comments were aimed at the CIA. The commission said that in future similar situations there should be a specialist intelligence team set up, 'harnessing selected elements of the US intelligence community and bringing them together as an integrated supported mechanism'. This would 'greatly facilitate achievement of acceptable readiness and forward deployment of forces where time is a critical factor'.[17]

THE FAILURE OF OPERATION Eagle Claw was a major embarrassment for the American military, with Iranian television showing pictures of burned bodies of dead US servicemen, footage that was rebroadcast on the US networks' nightly news programmes. To the American people, watching their television sets daily for any news of the hostages, it seemed that all hopes of rescue had been abandoned. But in fact planning for the second mission, codenamed Snow Bird, began almost immediately. General Vaught's response to the debacle at Desert One was to set up a special operations intelligence team to help Delta to mount Operation Snow Bird. This time, the CIA was not to be given the chance to hold back the key pieces of intelligence until the party was just about to begin. Jerry King was put in charge of the new aggressive, proactive special operations intelligence unit capable of gathering the information the rescue team needed on the ground in Iran. He was told to get his people inside Tehran in numbers and to do it damn quick.

'Field Operations Group was the name of the element I was tasked to put together as planning for the second Iran rescue mission,' King recalled. 'Actually the acronym FOG came first. Every time I attempted to define what we were expected to do, the mission changed. We were tasked to conduct intelligence operations inside Iran, to take out Iranian military command communications capability, to surreptitiously destroy or render inoperative several radar sites, to tap selected telephone communications, to be prepared to free-fall parachute onto key buildings, to mark landing and drop zones, to be prepared to conduct diversion missions, to collect and extract personnel left behind, and other assigned missions. You can see why FOG came to mind, hazy, ever-changing, hard to get a grip upon and often unpredictable.

'General Vaught formed this ad hoc unit because of the poor performance of the CIA in the first evolution. He wanted a force he trusted and could rely upon for difficult tasks. Why did he give me the task? Firstly he trusted me, secondly he perceived that I was determined, thirdly he knew I had imagination, and lastly I was comfortable with mission orders and didn't require supervision. Trying to recruit and train a force for such wide-ranging missions was difficult. The core was recruited from Army Special Forces. They may not have the skills, but I was convinced they had the ability to learn and master those needed for virtually any mission. In time, navy and air force personnel joined FOG.'[18]

The FOG traced its roots back far further, to the Jedburgh and

Sussex teams that parachuted into northern France during the 1944 D-Day landings to gather intelligence and organise local resistance groups. Its title was strikingly similar to the unit set up in Vietnam, the SOG, Special Operations Group, which specialised in reconnaissance and surveillance missions aimed at collecting tactical intelligence about Viet Cong bases and supply dumps; infiltrating secret agents across the border into North Vietnam, carrying out psychological warfare, including so-called 'dirty tricks'; mounting hit-and-run raids on the North Vietnamese coast from the sea; and interdicting enemy traffic on the Ho Chi Minh Trail.

The most effective of the SOG operations were those mounted by OPS-35, its reconnaissance and cross-border surveillance element. 'SOG recon teams developed priceless intelligence available from no other source,' one Special Forces officer said. The teams, which also rescued US and allied troops who were captured or missing in action, were made up of between six and a dozen men; most were specially trained local forces but they were led by US Army Special Forces, who formed around a third of each team. The SOG repeatedly fell foul of the traditionalists within the army – who saw special operations as what one former Special Forces officer described as 'a bastard stepchild' – and the politically cautious State Department, which worried about the legality of its cross-border operations into Laos and Cambodia.

This was a problem that would bedevil US special operations forces throughout the second half of the 20th century. The SOG was set up during a brief period of resurgence under President Kennedy. He saw the politically savvy, culturally aware and militarily adaptable Special Forces as the answer to his insistence that the post-war world required 'a whole new kind of strategy, a wholly different kind of force, a new and wholly different kind of military training.' In a letter to army chiefs, Kennedy outlined a force whose tactics would effectively mirror the 'hearts and minds' tactics adopted by the SAS in the battle against communist insurgents in Malaya a decade earlier. 'Pure military skill is not enough,' Kennedy said. 'A full spectrum of military, paramilitary and civil action must be combined to produce success. The enemy uses economic and political warfare, propaganda and naked military aggression in an endless combination. Our officers and men must understand and combine the political, economic and civil actions with skilled military efforts.' Despite the presidential backing, the army chiefs sneered at the type of warfare Kennedy had in mind as: 'just a form of small war, a guerrilla operation in which we have a long record against the Indians. Any well-trained organization can shift the tempo to that which might be required for this kind of situation. All this cloud of dust that's coming out of the White House really isn't necessary.'[19]

Kennedy's untimely death ensured that the SOG never had the unequivocal support it needed to be as effective as possible and it was eventually declared illegal. 'Support forthcoming from on high was stone cold at worst and lukewarm at best,' one former Special Forces officer said. 'Traditionalists in the Pentagon and Military Assistance Command Vietnam viewed covert action as a sideshow. The Department of State and the antsy US ambassador in Laos laid on political restrictions that all but declared the Ho Chi Minh Trail "off limits" for the first two years.'[20]

The US ambassador, William H Sullivan, had total control over whether or not SOG missions inside Laos went ahead. 'Bill Sullivan had a tendency to impose his own restriction over and above those laid on by the Department of State,' said General William C Westmoreland, who commanded US forces in Vietnam between 1964 and 1968. 'We sometimes referred to the Ho Chi Minh Trail as Sullivan's Freeway.' Often the SOG would be told they could not go somewhere because the CIA already had teams there but when they asked for the intelligence – just as with Eagle Claw – they were told none was available.[21]

But despite all the problems and the opposition to special operations among many of the US Army's most senior officers, a Pentagon study of 'lessons learned' in Vietnam said: 'SOG operations provided a considerable amount of intelligence data to Washington and Saigon on North Vietnamese troop movements along those portions of the Ho Chi Minh Trail that were patrolled by the OPS-35 forces. Because of these reconnaissance efforts, U.S. planners had a fairly clear picture of enemy forces in the sanctuaries and along the trail by early 1969.' [22]

THE SNOW BIRD mission team put together more than 2,000 men and lots of new equipment to ensure that this time they had the right tools for the job. As part of the attempt to maintain total operational security, $200 million was funnelled out of official unclassified programmes into top secret unofficial 'black accounts' and used to procure the latest state of the art communications and electronic warfare equipment for the Black Hawk long-range helicopters the mission planned to use.[23] Jerry King's new unit put people back into Tehran, including the two Special Forces sergeants from Berlin, and gathered more intelligence than they had for the first rescue attempt. It even devised an imaginative plan to send agents into Tehran under cover of being members of an independent film company attempting to gain access to the hostages for a documentary, only to see the idea vetoed by the Pentagon legal department.[24]

But after the failure of Eagle Claw, the Iranians split the hostages up to make another rescue attempt more difficult. Despite being put together on the hoof, and being asked to fulfil often contradictory objectives, the Field Operations Group did some good work but could not pin down the precise location of all the hostages. In the end, they were freed and Snow Bird was never needed.[25] But there were now influential voices in the army who were prepared to fight the entrenched prejudice against special operations forces. They knew that throwing together special mission teams who had never trained together before in order to mount counter-terrorism operations, as General Vaught and Jerry King had been forced to do for Eagle Claw, made no sense.

The Holloway Commission had recommended the creation of 'a Counter-Terrorist Joint Task Force as a field agency of the Joint Chiefs of Staff with permanently assigned staff personnel and certain assigned forces' to ensure it never had to happen again. 'The CTJTF would plan, train for, and conduct operations to counter-terrorist activities directed against US interests, citizens, and or property outside the United States,' the commission said. 'The commander would be responsible directly to the Joint Chiefs of Staff. The CTJTF staff should be filled with individuals of all four services, selected on the basis of their specialized capabilities in the field of special operations of various types. The organic forces permanently assigned to the JTF should be small and limited to those which have a unique capability in special operations.'[26]

Even before the hostages were released, the proponents of special operations, led by General Ed 'Shy' Meyer, the army chief of staff and a long-time supporter of the merits of special operations forces, set up a Joint Special Operations Command (JSOC – pronounced 'Jay-Sock'), next door to Delta in the south-east corner of the Pope air force base. Its publicly avowed mission was 'to study the special operations requirements of all US military services to ensure standardization'. But its real, top secret role was to coordinate the activities of the counter-terrorist 'special mission units' which could be used to form the basis for any future Joint Special Operations Task Force.[27]

For America's special operations forces, it looked like the tide had at last begun to turn. During the 1970s, their capabilities had been allowed to wither on the vine. The special operations budget, which had hit a peak of $1 billion at the height of the Vietnam War, had plummeted to less than $100 million in 1975. At last it seemed Spec Ops was on the way back up. The progress would be slow, and often halting, but progress there would be. JSOC's special mission units would eventually include Special Forces Operational Detachment –

Delta; a US Navy SEAL counter-terrorist unit, SEAL Team Six; an army helicopter unit called Task Force 160; and a US Air Force unit, previously known only as 'Brand X', which was given the deliberately bland and unrevealing name Detachment One, Military Airlift Command Operations Staff (Det 1 MACOS) to hide its real purpose. John Carney, a founding member of Brand X, said that according to the JSOC commander 'we had the best cover of any of his six special mission units because no one could figure out what our name stood for.'[28]

The FOG was not to be subordinate to JSOC, but there was no doubt it would continue to exist. Ed Meyer and his allies knew that their joint special operations task forces would need specifically targeted intelligence and they were not inclined to ditch King's Field Operations Group and go back to relying on the CIA. On 10 December 1980, the Joint Chiefs' Director of Operations, Lieutenant-General Philip C Gast, wrote a top secret memorandum to the Director of the Defense Intelligence Agency, Lieutenant-General Eugene Tighe, urging that the Pentagon create a permanent unit to provide the intelligence capability supplied by the FOG. 'A review of the intelligence collected during the past year to support Iranian contingency planning revealed a serious and persistent information deficiency,' he said. 'This deficiency revolves around the need of military planners to have accurate and timely situation oriented operational and environmental detail. Although technical systems can and did provide some of the information needed, the nature of the required data puts the burden of collection on reliable human observers. The current DOD/Service Humint structure is not organized to satisfy these requirements.'[29]

Ed Meyer was determined not to rub the CIA up the wrong way by giving it the impression he was creating a rival intelligence unit, and he knew that Bill Casey, the new Director of Central Intelligence, had the President's ear. If the Agency regarded his special operations intelligence and operations unit as a rival, it might leave the military getting even less intelligence from the Agency than it already was. So in January 1981, he went to see Casey and asked him if he wanted the new unit to be part of the CIA. He had a team of intelligence operatives and wanted them to form a new completely 'black' unit, a totally deniable covert operations force. 'This is not necessarily a mission that the army should do,' he said. 'It's a national mission. But I am not going to dissolve it now that Iran is over because we may need it in the future. You decide what you're going to do with it, whether you want it or you want us to keep it.' Casey said it was a military intelligence unit, the military should keep control over it.[30]

On 29 January 1981, Ed Meyer officially authorised the creation of the US Army Intelligence Support Activity (USAISA). Two months later, on 3 March 1981, the FOG was renamed the Intelligence Support Activity, with Jerry King as its first commander.[31] At this point, the unit had just twenty-five 'operatives', the majority of whom had served in the FOG. But few of those had the necessary language or tradecraft skills and King estimated it would take at least a year to train up the fifty men the army had told him to recruit. He asked for eighteen months to set the unit up. He was given just forty days. The ISA was deliberately kept out of JSOC because it would be doing a lot more than just fighting terrorists, which at that stage was the only role units like Delta and SEAL Team Six were expected to carry out. Meyer had already proposed a Strategic Services Command, which he intended to include all special operations forces other than those specifically dealing with terrorism, and he wanted the USAISA to be one of its first component parts. But there was so little support for a separate command for special operations – even among Meyer's own staff – that the idea stuttered and died. So for the first few years of its life, the ISA would not be part of any military command. It was made directly subordinate to the army's Assistant Deputy Chief of Staff for Intelligence, Lieutenant-General William E Odom.[32]

A top secret history of the unit said the ISA was set up in response to the 'institutional shortfalls in US national intelligence and special operations capabilities' revealed by the failure of Operation Eagle Claw and because 'there existed nowhere in the national capability an organization to provide this vital support'. Once the first rescue mission failed, 'the Joint Chiefs of Staff responded to satisfy the critical need for detailed military intelligence by creating USAISA's predecessor, a joint organization known as Field Operations Group,' the top secret history said. 'This was an ad hoc organization composed of selected personnel who were trained to fill critical intelligence and operational needs. The Joint Chiefs of Staff directed the Army to ration the unique capability developed during the Iranian hostage crisis. The Chief of Staff, Army, authorized creation of the US Army Intelligence Support Activity on 29 January 1981.' The Intelligence Support Activity was only supposed to be a holding name until the establishment and funding for a formal unit could be set up. But it stuck and, to the few insiders who knew the unit existed, it swiftly became known simply as the Activity. It was designed to meet 'unique military intelligence and special operations needs,' the top secret history said, adding that those unique needs were 'a combination of intelligence collection and operational support to a striking force'. Put simply, it was to be one of the military's most elite units, with a brief to seek out America's enemies wherever they were. What would follow was less clear. President Ford had signed a presidential order banning assassinations, whether carried out by US special operations forces or the CIA, and President Reagan reinforced that ban. But none of the people the ISA's covert operations would rub up against would be likely to surrender quietly. If its shooters found themselves in a firefight, they knew they had a choice of kill or be killed.[33]

2 OPERATION WINTER HARVEST

JUDITH DOZIER WAS BUSY in the kitchen preparing the evening meal when the workmen rang the bell. It was Thursday 17 December 1981. Judith's husband Jim, who was relaxing in the front room of their sixth-floor apartment in the Italian city of Verona, answered it. 'I just got up and walked to the door and asked who was there,' Jim Dozier said. One of the two scruffy-looking workmen explained in broken English that they were plumbers and there was nothing in the dirty overalls they were wearing to suggest anything different. They were working on a leak in the downstairs apartment. Water was seeping through the ceiling, could they look to see where it was coming from? It was the kind of routine domestic occurrence that might happen anywhere, any time. But this was different – really different.

Jim was General James Lee Dozier, the most senior US officer in Nato's southern command, and the plumbers were members of the Italian Red Brigades, left-wing terrorists who had already kidnapped and murdered a number of prominent hostages, including the former Italian Prime Minister Aldo Moro. Jim Dozier had been warned that he was a potential terrorist target. But after the Iran hostage crisis, everybody was warning of the dangers of this or that. Verona wasn't Tehran and Dozier wasn't alone among his colleagues in thinking the security boys were exaggerating the risks. These guys didn't strike the 50-year-old Dozier as terrorists, they just looked like ordinary workmen. 'They looked like plumbers and they acted like plumbers,' he said. 'So I let them in.' He showed them into the utility room, the most likely source of any leak, and was just about to go and get an Italian-English dictionary so he could better understand what they were trying to say when they made their move. 'The next thing I knew I was spun around and looking down the barrels of two silenced pistols,' Dozier said. One of the two men pistol-whipped him. He tried to get up to fight back but when he spotted a third terrorist holding a gun to his wife's head he backed off. 'Honey,' he told her. 'Do whatever they say.' The self-styled *brigatisti* then beat him senseless, bundled him into a trunk, dragged it down the stairs, loaded it into an anonymous blue Fiat delivery van and drove off.

Meanwhile, two other members of the cell were chaining Judith Dozier to a chair. 'They put me face down on the floor,' she said. 'They chained me, hand and foot. They covered my face, one threatened me with a knife.' The terrorists dumped her in a utility room and kept coming back to check on her. It was not until several hours later, when she finally felt safe to start banging against the washing machine and shouting for help, that anyone realised a US general had been kidnapped by terrorists. The *brigatisti* had plenty of time to get away. That night they announced to the world that Dozier had been taken to 'a people's prison' where he would be 'submitted to proletarian justice'. Two days later, they issued the first of a series of communiqués in which they said: 'an armed unit of our organization captured and put in a people's prison a Yankee pig of the American occupation army.' They called for a terrorist alliance with other groups like the IRA, 'an anti-imperialist combatant front for a new internationalism'. The Red Brigades were throwing down the gauntlet to the Reagan administration and its promise to take a hard line with terrorists who targeted Americans whoever or wherever they might be.[1]

Despite all the tough-talking rhetoric, the new administration's initial response was no better coordinated than that of its predecessor during the Iran hostages crisis. Having been specifically set up to take charge of any future terrorist incidents wherever they occurred, JSOC immediately swung into action. On orders from Caspar Weinberger, the US Defense Secretary, it sent in a six-man liaison team, including members of Delta and the Activity, led by Colonel Jesse Johnson, a senior Delta officer, to see if there was any 'technical assistance' they could offer the Italians. That sparked an immediate turf war with EUCOM, the US army command that controlled all US military operations in Europe. It had already sent in its own special operations team, Support Operations Task Force Europe, to the nearby Nato base at Vicenza. JSOC may have been put in charge of all counter-terrorism operations wherever they occurred, but nobody appeared to have bothered mentioning it to the regional commands which traditionally governed all US military operations carried out in their theatre. EUCOM simply refused to accept that dealing with terrorism was JSOC's call. Asked to arbitrate in the dispute over who was in charge, the joint chiefs made soothing noises and sat on their hands while, just as with Eagle Claw, virtually every section of the US military tried to get in on the act. The US Air Force even wanted to send in psychics, part of a top secret intelligence programme it was running called 'Distant Viewing', and apparently provided the Italians with endless pieces of 'intelligence' dreamed up by the psychics, none of which was any use at all. All of them were trumped by the US Ambassador Maxwell Rabb, a close friend of both President Reagan and CIA Director Bill Casey, who insisted he was in charge and told the military to butt out. 'They were coming through the windows, coming through the doors,' Rabb recalled. 'Everybody in the intelligence agencies wanted in.'[2]

But as far as JSOC was concerned, butting out wasn't an option. Thousands of Italian *carabinieri* and anti-terrorist police had combed the area around Verona without finding a single lead. A US general had been kidnapped by left-wing terrorists. It was absolutely essential that he should be rescued. The Americans needed to keep up the pressure on the Italian authorities to find the general. The terrorists could not be seen to win this battle. 'We wanted to keep their nose to the grindstone,' one US official said. The Italians had to be made aware 'that we wanted Dozier very badly, that they couldn't allow a repeat of the Moro killing.' But there was no denying the need for more subtlety. No one wanted to upset the Italians by suggesting they weren't up to the job. The JSOC team worked out a compromise with Rabb, a lawyer whose contacts on the ground and ability to get people on side were to be vital in the hunt for Dozier. 'The house rules were don't piss the Italians off,' said Noel Koch, who as Deputy Assistant Secretary of Defense for International Security and Affairs had political control over counter-terrorism operations. 'We had to make sure that we didn't offend the Italians and cause them to throw up their hands and say, "OK. You guys are so smart. You do it." Our contribution was to keep the pressure on the Italians by offering to help, shoveling information and gadgets at them.' EUCOM's team weren't prepared to compromise and found themselves elbowed aside.[3]

Jesse Johnson and his liaison team looked at what the Italians had and what the Americans could provide that the Italians hadn't got. There was one area where no one could match the US forces, electronic monitoring measures, their ability to latch on to any radio signal and track down its location. The chances were that the Red Brigades cell that had Dozier would need to talk to other cells, even if only to sort out the release of their 'communiqués' on Dozier's so-called prosecution by the phoney 'people's court'. If they surfaced, the highly advanced US listening capability would be able to find them. Johnson's liaison team reported back to JSOC headquarters at Pope air base that this was an ideal job for the Activity and Operation Winter Harvest swung into action.[4]

IN MARCH 1981 Ed Meyer had handed Jerry King a $7 million budget, and a set of unassuming, rundown offices opposite the Arlington Hall headquarters of the Intelligence and Security Command, and told him to put together a 50-strong team capable of collecting secret intelligence independent of the rest of the US intelligence community. The ISA's mission was to collect 'actionable intelligence' and to carry out what is now known as 'operational preparation of the battlespace', to get in first and provide the intel for those who would follow. When King said he had nowhere near enough men, he was told the unit would have to prove itself before it could be given the resources needed for increased personnel. Eventually the number of personnel was increased to 250. In an attempt to ensure that the ISA's existence remained top secret, it was given an anonymous sounding covername, the Tactical Concept Activity. 'Another name considered but reluctantly set aside was the Strategic Operations Brigade,' one former member of the unit said. 'This would have disguised the true strength of the unit and hopefully, made other intelligence services spend a great deal of time trying to figure out the organization and mission.' The title of Strategic Operations Brigade had another advantage that appealed to the unit's members. The unit abbreviation would have been a highly appropriate SOB. The Activity's funding and any reference to it in official documents that were not classified top secret were hidden behind a so-called 'Special Access Programme' with a colourful but anonymous codename, initially Royal Cape, that would be replaced on a regular basis.[5]

Once the ISA was officially activated as a unit, it sent out teams to check out the most vulnerable US embassies around the world, particularly in Latin America and the Middle East. They took photographs from every angle, mapped the layout of the buildings, compounds and approach roads, carefully logged details of potential entry and exit points and noted any possible obstacles. In essence, they collected all the information that would have been so vital to any successful attempt to rescue the Iran hostages but was missing from the intel the CIA provided. Way ahead of their time, they sought to develop a virtual computer program that incorporated still and video pictures and would allow a rescue team to walk 'virtually' down a given hallway and look into each office or room along that hall.[6]

One of the first embassies they looked at, amid fears that Nicaragua's Sandinista government might copy the Iranians and take US diplomats hostage in retaliation for Washington's support for the Contras, was the US mission in Managua. The Activity also carried out 'pathfinding' missions, checking out the routes that special operations rescue teams might use to get into what had to be assumed would be hostile territory and the best routes to use to get trapped US citizens out, mapping out potential drop zones for airborne forces and preparing to act as guides for any special operations missions against key installations in the capitals they surveyed. It was the type of mission the British SAS had routinely carried out for years, periodically revisiting countries and carefully logging the data for possible future use. But until the Activity came along, no one in the US military had thought to do it in anything like such a systematic fashion. King also rebuilt bridges with the CIA. 'Over time our relationship with the CIA, at least on the senior level, improved,' one former Activity officer said. 'However, we continued to encounter some naysayers, especially in the paramilitary [special activities] division. Our stock went up quite a bit when two sergeants attended the CIA course at the Farm [the CIA Operations Directorate training base at Camp Perry, near Williamsburg in Virginia]. Their instructions upon departure were: "You are expected to graduate number 1 and 2 in the class. You can sort out between yourselves who will be number one." They did exactly that. Five ex-CIA station chiefs were invited to observe the first course's final, overseas exercise. At the conclusion, they all submitted laudatory appraisals.[7]

Every one of the unit's members had to be a volunteer and they had to be personally vetted by Jerry King himself. Each was picked on the basis of a specific capability deemed to be useful to the unit, using the same technique that came up with the Farsi-speakers for the Iran rescue mission. All the qualifications they needed for each job were fed into the computer at the army's military personnel centre, which churned out a list of every soldier with those attributes. The men, and women, were chosen by the heads of the Activity directorate in which they were to serve from the lists the computer threw up and then checked out by King. Once they were selected, their names disappeared from the listings of servicemen and women. From the time they joined the ISA until they left, their names would only show up on the Army Special Roster, which lists members of top secret units like Delta and the Activity.[8]

There was no sexual discrimination, at any event not against women. The unit commanders concluded very early on that some women, with proper training, could get away with a lot more than men. 'Women went through the same program as men,' one former officer in the unit said. 'It still took time for the men to really accept women as full fledged partners. Unfortunately, we had to evaluate women somewhat differently. One female captain, a West Point graduate who had done exceedingly well in assessment, was dropped because she was an extremely attractive, tall blonde.' For an undercover operator, the more anonymous you are the better. The ability to merge into the background, to be instantly forgettable, is everything. 'Wherever the blonde went she would have stood out in the crowd and the eyes of any man in her vicinity would have been drawn to her instantly,' the former officer said. She had to go. She was so good at the job it seemed unfair but there was general agreement that it was right to turn her down.[9]

One of the things the computer was tasked to look for was membership of an ethnic minority, particularly candidates who had an Hispanic, Oriental or Middle Eastern appearance – perfect for operations in Latin America, south-east Asia, or the Middle East – and soldiers with dual nationality, who would have a genuine non-US passport they could use in undercover operations. Others were intelligence experts skilled in agent-running, analysis or signals intelligence; computer hackers; linguists; communications experts; and men who had proven themselves in low-intensity combat operations. 'After identifying individuals within the army who possessed a language capability, a team was sent to conduct an interview,' one former ISA officer said. 'In addition to administrative personnel, the team usually included two senior NCOs and the unit psychologist, who administered a preliminary psych test. Based on the interview team recommendations and command review, individuals were selected to attend assessment and selection. Each was told that they might not ever be promoted again and would not receive any official recognition, not even for acts of valor. Anyone could ask to be reassigned and his/her request would be honored within 24 hours. If they had done a good job, an attempt was made to get their desired assignment. If they were leaving under undesirable conditions, they might have ended up in Iceland.'[10]

One of those recruited by feeding the required capabilities into the army personnel computer records was Lieutenant-Colonel Calvin Sasai, the unit deputy, an Hawaiian officer with extensive Humint experience, including a tour in Vietnam, working as a case officer for the SOG. 'Cal was selected after reviewing all the personnel records of colonels and lieutenant-colonels with extensive backgrounds in Humint operations,' one former ISA member said. 'He was an outstanding officer who skillfully applied his knowledge and skills to all aspects of the unit.'

Jerry King believed that one of the commander and his deputy should be an experienced intelligence specialist and the other an experienced special operations man to provide a proper balance. The deputy would take over from the commander when he left, thereby ensuring continuity. In Cal Sasai's case he would then appoint a special operations specialist as his deputy to ensure the balance was maintained. The idea was that no outsider should step straight in to take charge of the unit. 'Familiarity with all aspects of the command and its missions was essential,' a former ISA officer said. 'The commander did not have the luxury of time to get up to speed.' Regardless of the extent of the new recruit's previous experience and training every one of them still had to get through the same course. 'Requiring operational personnel to go through assessment not only provided a good insight into the individual but also provided a bond of commonality and confidence,' another former member of the unit said. 'Each had to walk the same lanes, up the same mountains with the same weight.' Since King was renowned for not suffering fools gladly, they also had to be damn good.[11]

Training was always going to be the key to ensuring the Activity could do its job and the courses Jerry King and his command team devised were extraordinarily difficult. They had to be. The last thing you needed on the type of mission the ISA was carrying out was someone who didn't know what they were doing. One bad operator could get everybody killed. 'Training is among the most intensive in the US Army,' the top secret history said. It began with Assessment and Selection, known simply as A&S. This was 'a rigorous program designed to place the candidate for assignment to US Army Intelligence and Support Activity in a sufficient number of different physically and mentally stressful situations to provide assessment data to form the basis for a selection decision by the commander,' the top secret history said. One former member of the unit recalled that there was a deliberate policy of keeping the potential recruits on their toes at all times. 'Unlike regular units a training schedule was never posted,' he said. 'We didn't know what we would be confronted with from one hour to the next, a seemingly insignificant approach but one that began conditioning us to expect the unexpected.'[12]

First the volunteers were dumped in the middle of the desert with no food, water or means of communication and handed a list of near impossible intelligence requests. They had to gather the 'intel' and find a secure way of passing it back to the command post. Having done that, they were forced to go without sleep for several days before being dropped off in a strange city and ordered to carry out a series of complicated operations that would test their fieldcraft and ingenuity, like following a suspect while avoiding other agents who were on their trail. 'Physical condition was secondary to mental ability, especially mental toughness and determination,' one former member said. 'Admittedly, assessment required a certain level of physical conditioning. ISA teams were routinely able to cover up to 50 miles in 24 hours. Because candidates came from divergent fields, they were given heavy doses of physical training and land navigation. They also received, albeit introductory, training in other aspects that they were required to perform.'[13]

Once they had passed A&S, the volunteers were put through the main training course, described in the top secret history as 'a comprehensive course designed to train newly assigned A&S graduates prior to assignment to operational units, prepared to deploy to satisfy the US Army Intelligence Support Activity operational mission.' It included survival skills, parachuting, weapons training and espionage tradecraft such as agent-running. Training continued throughout the operator's time with the unit, which repeatedly carried out rehearsals and exercises to test its various capabilities, with the emphasis on the ability to adapt to any given situation. 'The unit structure provides for the extraordinary command and control manoeuvres required to oversee the proper functioning of this unique [unit],' the top secret history said.[14]

The Activity had to be able to get any kind of intel that might be needed for JSOC's 'special missions'. It also had to be capable of operating as a stand-alone special mission unit, using its own team of 'shooters' – special operations commandos trained to carry out 'direct action' – to follow through on the basis of the intelligence their colleagues produced. King had started with around twenty-five men, largely made up of Army Special Forces operators with a number of intelligence specialists and a few administrative and logistical staff. That gave him the basis of the intelligence analysts and 'shooters' he would need. The make-up of the unit would evolve as it went along, with King and his commanders adding new capabilities to the unit to match the various situations they came up against. Pretty soon the number of people in the unit was above 200. Jerry King began by adding a specialist agent-running team – the 'spooks' – to provide the human intelligence the CIA had failed to come up with, and an electronic surveillance team – the 'knob-turners' – to monitor radio communications and bug telephones, collecting what is known in the jargon of the spooks as signals intelligence, or Sigint for short. It was the 'knob-turners' who made up the bulk of the twenty-five-man team that he sent to Verona to help the Italians find the Red Brigades terrorists.[15]

Two days after Christmas and ten days after Dozier was kidnapped, the Red Brigades issued a second communiqué together with a photograph of him sat in front of a banner showing the five-pointed star the terror group used as its emblem. The communiqué denounced the general as an 'assassin and hero of the American massacres in Vietnam' and announced that his 'proletarian trial' had begun. His left eye was badly swollen. It appeared to be a foretaste of what was to come. None of the hostages taken by the Red Brigades in the past seven years had been found alive. The race was now on to find the US general before the terrorists condemned him to death and executed him.[16]

While the *carabinieri* swamped the area between Verona and Venice with roadblocks, the Activity's Sigint specialists got to work trying to track down the Red Brigades' communications networks. 'The boys in the dark glasses are here and they are going to do things their own way,' one US official told reporters. A Bell UH1 Huey helicopter, fitted out by ISA's own knob-turners with the latest frequency-scanning radio sets and electronic direction-finding equipment, flew circuits up and down looking for the walkie-talkie-style radio sets the *brigatisti* were believed to be using. 'The helicopter was a standard Huey,' one former member of the intelligence team said. 'The equipment was a test-set build within the unit. The approach was recommended, and developed by one of our warrant officers. A portable package that could be quickly put into an available aircraft was the goal. The army and intel community lacked such a capability.' The ethos of the unit was one of lateral thinking, finding new ways of doing the job that best fitted the requirements for each particular mission. 'It continued the approach that evolved in FOG,' one former officer said. 'Improve upon existing tactics, techniques and equipment by identifying the need, using our ingenuity, incorporating off-the-shelf equipment.'[17]

The scanners on board the Huey helicopter raced through the frequencies looking for the ones the terrorists were on. Once they found them they could lock on to them and follow the Red Brigades' radio nets up and down the wavebands as they changed frequency. Other members of the Sigint team were on the ground in vehicles and in static locations looking for the terrorists' communications links, searching through any type of means of communication that might be in use. Details of all the frequencies, and the terrorist networks that were using them, were passed back to the National Security Agency at Fort Meade, Maryland, which tasked an Aquacade spy satellite above the Mediterranean to monitor the signals and help to pinpoint the Red Brigades' *covos*, their safe houses.[18]

At first the terrorists seemed to be in the ascendancy, freeing four female *brigatisti* in a spectacular breakout from a high-security prison at Rovigo, 45 miles south-east of Verona. But slowly the combined operation began to bear fruit. Early in January 1982, the police arrested four Red Brigades members in Milan and three in Padua.

On Monday 4 January, the Rome police arrested two of the group near the city's Spanish Steps. In their car they found a sub-machine gun, hand grenades, a sawn-off shotgun, and incriminating documents, as well as chain, locks and ether, a chemical the group used to immobilise its hostages. Two days later, Red Brigades terrorists tried to kidnap the deputy chief of Italy's anti-terrorist police, Nicola Simone, persuading him to open the door of his apartment in a repeat of the Dozier kidnapping. When he realised what was happening and pulled back, slamming the door, they shot through it, wounding him twice in the face, before fleeing. But the arrests led to more information, some in captured documents and some of it obtained under interrogation, a process the *brigatisti* sought fruitlessly to avoid by pronouncing themselves 'political prisoners'. Further arrests followed and, in the early hours of Saturday 9 January, the search team made their first major breakthrough. Police raided two Red Brigades hide-outs in a Rome suburb, arresting ten suspected terrorists, including Giovanni Senzani, a 42-year-old academic, an expert on criminology and the Italian legal system, who led one of the two factions within the Red Brigades. The other, more hardline, faction, led by Antonio Savasta, a former law student, had kidnapped Dozier, but crucially Savasta had sought Senzani's advice over how to interrogate the US general, even suggesting that the academic take charge of the 'people's trial'. Senzani had acted as the Red Brigades' chief interrogator in three of the gang's political kidnappings over the previous fifteen months. The police found a letter from him in which he suggested what tactics Savasta should use, while one of the other nine arrested was 28-year-old Franca Musi, who acted as a courier between the two factions. Three days later, the police arrested 27-year-old Massimiliano Corsi, an architecture student who had taken part in the attempt to kidnap the deputy chief of the anti-terrorist police and belonged to the same faction as Dozier's kidnappers. Declaring himself a 'political prisoner', Corsi refused to answer any questions. But with fourteen *brigatisti* arrested in the space of a few days, hopes were rising that they might soon find Dozier. Arrest followed arrest, dealing the biggest blow to the Red Brigades in their ten-year history.[19]

But the widespread police clampdown was producing evidence of far more than the Red Brigades' terror campaign. The police began to uncover signs that the terrorists had links to the Mafia's international weapons smuggling operations. This might well have been what led the Mafia to decide to help the Italian authorities to track Dozier down, with Franchino Restelli, the mafia godfather in the northern Italian city of Milan, allegedly ordering his cohorts, from his cell in the city's high-security San Vittore jail, to do everything they could to find the kidnappers' hide-out. Whatever the truth of the story, Restelli was later moved to a much more comfortable prison.[20]

By now the net was closing in on Savasta and his fellow kidnappers. A combination of information gathered during the arrests and an intelligence analysis produced by the Activity had narrowed the search down to three separate areas in the narrow triangle formed by the three northern Italian cities of Padua, Verona and Vicenza. There were Red Brigades transmitters active in all three areas. They were talking in veiled speech, using simple and fairly obvious references to try to disguise references to Dozier but they were very easy for the ISA crews to lock onto and locate. Then the Activity team tracked a transmitter on a yacht off Venice that was in regular contact with suspected Red Brigades terrorists in one of the areas pinpointed by the knob-turners – the drab Guizza district of Padua, just 48 miles away from where Dozier was kidnapped and home to many of the city's students. The yacht turned out to be owned by Dr Mario Frascella, a respected local physician who specialised in lung diseases.

Given the rough locations of districts where the US general might be held, the Activity's intelligence analysts carried out a study of electricity usage in recent months in all of the local houses and apartments, tapping the telephones of any house or apartment using unusual amounts of electricity. Eventually, on Tuesday 25 January, they found an apartment in Guizza where the power usage had suddenly increased on the day Dozier was kidnapped.[21]

After a few basic enquiries by the Italian police, the Activity team was certain they had found their man. The second-floor apartment, above a supermarket at No 2 Via Pindemonte, had been rented by Mario Frascella, the same doctor whose yacht was in radio contact with the suspected terrorists. Frascella had rented it for his 21-year-old daughter Emanuela, who was studying history at the University of Padua. Neighbours had been surprised by the large amounts of food the slim, single young woman seemed to buy and a newspaper vendor said that for the past six weeks or so she had purchased a large selection of different newspapers from him every morning. There was no doubt in the minds of those coordinating the search team that they had found the place where Jim Dozier was being held. The only question now was what approach to take on the rescue mission. The raid on the apartment was to be carried out by the *Nucleo Operativo Centrale di Sicurezza*, a crack police anti-terrorist snatch team set up three years earlier in the wake of the Moro killing and known as the Leatherheads after the all-leather balaclava-style helmets they wore. At first there was a suggestion they should go in that night but it was eventually decided to wait until morning.

As the neighbourhood around the eight-storey apartment block began to wake up and shoppers crowded into the supermarket, plain clothes police officers moved in, taking up strategic positions, blending into the local population, waiting for the Leatherheads. Shortly after eleven o'clock, undercover police disguised as construction workers began digging up the road outside the building, starting up a noisy bulldozer, causing a distraction. At precisely half past eleven, the Leatherheads moved in, dressed in scruffy jeans, masked in leather, protected by body armour and carrying their weapon of choice, the

Italian-made Beretta M-12 machine pistol. Half a dozen went through the front entrance and up the stairs, others scrambled up the fire escape at the rear of the building while several more armed police blocked any exit via the supermarket.

The raid was over inside a couple of minutes. As the Leatherhead assault team forced their way into the apartment, they encountered Giovanni Ciucci, a 32-year-old former railway worker who had just returned from the supermarket and was holding two plastic bags full of groceries. He was felled with a single karate chop. Savasta, alerted by the noise, ran to the small 6-foot-square tent in which Dozier had been kept chained and placed a silenced pistol to his head. But a police commando who had scrambled in through a rear window pistol-whipped the terrorist leader from behind before he could shoot and he fell to the floor dropping his gun. The three other terrorists, Emanuela Frascella; 26-year-old Rome nurse Emilia Libera, who was Savasta's girlfriend; and Cesare di Lenardo, a 22-year-old former construction worker, surrendered immediately. Not a shot had been fired. The execution of the mission by the Italian commandos was breathtakingly good. It was major triumph and only the second time in the Red Brigades' decade-long reign of terror that a hostage had been safely rescued by police. Afterwards, US officials were careful to attach all the credit to the Italian police, and not without justification. The Activity had been an important part of the rescue operation. But in keeping with the secrecy surrounding its missions, its role went unrecognized, in public at least.[22]

SIX WEEKS AFTER being snatched from his home by terrorists, the missing US general had been rescued unharmed. It was the Activity's first major success. But the same problems over who was in charge of special operations that had bedevilled the Iran rescue mission had clearly not gone away. The ridiculous turf war that preceded Operation Winter Harvest must not be allowed to happen again. 'We realized we had a fucking mess,' said Noel Koch, one of the few firm supporters of special operations forces inside the Pentagon. 'I raised hell [and said] we've got to change the way we're structured.'[23]

Koch began lobbying Weinberger to give special operations more clout. It was an uphill struggle. But a few months later, the budgets for special operations were increased with Ed Meyer and John Marsh, the Secretary for the Army, telling Congress that the terrorist threat required the army to ready 'specialized units to stop such lawless and inhumane activities as kidnapping and assassination'. Marsh said the emphasis would be on 'special operations forces, Ranger and airborne units and on our Special Forces in order to improve capabilities in the area of unconventional warfare.'[24]

The Activity was on the up and up but it wasn't just focusing on the terrorists. The Soviet threat remained at the heart of everything the US military did. Quite by chance, Jerry King's team were given the opportunity of obtaining all the intel the army needed on the Red Army's most important weapon, the T72 main battle tank. The US Army's troops were lined up in West Germany ready to face a Soviet invasion in which the T72 would be among the main threats. So Jerry King and his senior intelligence officer Tom O'Connell devised Operation Great Falcon, a scheme to persuade Iraq's Saddam Hussein to part with one of the T72s that he had been given by the Soviet Union. Iraq had received large stocks of weapons from Moscow but, after launching an attack on southern Iran, had become bogged down in a long war of attrition. It desperately needed more modern weapons but Moscow was refusing to play ball. Saddam was infuriated and when the opportunity suddenly presented itself, the Activity moved in.

'A source had been for possible recruitment and it was discovered that he had contacts in Iraq,' one former member of the unit said. 'Through him, Iraq's perceived critical need for long-range artillery was identified.' The contacts turned out to be at the highest level, Uday Hussein, the eldest son of the Iraqi dictator Saddam Hussein.

At a series of secret meetings in Washington and Europe, members of Jerry King's team met Iraqi representatives to haggle over a deal. The Iraqis desperately needed long-range artillery. So the Activity negotiators offered them the American M107 175mm self-propelled heavy howitzer, which could bring down heavy fire on positions 20 miles away and was ideal for what the Iraqis had in mind. 'It was common knowledge that the US Army had withdrawn the 175 from active service and was preparing to destroy or recycle them,' the former member of the unit said. 'The idea was born to "sell" the Iraqis the 175s with associated equipment. In exchange for the price of a couple of billion dollars, they would provide a T72.'

The Iraqis were so pleased with the deal, which was rubber-stamped by the US Joint Chiefs of Staff and Caspar Weinberger, the US Defense Secretary, that they also offered to throw in a Hind D helicopter gunship and a MiG25 fighter aircraft. The Hind gunship was being used by the Russians to good effect in Afghanistan. Obtaining one would have allowed the Americans to work out the best way of bringing them down, information that could have been passed on to the mujahideen by the CIA and its British equivalent MI6. But at the last minute, Saddam pulled out, afraid that it might be a double-deal too far for his Soviet sponsors. 'Other items were discussed but not agreed upon,' the former ISA member said. 'When it appeared the Iraqis were hesitating to fulfill their end of the bargain, the CO recommended to the Secretary of Defense for Intelligence, with representatives from CIA, that the operation be terminated. The CIA pushed hard that the channel to Iraq through Uday should not be severed and should be kept running. Based on their statements, they did not have any contacts in Iraq, especially at the level we were dealing, Saddam's elder son. Subsequently, this provided the US entrée into the regime.'[25]

JERRY KING WAS EAGER to get more missions for his team, whose unit crest carried the enthusiastic directive: 'Send me'. There were no shoulder flashes and, according to one former member of the unit, they rarely wore uniform. 'Generally, unit members wore civilian clothes,' he said. 'Uniforms were worn when the occasion called for them.' The Activity's motto was *Veritas Omnia Vincula Vincit*, Latin for 'Truth Conquers All Chains', and its crest depicted an eagle grasping a claymore – the traditional broadsword used by the medieval Scottish highlanders to repel the English invaders – and wrapped in a metal chain. The crest came about because a number of the leading members of the unit, including Jerry King, had Scottish ancestry. The outer frame of the crest was in the form of a leather belt normally worn around a kilt. One of the nine links in the chain was broken as a reminder of the failed Eagle Claw mission. Each of the eight other complete links represented one of the eight men who died at Desert One. The words 'Send Me' were inscribed on the blade of the claymore. It was a quotation from the Bible, Isaiah 6: 8: 'Also I heard the voice of the Lord, saying, "Whom shall I send, and who will go for us?" Then said I, "Here am I; send me".'[26]

Another early special mission the Activity took part in brought it into conflict with a man who would become a thorn in Jerry King's side. Lieutenant-Colonel James Longhofer was another member of the senior hierarchy for Operation Snow Bird. Short and squat, and pushy as hell, Longhofer was a distinguished helicopter pilot who had received a number of decorations for his service in Vietnam, including a Silver Star and three Distinguished Flying Crosses. He was appointed to head a new US Army staff department inside the Pentagon called the Army Special Operations Division, which despite its grand sounding name was intended to be just a small planning department. His new job was a reward for the good work he had done on Honey Badger, the air planning side of Snow Bird, the second Iran hostages mission. Longhofer had worked under General Vaught in the 24th Division and was brought into the planning for the second Iran rescue operation to look at the helicopter options available to get round the 'air lift' problem that led to the failure of the first mission. He helped to set up Task Force 160, getting hold of the MH60 Black Hawk helicopters used by the army's heliborne 101st Airborne Division and having them fitted with long-range fuel tanks that gave them a 1,200-mile range, 400 miles further than the Sea Stallions used in Eagle Claw. Like any front-line operator who gets assigned to a headquarters, he wasn't happy sitting behind a desk. But while most accept that someone has to do it, Jim Longhofer couldn't help but get involved on the ground in the missions he was supposed to be directing from a distance.

His brief as head of the Army Special Operations Division was to bypass the opponents of special operations and to get the job done, whatever it took. One of his team recalled that they had interpreted this as blanket clearance to do, within limits, whatever they thought necessary to achieve the mission. 'Push legalities to the outer limits. Stay generally within the rules and regulations if you can but first get the job done. We intentionally ignored the bureaucracy. We had to because whenever we dealt with the normal bureaucracy, it was immediately a giant roadblock. We were told: "We want twenty-seven signatures" and: "You can't do this." The impetus was why something could not be done as opposed to how to make it happen. Of course we were pissing off the internal army bureaucracy because we were totally avoiding them. We'd get a piece of paper signed by General Meyer and, wham, we'd stick this up some comptroller's ass. He'd invariably ask: "What's your justification for this?" And we'd simply say: "Fuck you. This piece of paper has the chief of staff's signature. You don't have to know. You just have to do this for me."'[27]

That attitude might have seemed to be justified by the otherwise impenetrable barriers put up by the army traditionalists, who opposed what they saw as the elitist, maverick behaviour of the special operations forces. But in practice it only served to reinforce, and in a sense justify, those prejudices. Hidden away in the basement underneath the army's operations centre at the end of the Pentagon's seventh corridor,

Longhofer's team called their offices 'the Zoo'. But to those who had to deal with them, they became known as 'the Crazies in the Basement'.[28]

The Night Stalkers of Task Force 160 which – aside from its thirty Black Hawks – had sixteen CH47 Chinook transport helicopters, twenty-eight OH6 Cayuse scout helicopters, and an AH6 Little Bird helicopter gunship, gave Longhofer all the lift he needed for conventional special operations missions. But he wanted a more covert force that could help to mount operations that only a selected few would know about. So he set up a top secret unit, called officially the First Rotary Wing Test Activity, but referred to during operations by the codename Sea Spray. He equipped it with a mix of civilian and military aircraft. This unit was originally to have been part of the Activity but Longhofer took it under his control. 'The first proposed organizational diagram for the Activity included an aviation component,' one former officer said. 'General Vaught, apparently with Longhofer's encouragement, elected to start the aviation element separately and stated it would be assigned to the Activity later. Sea Spray was a good idea but Longhofer failed to provide them with the manpower and tools to plan and conduct operations properly. As long as they lacked them, then Longhofer and his Department of Army cronies could act as the de facto commander and staff.'[29]

There was only one problem. Under a presidential executive order signed by Jimmy Carter in 1978, only the CIA was allowed to run operations that used bogus companies for covert missions. Ed Meyer's decision to keep Bill Casey on side now paid dividends. The Agency agreed to share Sea Spray. The army paid for the aircraft, using unofficial so-called 'black' funding siphoned off from conventional army budgets. But it was the CIA that actually bought them and provided Sea Spray with its cover in the form of a civilian proprietary company Aviation Tech Services. The bogus front company would eventually obtain a number of civilian Cessna and Beechcraft King Air light fixed-wing aircraft, which were all available for the use of either Longhofer's men or the CIA. Sea Spray's aircraft also included a number of Hughes 500MD Scout Defenders, based on the baby OH6 Cayuse reconnaissance helicopters that had been developed for the war in Vietnam. They were armed with machine guns and air-to-ground missiles and fitted with silenced tail rotors and collapsible skids capable of carrying four special operations 'shooters' on each side. The skids had been devised by King's planning team for the second Iranian hostage rescue. The Scout Defenders could fly at 140 miles an hour in total darkness, skimming above the trees using sophisticated forward-looking infra-red radar to see where they were going. The Sea Spray aircraft were largely based at Fort Eustis, Virginia, with others kept in Tampa ready for the military and CIA covert operations in Latin America that would proliferate during Reagan's presidency.[30]

It was Sea Spray that provided the Activity with another of its early missions. Bashir Gemayel, the most powerful Christian leader among Lebanon's warring factions, flew to Washington DC for secret talks with the CIA in August 1981. Civil war had broken out in Lebanon six years earlier between the Christian minority, who under French occupation had occupied most of the important seats in government, and the Muslims, leaving the once cosmopolitan capital Beirut in ruins. By early 1981, Gemayel had ruthlessly eliminated any Christian leader who posed a threat to his leadership and had provoked a quarrel with Syria. With Phalangist troops using weapons provided by Israel to fight Syrian troops and PLO forces based in southern Lebanon attacking Israel with Katyusha rockets, there was a risk of the civil war escalating into a full-scale Middle East conflict. So America stepped in and, using the CIA and others, began holding secret talks with all sides. There were now credible reports that the Syrians were planning to assassinate Gemayel. Having got him to agree to an interim ceasefire in return for money, arms and support, no one at Langley was anxious to see him killed off. The plan was that he should fly first to Cairo on board a US Army Gulfstream executive jet normally used for transporting generals. Sea Spray would then take over, flying Gemayel and his entourage to Junieh, the Phalangist stronghold north of Beirut, in two heavily armed Scout Defender helicopters.

The mission, codenamed Project Otto, involved complicated co-ordination with both the Egyptians and the Israelis while the Activity's Sigint experts searched the wave bands for anyone seeking to attack the helicopters. Activity communications experts were also assigned to the mission because Sea Spray lacked any form of command communication. Despite the fact that he was supposed to be driving a desk back in his basement offices in the Pentagon, Longhofer took active control on the ground, sending one of his officers to Tel Aviv to liaise with the Israelis, and another to the Egyptian Air Force base at al-Arish, close to the border with Israel, where the helicopters would be refuelled. He meanwhile monitored the entire operation from the roof of the US embassy in Cairo with an Activity liaison officer alongside him to keep him up to date with what was going on. The ISA man had satellite communications to stay in touch with the latest intel and was recording all the comms, a standard operating procedure. Taping all of the radio communications would allow swift verification of what was said and would also be useful for after-action reviews. Longhofer's response when he saw the tape recorder appears to have been sparked by a paranoid belief that Jerry King was out to get him and was likely to use the tape against him if anything went wrong. He refused to listen to the argument from the Activity communications officer that it was no more than a routine procedure and insisted it be turned off. 'Young man,' he said. 'This is a CIA operation. You can either turn off that tape recorder or I'll throw it off the roof.' Longhofer also insisted that the ISA comms were shut down once Gemayel was dropped off at Junieh, a move King regarded as designed to prevent his team from doing their job. It was the start of what would, for Longhofer and his 'Crazies in the Basement', become a bitter and obsessive rivalry with the Activity in general and Jerry King in particular.[31]

3 INAPPROPRIATE ACTION

EVERYONE IN LA CEIBA knew the place where the US aerial survey team lived was well guarded and no one was stupid enough to try to break in. The people of the northern Honduran port were used to *norteamericanos* – there were more than 100 working there in the local banana industry. But none of those were quite so well guarded as the men living in 'Quebec', a large six-bedroomed house on the edge of the city. Armed guards wearing blue windcheaters and baseball caps and carrying Uzi machine guns patrolled the grounds 24/7. But the members of the survey team didn't seem too worried about their own security. There were beach barbecues with lobster, steaks and beer flown in from the States, and regular trips up into the Nombre de Dios mountains that towered above La Ceiba, rising steeply from the Caribbean coast. The security clearly wasn't for the *norteamericanos*. The local consensus was that the Uzi-toting guards were protecting something else, something inside the house.[1]

The local consensus was right. The house was full of top secret equipment. The *norteamericanos*, and the Beechcraft King Air 100 aircraft they flew in endless figure eights across southern Honduras, were not conducting aerial surveys at all. They were US intelligence operators, members of Jerry King's Intelligence Support Activity, knob-turners from his electronic surveillance team, while their guards were from Delta. No one was interested in mapping out Honduran territory. This was a covert operation by a unit that in theory didn't even exist. The knob-turners were monitoring the communications of the Salvadoran left-wing rebel coalition, the Faribundo Marti Liberation Front (FMLN), which was undermining the government of President José Napoleón Duarte, a Christian Democrat who although originally part of a junta subsequently won surprisingly free and fair presidential elections. The Reagan administration was determined El Salvador must not become another Soviet satellite state. So someone had to provide Duarte's men with the intel that would help them to beat the rebels. The CIA and the NSA couldn't help. But the boys from the Activity could. Hidden from everyone, their existence unknown even to Congress, they were producing some incredible stuff, intercepting plans for virtually every rebel attack and ambush, which were then passed on to the US Army Special Forces who were advising the Salvadoran military commanders.

The attention of the American people had first focused on El Salvador fourteen months earlier, in December 1981, when four American women, three nuns and a lay missionary, were murdered by right-wing death squads just outside the capital San Salvador. The murder of the four American women led the Carter administration temporarily to cut off military aid to the Duarte government. A month later, two US lawyers working for the Salvadoran government were killed when gunmen walked into the restaurant of the Sheraton Hotel and shot them. Robert White, the US ambassador to El Salvador, was unequivocal that the death squads were to blame. 'I don't believe a reasonable man can come up with any other conclusion than that right-wing hit squads enjoy some kind of relationship with some people in the security forces who, at least until now, have given them some kind of immunity,' he said. On 11 January, with the Reagan administration waiting to take over the reins of power, the FMLN announced a 'final offensive' designed to topple the government and launched a series of attacks in which hundreds of people were killed. Duarte responded by declaring martial law and the Carter administration, still in power if only just, approved the shipment of $5 million in 'urgently needed arms and ammunition' to the Duarte government.[2]

Once the Reagan administration was sworn in, it published a dossier accusing the Soviet Union, Cuba and Nicaragua of giving 'clandestine military support' and 200 tons of arms to the FMLN. 'Their objective in El Salvador, as elsewhere, is to bring about – at little cost to themselves – the overthrow of the established government and the imposition of a Communist regime in defiance of the will of the Salvadoran people,' the dossier said. 'The foregoing record leaves little doubt that the Salvadoran insurgency has become the object of a large-scale commitment by Communist states outside Latin America. In short, over the past year, the insurgency in El Salvador has been progressively transformed into a textbook case of indirect armed aggression by Communist powers through Cuba.'[3]

That a US administration should show such great interest in the future of a foreign country the size of Massachusetts was not as surprising as it might at first seem. America has regarded control over Latin America as vital to its security interests since the 1823 proclamation of the Monroe Doctrine, which warned European countries not to interfere in the continent's affairs. That had re-emerged during the 1980 presidential elections with the failure of the Carter administration to prevent the Sandinista takeover in Nicaragua, and the idea that this was another domino falling to Soviet influence, forming a key plank of Ronald Reagan's election campaign. Hardliners within the Reagan camp were arguing that there was no point in supporting the Duarte regime, which was deemed to be weak. The hawks believed that the death squads, controlled by Roberto d'Aubuisson, a former Salvadoran national guard intelligence officer, had more chance of seeing off the left-wing rebels. But the killings of the seven Americans by the death squads and Duarte's commitment to democracy meant that backing d'Aubuisson was out of the question. Bill Casey persuaded President Reagan to sign a National Security Decision Directive authorising the CIA to start pouring funds into Duarte's Christian Democratic party and the pro-Duarte unions and cooperatives in order to strengthen the Salvadoran president's hand ahead of the democratic elections promised for March 1982. The White House also sent more than fifty troops to El Salvador, mainly Army Special Forces and Delta instructors to train up the government troops. President Reagan said he was determined to stop the dominos from falling before they reached America itself. 'The terrorists aren't just aiming at El Salvador,' he said. 'They are aiming at the whole of Central and possibly later South America and, I'm sure, eventually North America. What we're doing is trying to stop this destabilizing force of guerrilla warfare and revolution from being exported in here.'[4]

US military involvement in El Salvador was not popular at home, in part because of the legacy of the Vietnam War – the US involvement there had begun with the dispatch of a small number of military advisers – but largely as a result of the ruthlessness of d'Aubuisson's death squads, whose murders far outweighed those committed by the FMLN. Nevertheless, the conflict played a crucial part in the rebirth of US special operations forces. The special operations missions carried out in El Salvador allowed the lessons learned in Vietnam to be put into practice and crucial new lessons to be learned. Sometimes, as a result of the damage done to special operations in the years since Vietnam, old lessons had also to be relearned. It was a crucial – and it is sometimes forgotten, ultimately highly successful – campaign that formed a useful template for what the US military calls Foreign Internal Defense (FID) missions, essentially assisting an allied country in counter-insurgency operations, a key role for US special operations forces. FID is much more than simply about providing the military of the country that is being supported with weapons. The British had shown in Malaya in the 1950s and in Oman during the 1970s that the key to winning the battle against an insurgency was much more to do with psychology – or as the British SAS put it 'winning hearts and minds' – as it was to do with military firepower. The main thrust of a counter-insurgency operation should be aimed at denying the guerrillas the access to the local population they need to provide them with support, particularly in the form of food and shelter, while at the same time improving the lot of the local people in order to wean them away from their support for the rebels and the widespread belief that a defeat for government forces would somehow make life better for them.[5]

The FMLN deliberately set out to capitalise on the poor living standards enjoyed by the Salvadoran population, and the experience of repression under a succession of military juntas, using their attacks to exacerbate the situation and at all times seeking to reinforce the impression that since the terrorist attacks were a result of the government policy they were therefore the fault of the government. The FMLN aim was not to capture territory but rather to capture the minds of 'the masses'. Once the revolution was complete all the problems of society would go away. The rebels were operating in fertile territory. The infant mortality rate was high, and thousands of Salvadorans had been forced to cross into Honduras to find a means of earning a living. The right-wing death squads were increasing the feeling of repression and in reality were the terrorists' greatest ally. They needed to be eradicated, not supported as some in the Reagan administration suggested. They were part of the problem, not part of the solution. Worse, they included many members of the armed forces. In short, El Salvador was an intractable problem.[6]

The main thrust of the overt US support was provided by US Army Special Forces and Delta officers and NCOs. This took the form of a two-pronged approach involving training of Salvadoran soldiers in counter-insurgency tactics, both inside El Salvador and at bases in Honduras, Panama and the United States itself, and the positioning of Special Forces officers in the actual army command structure as Operations, Plans, and Training (OPAT) advisors. Ostensibly, there was a limit of fifty-five placed by Congress on the number of US soldiers in El Salvador. But in fact many more were involved because mobile training teams could come in and out of the country, staying for up to three months without counting in the figure of fifty-five. They provided training for the Salvadoran Army, which was in an appalling state. There were around 9,000 troops, mostly infantry, organised into four brigades. The officer corps was split between those who backed Duarte and the need for reforms and those who supported the death squads. The enlisted men, many of whom had been press-ganged, had virtually no training at all and what they did have was entirely based around conventional army tactics. They had no com-prehension of how to deal with an insurgency.[7]

The Salvadoran forces tended towards a nine-to-five mentality and the use of indiscriminate force in large-scale 'jungle-bashing' opera-tions. There was a huge temptation, given the relative lack of firepower of the FMLN, to use overwhelming force to attack the guerrillas. 'We initially adopted a traditional military approach of meeting force with greater force,' one US Army Special Forces officer said. 'This was like driving your fist into a bucket of water. You put your fist in, twirl it around and when you'd withdrawn it there was no evidence that you had ever been there. We then changed our policy to develop a more political campaign where influencing the people was seen as the key.' The US trainers began to place emphasis on large numbers of small-scale 24-hour-a-day heliborne patrols – which denied the FMLN access to the local population – and on the need to avoid excessive force and collateral damage that would alienate the ordinary people.[8]

A key factor at the start of the battle to win hearts and minds was Duarte's promise to hold elections in March 1982 followed by economic reforms that would improve living standards. But the continuing FMLN attacks and the activities of the death squads were undermining electoral support for the president and threatening to push the majority towards d'Aubuisson. There was also a need to cut the rebels off from their source of weapons supplies, which according to the Reagan administration were coming across the border from Nicaragua, where the Sandinistas were also providing safe bases from which the FMLN could mount cross-border raids. Thomas Enders, Assistant Secretary of State for Latin American Affairs, said in early 1982 that clandestine infiltration of arms and munitions was 'again approaching the high levels recorded before last year's offensive'. In the face of criticism from Democratic congressmen, he was adamant that America had to act. 'There is no mistaking that the decisive battle for Central America is underway in El Salvador,' he said. 'If after Nicaragua, El Salvador is captured by a violent minority, who in Central America would not live in fear? How long would it be before major strategic United States interests – the Panama Canal, sea lanes, oil supplies – were at risk?'[9]

The CIA had a large number of men on the ground in El Salvador but no technical resources to intercept the rebel radio communications. So it turned to the National Security Agency at Fort Meade. The success of the British SAS in turning around the guerrilla war in Oman had relied on good intelligence supplied by small teams of British army human intelligence and signals intelligence operators. A lot of guerrilla communications were low power, and therefore difficult to intercept without close-in signals intelligence operators like the SAS had in Oman. The guerrillas also had little understanding of communications security. So any intercept operation would uncover extensive details of their operations and hideaways, producing an intelligence bonanza for the Salvadoran Army that would be likely to swing the war back in Duarte's favour, with the added bonus of providing intelligence on Nicaragua that could be passed to the Contras, the CIA-backed rebels who were fighting the Sandinista government. But the NSA couldn't help. It relied on armed forces units to provide the kind of close-in monitoring that was required to track the FMLN and so it passed the request on to Bill Odom, Assistant Chief of Staff for Intelligence, who had direct operational control over the Activity and ordered Jerry King to get a Sigint operation up and running.[10]

The best way of tracking the FMLN and Sandinista communications was to use an aerial platform, so King had to turn to Sea Spray, which leased a fixed-wing Beechcraft King Air 100 aircraft, respraying it and covering it in the logos of a civilian aerial survey company. The Beechcraft was then fitted out with the latest interception equipment, including frequency-scanning radios and direction-finding equipment, by Sanders Associates, a specialist producer of electronic warfare systems based in Nashua, New Hampshire. The Activity, referred to only by the codename for its special access programme Royal Cape, worked with Sanders Associates to eliminate problems that had cropped up during Operation Winter Harvest, the mission to rescue Jim Dozier from the Italian Red Brigades. Using Sea Spray aircraft left the Activity reliant on Jim Longhofer, which given his attitude towards the unit was not ideal and would later cause problems, but without its own integral air element, it had no choice.

Jerry King's men were expanding their operations in Central America and another signals intelligence operation there, codenamed Graphic Book, was ongoing. Since Queen's Hunter was only expected to last for thirty days to cover the run-up to the elections, Cal Sasai switched some of the operators from Graphic Book to carry it out. They initially operated out of a rented house in San Pedro Sula, the second biggest city in Honduras, with the Sea Spray pilots based in a hotel. But the operation was spectacularly successful, revealing a large number of rebel hide-outs; the arms smuggling routes into El Salvador; details of a number of planned rebel attacks and much more. The knob-turners found a wealth of highly productive radio nets across the wavebands that also included those not only of the Sandinista troops assisting the FMLN but also those fighting the US-backed Contras. They also turned up a lot of intelligence on the few small and largely ineffective rebel organisations operating inside Honduras itself. Members of the team were irritated that this success was later claimed by Sea Spray, which merely provided the aircraft and pilots. But they had all been warned before they joined the Activity that their exploits would never be publicly recognised and those that mattered within the US intelligence community knew that the success was down to Royal Cape, even if many of them didn't know precisely what Royal Cape was.

THE NSA WAS extremely pleased with what it called 'the take' from Queen's Hunter, which was extended first for another sixty days and then – once the scope of its intercept operations, in particular against the Sandinistas, was realised – expanded to include a number of other Beechcraft King Air 100s. The operation also had to be moved north to La Ceiba to prevent too many questions being asked and was given a new codename, Quiet Falcon. The aircraft flew criss-crossing the borders with El Salvador and Nicaragua for at least six hours a day with some averaging 1,500 hours in the air a year. The 'take' was passed on to the Salvadoran and Honduran armed forces and to CIA and Special Forces officers on the ground in both countries – preventing at least fifteen rebel ambushes. The CIA also passed relevant intelligence on Nicaragua to the Contras until the Boland Amendment, which banned intelligence support to the anti-Sandinista forces, was passed in December 1982. All the Activity's El Salvador 'take' was relayed back to the Fort Meade headquarters of the National Security Agency. 'The unit enjoyed a very good working relation with the NSA,' one former member said. 'Following one operation, NSA reported that the small team collected 95 per cent of the tactical intelligence on Nicaragua, and it was done for less than the cost of three flights of a conventional asset. Not bad for a bunch of upstarts.'[11]

That 'upstart' attitude from other parts of the US military undoubtedly served to bond the members of the Activity together as a team. There is always rivalry between elite units – Delta and the US

Rangers referred to the Activity as 'the Secret Army of North Virginia' because of the intense secrecy surrounding its operations and the closeness of its base to Washington and the Pentagon, deemed essential if it was to react and deploy as swiftly as it often needed to do. The members of the Activity revelled in the back-handed compliment that such rivalry represented. But its senior officers were concerned at the far more serious attitude of Jim Longhofer and his cohorts in the Army Special Operations Division. It was not just damaging and corrosive. It was downright dangerous and, given that the Activity had to work with Longhofer and his men very closely, quite likely to get someone killed.

The simmering dispute blew up into a major row when the Army Special Operations Division decided to have a $7,500, 15-foot satellite television dish set up in the grounds of the new house outside La Ceiba. Having moved out of their hotel, the Sea Spray pilots were upset they could no longer watch US television shows. The Activity team at La Ceiba were astonished. They were operating one of the most secret and clandestine missions being carried out by anyone in the US military and a 15-foot satellite dish that was bound to show up on the imagery from the Soviet surveillance satellites had been erected right beside the house. It was like a big signpost saying: 'Look, a secret US signals interception team is based here.' Not only that, it wasn't even required for operational communications. It was to allow the Sea Spray pilots to keep up to date with what was going on in the latest episode of *Dallas*. Jerry King blew his top and confronted Longhofer with the stupidity of his action. When the Army Special Operations Division chief refused to back down, King took it to the generals, along with the US satellite imagery of La Ceiba. Before the satellite dish was brought in, you couldn't tell the Activity's base from any of the other houses along the coastal road. Afterwards, the satellite dish showed up as a big round white circle. It was unmistakable. 'When they saw the overhead photos, they ordered its immediate removal,' one former ISA officer said. 'Unfortunately the damage had already been done.'[12]

JERRY KING DIDN'T need this. He already had enough on his plate. The ISA was under investigation by the Pentagon Inspector-General while at the same time he was getting a hard time over its involvement in a scheme to try to find missing American soldiers allegedly still held as POWs in Laos and Vietnam. It was an affair that would lead the carefully constructed covert existence of the Activity to unravel. During testimony to a Congressional committee just over a year later, Lieutenant-Colonel 'Bo' Gritz, a heavily decorated veteran of Special Forces operations in Vietnam, explained how he had been recruited, by an organisation he would name only as 'the Activity', to go into Laos and look for US POWs still being held there.[13]

'I was approached by a member of a special intelligence activity,' he said. 'I was advised that the Activity shortly hoped to obtain the charter for the rescue of American POWS and was invited to participate in its operation. The Activity was a field unit and would have put an American across into Laos to verify, using various recording means, the presence of Americans thought to be at specified locations.' Admiral Allen G Paulson, Assistant Vice-Director of Collection Management at the Defense Intelligence Agency, confirmed to the hearing that a military organisation had at one point 'proposed an operation, using Mr Gritz in a collection capacity'.[14]

Gritz, who had achieved a good deal of notoriety as a result of a series of private missions to south-east Asia to look for MIAs (US soldiers missing in action), claimed that it all began back in October 1978, when he was serving at the Pentagon. Lieutenant-General Harold Aaron, the Deputy Director of the Defense Intelligence Agency, had come into his office and said: 'Bo, we have overwhelming evidence now that Americans are being held against their will by the communists in Asia. I want you to consider early retirement so that you might do through the private sector what we have been politically handcuffed from doing by the Carter administration.' It was that conversation that led to his private missions to rescue the US POWs, Gritz said.[15]

Reports of missing Americans still held prisoner in south-east Asia had divided the military community with many believing fervently that both politicians and senior officers would rather the boys stayed behind the wire rather than have them rescued and rekindle bad memories of the war in Vietnam. Most of the reports of POWs still held captive were in any event lacking in detail. But in 1979, a DIA agent in Laos claimed that eighteen captured Americans had been moved to a cave north of the Laotian town of Nhommarath. At least one was believed to be a captured US pilot. His account was convincing, it appeared to be confirmed by satellite imagery, and he passed a lie detector test. It was nowhere near enough to justify a rescue operation with all the opposition both within the senior military hierarchy and the Carter administration that this would entail, but then in December 1980, more evidence emerged of American MIAs being held prisoner at Nhommarath. A CIA agent codenamed W1, an elderly woman with close ties to the communist leadership in the Laotian capital Vientiane, reported that about thirty US pilots were working on a road gang near Nhommarath and that a POW camp had recently been built outside the town. Later that month, a Thai signals intelligence station intercepted a radio message that ordered officials in southern Laos to fly US POWs up to the central area.[16]

On the same day, satellite imagery of the Nhommarath camp, tasked as a direct result of W1's report, turned up what appeared to be a remarkable message, apparently spelled out in what were thought to be red tiles. The message allegedly read: 'B 52 SOS POW K', although accounts differed and the only consistent item in the various accounts of the message was the figure 52. The camp at Nhommarath became known as the '52 on the ground' camp. The B52, or simply 52 depending on which version you believed, was thought to be a reference to the downed crew of an aircraft, tying in with both the human intelligence reports of captured pilots. The message behind SOS and POW was obvious, the K was said to be the signal to tip off search aircraft that a pilot was down and alive.

Shortly after President Reagan came into office, he was briefed on the intelligence and shown the satellite photographs of the '52 on the ground' camp. He is reported to have said: 'We've got to get them home', and a top secret mission to retrieve the airmen was put in place. Gritz received a call from a senior DIA official telling him of official plans, sanctioned by the President, to use Delta to rescue the prisoners at Nhommarath and asking him to put his own private missions on hold so as not to interfere with them. A sceptical Gritz checked out with his own contacts at Delta as to whether or not Operation Velvet Hammer, as it was allegedly called, was in fact being prepared and they confirmed it was.[17] That an operation was put in place is not in doubt. Eric Haney was a member of the Delta team that began practising a mission to bring home the men believed to be held prisoner at Nhommarath. 'Delta Force initiated planning to conduct a rescue operation,' Haney said. 'We worked very rapidly. By the summer of 1981 we were ready to launch.' But then the senior DIA official called Gritz to tell him that Velvet Hammer had been called off after a reconnaissance mission by Laotian mercenaries working for the CIA failed to turn up any evidence that Americans were held at the Nhommarath camp.[18]

'At that point in time, Dan Myer, an agent, whom I had known for more than 20 years, approached me in Los Angeles and said that he couldn't identify his organization but they wanted me to continue the POW rescue mission under their authority,' Gritz claimed. 'He confided that his organization had been observing Velvet Hammer through the Joint Chiefs of Staff, and that they should have had it all along. He told me that they wanted me to continue the operation, working for them as a principal agent.'[19]

A former ISA officer dismissed this as 'bullshit'. Dan Myer was a member of the Activity at the time but he had been at a convention for ex-members of the Vietnam War SOG teams in Las Vegas when he heard Gritz talking about rescuing MIAs. 'Needless to say POWs were a hot topic with many in the military, especially with Special

Forces,' the ex-ISA officer said. 'We were privy to some reports and photos of certain sites in Laos but we were never told that JSOC was planning an operation.' There was some debate among the unit's senior officers over what to do. 'We discussed the matter at length. We were not trying to take over all responsibility for POW rescues in south-east Asia. We concluded that an ad hoc effort, such as that being bantered about by Gritz, did not have a high probability for success. If such an attempt was to be mounted it should be done with the full support of the US Government and the best troops and equipment available. Oh, deep down, we would like to be the ones to launch a rescue but we fully realized that Delta was the better candidate for such an undertaking. Several members of the unit knew of Gritz and did not hold him in high esteem. It was decided that we needed to preclude him from blowing a potential operation with a premature solo effort, secondly, we were extremely interested in Gritz's alleged numerous contacts in the region. It was our intention to learn the identities of his contacts, evaluate them and, if promising, take them over.'[20]

Dan Myer then spoke again to Gritz, who was suspicious of the approach but discussed it with contacts in Washington. They confirmed that Myer was on the level and worked for a secret military intelligence unit. 'It was known as the ISA, Intelligence Support Activity,' Gritz said. 'Even the initials were Top Secret – Special Intelligence because Congress did not know about it. ISA was commanded by Jerry King. His code name was "Cranston". I met again with Dan Myer, the agent for ISA, who became my case officer. When I mentioned ISA to him he was literally dumbfounded. We were meeting in a motel room on Century Boulevard. He had been tape-recording all that we had said, as was routine. He told me: "I've got to erase this part of the tape because absolutely no one is supposed to know the initials of the organization outside of headquarters." I agreed to work through ISA.'[21]

Gritz claimed to have had frequent meetings with Jerry King, as well as with CIA liaison officers. One former ISA officer involved in the operation said King himself only attended one of the meetings and if Gritz had any meetings with CIA officers it was done without the knowledge of anyone in the Activity. But Gritz said there were a series of meetings 'in the Red Carpet room at the National Airport in Washington DC, in safe houses, apartments, and hotel rooms to plan the rescue of American prisoners of war'.[22]

'The meetings were used to map out an organization that would include agents within the Soviet Union, the People's Republic of China, North Korea, Vietnam, Laos, Cambodia, Malaysia, Indonesia, and Thailand,' Gritz said. 'I was to direct this organization to collect information.' In fact, the former ISA officer said, the discussions were all designed by the Activity to find out where Gritz's agents were and whether they might produce valid and useful intelligence on the POWs issue.[23]

In a colourful account of the alleged preparations for his mission to Laos, Gritz said that he was given the codename Bear and his wife Claudia, who was to play a bit part in the handover of documents and thousands of dollars, was codenamed Little Bear. 'She was to meet an ISA agent in a specified aisle in the Rosslyn suburb Safeway,' Gritz said. 'After an exchange of signs and counter-signs, the agent turned over a grocery sack full of documents and money. Beside the packages of banded $100 bills was a sealed envelope containing three US passports with my photo, but a different name.' Gritz also claimed that at a meeting in Tucson, Arizona, Myer had given him 'a huge red suitcase containing a do-it-yourself spy kit, including cameras, code machines and portable polygraph.' In total, he claimed to have been given $40,000; two cameras; polygraph equipment; radio communications equipment; 'ISA code machines using a Diana one-time pad system'; maps; classified aerial photographs; air tickets to Bangkok and several telephone numbers for the ISA, including one Washington number 'which I was instructed to call in the event of "difficulties".'[24]

But the former ISA officer dismissed suggestions that Gritz was ever given any false documents, much less $40,000. 'That's untrue,' he said. 'It's all bullshit. We would not trust Gritz with that much money. He was provided with one camera, with fixed focus, and a broken polygraph machine. Nothing else was provided to him. We were trying to buy time in the hope that he would better identify his contacts. But we had begun to believe that he did not have any contacts worthwhile in the region and increasingly thought he simply enjoyed the limelight and was trying to obtain funds from us.'[25]

The phoney ISA operation was given a codename, Grand Eagle, and was supposedly due to begin in December 1981, when Gritz would cross into Laos accompanied by Laotian mercenaries who had worked for the CIA. He was also obtaining funding from private individuals, allegedly including Ross Perot. (Others who would later provide financial backing for Gritz and his private missions included the actors Clint Eastwood and William Shatner.) But Jerry King and other members of the Activity were rapidly coming to realise that Gritz was 'a loose cannon' who could not be controlled.[26]

King attempted to have him brought back into the army so that he could at least have some degree of control over him. 'I don't recall the date, but we learned that Gritz was coming to DC to testify before a Congressional Committee or sub-committee,' a former ISA officer said. 'Jerry King informed Bill Odom and the next day Odom rang him and ordered him to terminate all contact with Gritz. Odom, who had been periodically updated on our efforts with Gritz, concluded, as we did, that Bo was a loose cannon. The CO warned Bill Odom that if we terminated Gritz ASAP, there was the distinct potential that he, Gritz, would go public. He requested permission that we be permitted to string Gritz along and sever our contact over time. Odom denied the request. At this point, the CO suggested another alternative: bring him back on active duty where he would be subject to military discipline. We thought the threat of a court martial would terminate his propensity to talk.'[27]

Gritz painted an entirely different picture of what was going on, claiming that King fully backed his missions, and alleging that the Activity commander told him: 'Bo, I've been ordered to put Operation Grand Eagle back on the shelf as if it never existed. There are too many bureaucrats here in Washington DC who don't want to see American prisoners of war come home alive.' He also claimed that King told him to continue with the search for missing POWs. 'Press on and stay in touch with us,' he quoted King as saying. 'We'll continue to do all we can to help you.'[28]

But former ISA officers dismiss any suggestion that they wanted the operation to continue or that King would have said any such thing. 'It was never our intent to send Gritz into Laos,' one said. 'Our plan was to cut him out once we knew and made contact with his alleged Thai contacts. The colonel informed him he had been directed to terminate all contact with him and requested he return the equipment that had been provided to him. He never did return it. The CO did not discuss any further activities with him and definitely did not offer support for an ad hoc endeavor.' Whatever the truth of the affair it was to have a devastating effect on the Activity's reputation, leading to an investigation that nearly brought its short life to a close.[29]

THE INSPECTOR-GENERAL'S REPORT into the Activity was a strange mix. It argued with some justification that the unit was 'watched insufficiently closely' for the first year of its existence, when it existed without a Presidential Finding, authorisation that it ought to have had under the law. But it also criticised the Activity for 'supporting ill-advised schemes'. This appeared to refer to equipment that the Inspector-General felt the Activity should never have wasted money on. But in fact it was an irrelevance. The 'ill-advised' acquisitions included a hot-air balloon, which had been discarded by an army unit, so could scarcely have been an abuse of funds by the Activity. 'The balloon belonged to the army and they were about to discard it,' a former ISA officer said. 'We wanted to see if we could use it as a lift device for parachute training. The British had a jump school training programme where a balloon was used for the first couple of practice jumps. It didn't work out, too unstable, and difficult to maintain a pre-determined altitude.'[30]

The other pieces of equipment the report complained about were a dune buggy – properly and indeed sensibly acquired during the FOG's preparations for a second Iran hostage rescue mission – similar buggies were used by allied special operations forces during the 1991 Gulf War – and, most controversially, a Rolls-Royce saloon. This had been obtained from the Drug Enforcement Agency, which had confiscated it from drugs smugglers. Arguably the Rolls should have been disposed of and the money put to better use. But there was a belief among some of the Activity's staff that it might be useful in the event of a counter-terrorist operation in an unfriendly country. The Rolls could have been disguised as the car of a prominent politician or personality and used to transport Delta troops surreptitiously to the scene of the anti-terrorist operation. Given that this was one of the plans put forward later for the rescue of terrorist hostages in Lebanon, it was scarcely as frivolous a possession as the Pentagon Inspector-General suggested. He could also not understand why the Activity needed to set up private companies like a refrigeration plant in Panama as cover for its activities. Despite the report's flaws, it was right in concluding that the Activity needed proper Congressional oversight of its missions and accounts, as would later emerge.[31]

The Inspector-General's report seriously damaged the Activity's reputation at the top of the Pentagon, leading Caspar Weinberger, the US Defense Secretary, to order the unit's disbandment within a month.[32] In a memorandum to the Deputy Under-Secretary for Policy dated 26 May 1982, Frank C Carlucci, Deputy Defense Secretary, set about the Activity, describing the Inspector-General's report as 'disturbing in the extreme'. However, intense lobbying by Bill Odom saved the ISA to fight another day, and his arguments in favour of Jerry King's team, who could scarcely be blamed for the main problem, the lack of presidential authorisation, were reflected, albeit tersely, in Carlucci's memo. But the Deputy Defense Secretary's tone elsewhere suggested that he had doubts as to whether it was all worth it and laid out some pretty firm conditions if the Activity was going to continue to exist.

'We seem to have created our own CIA,' he said. 'But like Topsy, uncoordinated and controlled. Unquestionably, ISA contains much talent, and probably even more dedication. There may also be a need, but that is less clear. But we should have learned the lessons of the 70's on controls over [three or four words missing, censored out]. Accountability is the essence and we have created an organisation that is unaccountable. Action will be taken to terminate all ISA operations within 30 days; or effect transfer thereof to other competent organizations. If it is desired to continue ISA in some form, the following will be submitted for my approval not later than 15 June.

A concept plan.

A list of requirements.

A command structure, indicating to whom it is accountable and how.

A list of controls to be established, particularly over [two or three words censored out].

A fiscal management and accountability plan.

A program for working with appropriate committees of Congress.

A funding plan, fully coordinated with the Comptroller.

The concurrence of the DCI and the General Counsel for all of the above.'[33]

THE GRITZ TESTIMONY and leaks by opponents within the military who hoped to hammer the final nails into the Activity's coffin led to the unit's existence bursting into the open. It emerged that by the time of Carlucci's memo, the Activity had carried out ten missions, of varying importance, two of which had been commissioned by Bill Casey, giving the lie to the, often conflicting, leaks from inside the Pentagon that the CIA had no knowledge of the unit, or did and was opposed to its existence.

The most significant missions were the signals intelligence operations in Italy and Honduras; the operation to get Bashir Gemayel back into Lebanon; the attempt to trade weapons for a Soviet T72 tank with Iraq; and the brief and damaging liaison with Gritz. The Activity had also carried out so-called 'black hat' penetration surveys of the US embassies in El Salvador, Guatemala and Nicaragua to test security, and developed 're-entry/relief support plans' to evacuate or rescue US personnel from the embassies if it became necessary; mounted an operation in Panama to monitor President Manuel Antonio Noriega using the refrigeration company as a cover; provided training, alongside Delta personnel, for a new Saudi Arabian National Guard 'Special Purpose Detachment' set up to conduct anti-terrorist and 'special security' operations and to provide additional protection for members of the Saudi royal family; and sent a small team of bomb disposal and security experts to Khartoum to set up a scheme to protect the Sudanese President Gaafar Numeiry from an expected assassination attempt ordered by Libyan leader Muammar Gaddafi. Delta also helped Numeiry's bodyguards, providing security training. In return for their contribution, the Activity received good intelligence on Libyan and Ethiopian troop movements.[34]

While these might seem to be relatively few operations for a unit with more than 250 members, the Activity was a trailblazer. Jerry King and Cal Sasai were carefully feeling their way in an area of covert operations that no one in the military had really explored before and they were up against a military hierarchy that included many who, in the wake of the traumas caused by the withdrawal from Vietnam, were reluctant to send US troops anywhere. 'It's important to remember that there weren't a lot of hot spots the US was focused on in those days,' one former ISA officer said. 'Moreover, there were plenty of spineless bastards in the Pentagon leadership who blanched at the idea of military guys going on covert or clandestine ops. My point is that we had plenty of folks to handle the missions we were given. We were never in a position of having to send large teams anywhere. The nature of ISA's presence in a foreign spot was small and secretive.'[35]

For the next few months, the Activity was briefly put into 'suspended animation' with no new tasks taken on, although all those which had already deployed continued as before, including the highly successful signals intelligence operation against the Salvadoran rebels and their Sandinista allies. If the Activity's opponents thought it was about to die, they were highly mistaken. In secret testimony before closed sessions of the Senate and House intelligence committees, King strongly defended the Activity's operations. He refuses now to be interviewed about the ISA or its operations, but he did say that the results of the congressional inquiries had disappointed some of those who 'were carrying wood to the foot of the cross that they just knew I was about to be burned on. They were sorely disappointed that I wasn't summarily executed but devastated when a letter of commendation from the Chairman of the Senate committee came down through the chain of command complimenting me. I had been handed the difficult task of establishing a unit that the majority of the military did not realize it needed or wanted. Yes, we made mistakes, but they were mistakes learned from trying to fulfill difficult undertakings, not from sitting on our collective glutus maximus.'[36]

By the middle of 1983, a unit charter for the Activity was in place. In a memo to John Marsh, the Secretary of the Army, Caspar Weinberger said 'we must be extremely cautious in assignment of any new tasks or missions' to the unit and that he expected to receive a monthly report on the missions it was carrying out. The charter, dated 5 July 1983, placed what the Top Secret history described as 'extraordinary controls on use of the unit'. It confirmed the previous status quo that

Bill Odom, as Assistant Chief of Staff for Intelligence, had operational control over the unit, which although multi-service came directly under headquarters Department of the Army. King, as ISA commander, would in future keep both Odom and the Deputy Chief of Staff for Operations and Plans 'fully and currently informed' of everything the unit was doing, and Odom would similarly do the same for all relevant congressional oversight committees.

Crucially, the charter authorised the ISA to engage in 'special activities', clandestine intelligence collection operations. Under Presidential Executive Order 12333, passed by President Reagan on 4 December 1981, only the CIA was to carry out 'special activities' unless the country was at war or 'the President determines that another agency is more likely to achieve a particular objective'. The Activity was also able to conduct covert military operations in support of both the armed forces and non-specified outside agencies. All intelligence collection missions, whether involving human or signals intelligence, had to be authorised by both the CIA and the DIA, while any signals intelligence operations would come under the operational and technical control of the National Security Agency. The charter also laid down that both the Secretary and Chief of Staff of the Army had to approve any missions involving members of the unit serving in combat overseas. They should also be informed of any missions likely to involve: 'substantial risk of embarrassment' to the United States; 'substantial risk of physical harm' to army personnel or 'substantial loss' to army resources; the use of 'a prominent or notorious person'; or targeting a US national. Perhaps the most telling point of the whole charter, and the one that summed up the whole raison d'être of the Activity, was that it would be 'directed to undertake activities only when other intelligence or operational support elements and resources are unavailable or inappropriate'. In short, if there was an extremely difficult intelligence collection operation that no one else could manage, the Activity would be called in to do the job.[37]

4 MAKE THE GROUND SHAKE

DUNDAS MCCULLOUGH was running a little late. The 25-year-old consular official from Berkeley, California, was talking to one of the Lebanese who regularly crowded into the visa section in the seven-storey US embassy in Beirut. It was lunchtime on Monday 18 April 1983. The Avenue de Paris, the palm-lined promenade separating the embassy from the Corniche, was busy with lunchtime strollers. McCullough was a stickler for routine and would normally be eating a sandwich at his desk at this time. For just a fraction of a second, the back of McCullough's brain registered the sound of rolling thunder. There had been squalls earlier that day and he initially thought that this was just another thunderclap. Then he realised it wasn't. There was a big flash of light, the room seemed to contort, first inwards and then outwards. He was knocked to the ground as a wall collapsed on top of him. The air was full of choking dust. 'There was complete darkness,' he recalled. 'I thought what might kill me, aside from the explosion, was suffocation. When the air cleared, there just wasn't much left.' The whole of the front of the building had disappeared, including his office where he would have been had his work schedule not been disrupted. He looked around and saw a woman lying under some rubble. 'I tried to pull the debris off her,' he said. 'Then I realized she was dead.'[1]

The dead woman was just one of sixty-three people killed, seventeen of them Americans, when a suicide bomber drove an orange General Motors pick-up truck packed with around 300 pounds of high-explosive straight across the circular embassy drive and into the horse-shoe shaped building, ripping apart its salmon-coloured façade and leaving the former hotel a tangled mass of concrete and steel. Among the dead were six CIA officers, including Robert Ames, director of the Agency's Office of Analysis for the Near East and South Asia, who was passing through on a visit, and Kenneth Haas, the station chief, and his deputy. The bulk of the dead Americans were US servicemen, eleven Marines and one member of Delta. Sergeant First Class Terry Gilden was standing outside the entrance to the embassy with the eleven Lebanese bodyguards he was training when the suicide bomber drove into it. He and his Lebanese colleagues were killed instantly.[2]

Shortly after the attack, the Christian radio station Radio Free Lebanon reported that Islamic Amal, an extremist breakaway group once part of Lebanon's Shi'ite Amal militia, had claimed responsibility for the suicide bombing. The leader of the terrorist group was Hussein Musawi, an Iranian-backed extremist, who would later go on to lead Hezbollah. 'We point out here that Hussein Musawi, who is backed by Iran and Syria, had threatened to carry out a series of operations against foreign embassies in Lebanon,' the radio announcer said. Islamic Amal was based in Baalbek, in the Beka'a Valley, which was occupied by the Syrian Army. But the Syrians had ceded control of the town of Baalbek itself to Iran and around five hundred Iranian Revolutionary Guards had set up shop there, training Islamist terrorists.[3]

LEBANON WAS A complex mosaic of different ethnic groupings made up largely of people whose ancestors had fled there to avoid persecution elsewhere. The Maronites, the largest of Lebanon's Christian sects, had fled Syria at the turn of the 8th century. The Druze, believers in a heretical offshoot of Islam, came from Egypt in the 11th century. The largest faction – the Shi'ite Muslims – was by far the poorest. There was also a substantial Sunni Muslim minority. Until the First World War, Lebanon was part of the Ottoman empire, but after the war it became a French protectorate in which the then dominant Christians were given most of the good jobs. Under the 1943 National Pact, a power-sharing arrangement based on a 1932 census, there were to be six Christians for every five Muslims in the government and civil service. The President would always be Christian, the Prime Minister, a Sunni Muslim, the Speaker of Parliament, a Shi'ite, and the Defence Minister, a Druze.

Beirut's position as the capital of the only democratic Arab country led to it becoming a major financial centre and the favoured holiday spot for wealthy Arabs, making it in everybody's interests not to rock the boat. But the much higher birth rate among the poorer, mainly Shi'ite, Muslims left the 1943 National Pact looking increasingly outdated. There was a brief civil war in 1958, which was stopped almost immediately by US intervention. But by the early 1970s, the increase in the numbers of poor Shi'ites and the influx of increasingly militant Palestinian refugees from Israel and Jordan was causing immense problems. Attacks on Israel by Palestinian militants on Lebanon's southern border led to Israeli retaliation, forcing thousands of poor Shi'ites to flee to Beirut where they built up shanty towns in the south of the city. A combination of extreme poverty and anger over the way in which they had been driven from their homes produced large numbers of willing and fanatical recruits to the increasing number of radical left-wing Muslim groups aligned with the Palestinian guerrillas.

The response was a major build-up of militia forces, led by the

12,000-strong Christian Phalangist Lebanese Front, which dominated East Beirut and an enclave to the north; the Druze Progressive Socialist Party, the second largest militia with around 4,000 men based in the Chouf mountains above Beirut; and the Shi'ite Amal, with around 3,000 men, controlling West Beirut and the sprawling southern suburbs and shanty towns. The tensions between the various groups erupted into civil war in April 1975. This essentially pitted Muslim against Christian, drawing in money and arms from Syria, Saudi Arabia, Iraq, Libya and Israel. The backing of the PLO gave the Muslims the upper hand but President Hafiz al-Asad, the Syrian president, feared that any result which left the PLO dominant would threaten Syria's own security and intervened on the side of the Christian Lebanese Front. That brought about fragile peace, broken by intermittent outbreaks of fighting. It also brought a Syrian occupation force of some 50,000 men into the north and east of Lebanon.

The number of military forces in Lebanon increased still further in March 1978, when a Palestinian terrorist attack on Israelis led the Israel Defence Force to take over the south of the country, forcing the Palestinians on the border to flee to refugee camps in Beirut. Israel withdrew a few months later, handing control of the border area over to its ally, the mainly Christian Army of South Lebanon. Four years later, in response to a Palestinian terrorist attack on its ambassador in London, Israel invaded Lebanon and forced the Palestinians to withdraw. President Reagan sent US Marines into Lebanon on 25 August 1982 as part of a multinational force designed to form a buffer between the Israelis and the PLO fighters, who were being evacuated from Beirut. 'We proposed that each departing individual be secretly photographed and if possible identified,' one former ISA officer said. 'Odom concluded that such a mission should be given to Inscom [Intelligence and Security Command]. As we expected, they studied the problem until it was overcome by events and the PLO had gone.' Three weeks later, the Marines were pulled out – only to be sent back again almost immedi-

ately after Bashir Gemayel was assassinated, leading to swift retaliation from the Christian militias, who massacred 2,000 Palestinians in the
Sabra and Shatila refugee camps, an operation carried out with Israeli
connivance. Those attacks and the increasing influence of Iran, allied
to Syria, led to the creation of a number of extremely radical Islamist
terrorist groups like Hezbollah and Islamic Amal, most of which
received training and weaponry from the Iranian Revolutionary Guards
at Baalbek.[4]

Noel Koch, the Deputy Assistant Secretary of Defense for International Security Affairs, the man ostensibly in charge of Pentagon
counter-terrorism policy, had spent the time since the US Marines
first deployed desperately trying to warn the Joint Chiefs and his
Pentagon bosses that the radical new terrorists based in Lebanon had
embarked on a series of suicide bombings. He could barely contain his
anger that his predictions, having been ignored, had now been shown
so conclusively to be right and at the expense of so many lives. Koch, a
vehement proponent of the use of special operations forces like the
Activity and Delta, had a similar hard-nosed attitude to that of Jerry
King and had made just as many enemies among the more traditionally
minded military hierarchy. He sent Caspar Weinberger a dangerously
intemperate message. 'I am outraged,' he said. 'This is just one more
example of what occurred under this no-fault-no-fix policy in the
Pentagon.' There were 1,500 US Marines in Beirut, sent there by
President Reagan against the advice of both Weinberger and the Joint
Chiefs. The Defense Secretary ordered a small five-man undercover
team from the Activity to Beirut, led by Jerry King's deputy, Cal Sasai,
to carry out a thorough review of the intelligence that was available to
the embassy and the Marines. Was it the best they could get and were
they making the best use of what they had?[5]

One member of Sasai's team was Lieutenant-Colonel Bill Cowan,
a US Marine officer who had spent nearly three and a half years on
combat assignments in Vietnam. Much of his time there had involved

special operations. He had experience of intelligence work and had operated alongside the CIA. Born in Sacramento, California, he was brought up in Alaska, learning the instincts of a tracker as a child. 'Alaska was and still is the formative basis of my character,' Cowan said. 'Days and, on occasion, weeks in the woods by myself, figuring out how to survive. My senses – smell, hearing, eyesight – became very acute, and those are skills that don't go away with time.' Once in Vietnam, while leading a small patrol, he had smelled the enemy, who often didn't shower or bathe for days on end. His Vietnamese troops didn't notice anything, but he put everyone on alert. 'After some careful snooping and pooping, we came upon a small base camp. No one was in it at the time, but the date etched into the mud over one of the bunkers was the previous day. It was strictly the smell that alerted me and took us there. It was the same as sniffing for bears or other large game in Alaska. It was all about survival.'[6]

COWAN ENLISTED IN the US Navy at the age of 17, and received an appointment to the Naval Academy from which, in 1966, he graduated as an officer in the US Marine Corps. He spent two stints in Vietnam. The first year was spent in the northern part of the country where he served as a platoon commander during the fierce battles along the DMZ (demilitarised zone) in the fall of 1967. His last five months were as the officer in charge of the Kit Carson Scout programme, training defectors from the Viet Cong and North Vietnamese Army to act as scouts for US forces. 'After a brief return to the States, I realized that as long as there was a war going on, and as long as I was a Marine, I needed to be where the action was,' Cowan said. 'I requested and was given orders back to Vietnam after 10 months back in the States.' He was sent to the Rung Sat Special Zone, one of two special zones in Vietnam. The Rung Sat zone controlled the shipping channel from the South China Sea to Saigon, Cowan said. 'The Viet Cong were intent on closing down the lanes, and attacks were becoming more frequent.

We worked with Vietnamese regional force companies, popular force platoons, and our own intel squads which we organized and trained. On the US side, the Rung Sat always had a SEAL platoon on six-month rotation. My focus was my Vietnamese forces. We would often conduct thirty-man daytime ops, twelve-man day or night-time ops, and I had an intel squad that often went out with five or seven men. The most important aspect of my Rung Sat experience was exposure to intel programmes unlike that which most Marines saw. We had intel from many sources, all of it intended to curb Viet Cong/North Vietnamese Army activity along the shipping channel. In my final eight months, I started running the Rung Sat's Provincial Reconstruction Unit (read CIA) ops. All of our effort was out in the jungle or the paddies. We never operated around villages, because that's not where our enemy was at the time. Our intel was often exceptional. Lots of kills, and lots of POWs. These experiences later made me somewhat unique in the Marine Corps and that's what led to me being selected for ISA.'[7]

In early 1983, Cowan was offered a plum job in the White House Science Advisor's office. 'This was serious business, rubbing elbows with senior folks in the Administration and in the corporate sector. They wanted someone with a strong intelligence background and with a technical degree. Besides my Marine Corps intel experience, I had worked quite a bit in Vietnam with CIA and army intel folks, and I had a masters in computer science.' But Cowan was destined not to go to the White House staff. The US Marine Corps representative in the Activity, the deputy operations officer, who had served with Cowan in Vietnam and knew him well, was due to leave in the summer of 1983. When the US embassy in Beirut was bombed and the Activity was looking for someone to go to Beirut, Cowan's friend recommended him for the job. The armed forces personnel computer showed he had all the qualifications the Activity needed in a deputy operations officer. 'He suggested that I'd be a good replacement – strong combat experience, especially on small unit stuff, and a good intel background. At the end of April, I was approached by one of the senior colonels in Marine Corps assignments branch and asked what I'd prefer to do – the White House or ISA. The differences were stark, but there was no question in my mind where my heart was – operations. I told him so, and that's where I went.'

Cowan was initially only attached to the ISA for the Beirut mission. He was immediately impressed by the training and calibre of the operators working in the Activity. These were obviously some of the army's best and most qualified people. The level of combat and intelligence experience from Vietnam was incredible and many of the operators had participated in the effort to rescue American hostages from Tehran in 1979. These were some of the military's finest commandos – true 'special operators' long before the term came into vogue. 'The ISA ran a very tough selection course for the majority of its operators and some of its staff. The course entailed being pushed physically, mentally, and emotionally to stress out candidates and see if they could withstand or adjust to harsh conditions. Those who didn't make it through didn't make it to the unit. Delta had their own selection course, the SEALs of course always had their own version. My understanding was that ISA's selection course was the toughest being run at the time.'[8]

Like most of the new recruits to the Activity, Cowan was also sent on a CIA indoctrination course. 'This was a standard course run by the CIA,' another former ISA officer said. 'We sent a number of so-called non-operational staff people, officers and NCOs to this course in hopes it would give them a better understanding of what those on the cutting edge did. I say "so-called non-operational" because most everyone was expected, if and when required, to go forward to provide support. Obviously, they were not all expected to become active clandestine or covert operatives, but frequently they had to operate in that mode or environment to support those operating "down-range". On the surface, there is nothing glamorous and heroic about the multitude of efforts being simultaneously conducted by the unit. Without a doubt, the conduct of our people down-range attracted the most attention. But every member of the unit contributed to the ultimate success of the operatives launched on a mission. Execution of the daily mundane requirements, from the junior personnel clerk, the armorer or supply clerk, made everything else possible.'[9]

Cowan had very little time to become acclimatised to the ethos of the Activity before he joined Sasai's team on the flight to Beirut, arriving in the Lebanese capital on 26 May. 'The primary purpose was to ascertain the intelligence situation,' Cowan said. 'That is, was there sufficient intelligence being acquired? How was it being acquired? Was it moving around? Were the right people seeing it. We in the United States had a lot of intelligence activities in Beirut at that time. They didn't all report to the same person. The real issue was, was all this intelligence coming to one place where it could be analyzed and put to good and immediate use?' Sasai and his team quickly realised that the answer was no. They ran into opposition straight away from the embassy, which had been repeatedly warned that its security was poor but had stalled on improving it, and initially from Bill Buckley, the new CIA station chief. No one saw any reason for someone from outside to tell them what they should be doing. All the old prejudices about secret military covert units were in evidence, particularly inside the CIA station. No one wanted them there and no one was willing to give them any help. Everyone who could have done something that might have helped to prevent the attack in the first place was in denial.[10]

Quite apart from anything else, three of the CIA Lebanon station's most experienced officers, each with their own contacts with, and links into, the various feuding Lebanese communities and the Syrian occupying forces, had been taken out of the equation by the bomb blast, Cowan said. 'The CIA station chief and a number of people who worked for him were killed when that happened. So for the most part, the CIA operations in Beirut were essentially terminated at that point.

When you lose people like that, you lose the connections to the sources, to their agents. All these things have to be reconstituted and put back together.'[11]

Sasai and his team asked all the questions that no one had thought to ask previously. They spent ten days talking to everyone, the embassy staff; the CIA; the US Marines, who were based in the airport and vulnerable to shelling from the mountains above Beirut; the Delta bodyguards; and embassy security personnel. They also talked to the Israelis, who had as good a handle on the situation as anybody, and to the Army Special Forces Mobile Training Teams who were working with the Lebanese Army. The Special Forces teams 'were identified as potentially great sources and the unit through various means had indirectly established essential elements of intelligence as part of their mission brief,' one former ISA officer said. 'All SF teams wrote lengthy after-action briefs upon mission completion. We, as was the army, were especially interested in the names and background of leaders or key individuals identified by the teams during their mission.'[12]

But they didn't just leave it there. They got out on the street, talking to the local people, finding out what the situation was on the ground, familiarising themselves with the city, its people, the various factions and all their different perspectives. Finding out what the local people thought about the Americans, where they were seen as falling short, what they did well, what they did badly. 'The way we operated in Beirut was very, very low key,' Cowan said. 'I mean the most important thing you can do in doing the kinds of things we were doing is to be unobservable. Stop and talk to people of all types, never act like you're doing something sinister. We would stop and talk to anybody who we could get eye contact with. We always said: "Alright, we talk to Muslims, we talk to Christians." We'd stop and have a cup of coffee. We would walk the streets. We would be laughing all the time. We would be having a good time. But the bottom line was, in all the things we were doing, we were collecting information.'[13]

General Carl Stiner, who was sent to Lebanon in August 1983 as a brigadier-general to act as the Joint Chiefs' man on the ground, recalled that for the US Marines in particular the intelligence situation in Beirut in the wake of the embassy bombing was very poor. 'The Marines were always eager to get intelligence and operational information about Beirut, but often complained about their vulnerable location, a situation made worse by the scarcity of accurate information about the areas around them,' Stiner said. 'The truth of the matter was there was very little intelligence information available about the nature of the threats to American forces.'[14]

The Activity intelligence specialists discovered that the lack of useful intelligence passed to the Marines was not the result of a lack of intelligence available to American sources as a whole. The intelligence picture was poor but there were people with access to some of the intel that was needed, it was just not being shared properly. There was no single cell with access to all the sources of intelligence that could ensure proper coordination and rapid dissemination of all means of collection: signals intelligence from the NSA in Fort Meade, Maryland, and from the British monitoring base just outside Famagusta in Cyprus, where teams of Arabic specialists worked round the clock intercepting the communications of the different Lebanese factions; imagery intelligence from the Keyhole satellites and SR71 Blackbird spy planes; and human intelligence collected on the ground by the CIA. 'Wherever I was, Embassy or residence, I read the latest intelligence traffic received by the station chief Bill Buckley,' Stiner said. 'Buckley was good at his job. He was successfully rebuilding the network of agents lost in the Embassy bombing, and we got along well, but – predictably – he was not always cooperative about sharing information with anyone outside his office.'[15]

Sasai and his team managed to get over Buckley's initial suspicions of their mission. They kept him informed of everything they were doing, passed him the information they obtained and, as he realised they knew what they were doing, built up a good relationship with him that would pay dividends later. They concluded that there needed to be much more coordination of intelligence in Beirut itself and that there should be a special 'fusion cell' set up to act as an analysis and distribution centre that would make sure everybody got the intelligence they needed, tailored to their specific requirements. They also warned of poor security at the Marines' barracks at the airport and pointed out that they represented a tempting terrorist target, probably the most tempting in Beirut.

'We sent back a report to Caspar Weinberger, the Secretary of Defense, that really we needed to have an intelligence operation over there that was more focused, where all the intelligence that was available came to one place,' Cowan said. 'We needed to be sure that it was analyzed properly, and that the intelligence went directly to the military forces inside Beirut so that they could be aware of threats and prepared to defend themselves if a threat came about. We said in the report that if there were not something done to improve the intelligence gathering and sharing of information in Beirut that in fact, a military presence was at risk.'[16]

The Activity team also briefed Marine commanders on the potential threats against their troops and position, specifically warning them about their vulnerability to car bombs, another former ISA officer said. 'They discussed the need to improve the roadblock leading into their position and the rules imposed on those at the roadblock. The Marines were not allowed to keep their weapons loaded. The arrangement of the roadblock allowed vehicles to drive through, at fairly high speed without stopping. In short, the roadblock was a roadblock in name only. I believe this was also included in our after-action report. We were livid when the Marine commander was later questioned, after the bombing, about this very point and he replied, that we had warned only about the threat of car bombings, not truck bombings. What the hell was the difference?'[17]

Cal Sasai returned home and submitted the team's report, assuming that their recommendations would be examined and acted on. But the omens were already bad. Jerry King told Sasai to come back via the Eucom (European Command) HQ in Stuttgart, which controlled operations in Lebanon, to brief them on the operation and the team's findings. 'Eucom, in turn, blew their stacks, because they had no knowledge that we were there,' the officer said. The DIA was supposed to have informed Eucom that the Activity team would be in theatre. 'They had not done so. Once again, we were blamed, by Eucom, for the failings of another agency.'[18]

Cowan was so impressed with the Activity that he accepted a permanent assignment to the unit. Shortly after returning from Beirut, he found himself on a two-week course – specially set up for the Activity – at jump school, learning how to parachute, including the use of stand-off parachuting, now known as HAHO (high altitude, high opening), at which the Activity was adept. 'In my early days the Marine Corps did not send many people to jump school, and I hadn't had the chance, so I went at age 40,' he said. HAHO was pioneered by the Activity, which introduced the technique to Delta and other special operations forces, another former ISA officer said. 'Delta organized a conference and demonstration of HAHO somewhere in Texas and along with 1st Ranger Battalion, and SEAL Team Six, we attended. Someone, I don't recall who, proposed a competition jump. We knew they had been frequently practising but we went along. End result, we embarrassed them rather badly. We were never again asked to compete.'

Two weeks after Sasai's team returned from Beirut, the training that Activity and Delta had provided to Sudanese President Gaafar Numeiry came into its own. Guerrillas from the Libyan-backed Southern Sudan Liberation Front stormed a mission compound at Boma on the border with Kenya and Ethiopia. They kidnapped John Haspels, a 36-year-old Presbyterian missionary from Lyons, Kansas, together with his family and six other westerners. Seven of those held hostage by the rebels were Americans. They were just in the wrong place at the wrong time. The two-dozen poorly clad rebels had arrived at Boma two weeks earlier, looking for a Sudanese Air Force pilot who had got lost and run out of fuel while helping to quell an army mutiny. The pilot had managed to land at the rough dirt runway next to the small mission station on the Boma National Park. The guerrillas were hoping to take him hostage and use him to bargain with the Sudanese government for money. But after having his aircraft refuelled, and persuading Phil Snyder, the national park's head warden to use his new earth grader to extend the runway, the Sudanese pilot had taken off and flown 200 miles west back to his base at Juba, the regional capital.

A few days later, the rebels arrived in Boma looking for him. They had endured a week-long trek through torrential rain, only to discover that their prey had escaped. Having lost one potential hostage, they decided the American missionaries would make a profitable alternative. The rebel leader Lekurnyang Lado, known as 'Double L', claimed to have been one of the guards to the Iran hostages and told his followers that there was money and publicity to be had from taking on the Americans. He assured them they could make the mighty 'Yankees' look impotent, just like the Iranians had. But he was wrong.

Despite undergoing extensive counter-revolutionary training in Libya, 'Double L' was little more than a two-bit hustler. A few days later, he freed Gwen Haspels and her children; plus a British zoologist who was suffering from dysentery; and the pilot who would fly the released hostages to Nairobi. They took with them Lado's pathetic demands. He wanted just under $100,000, some medical supplies and enough clothing and shoes for 150 men. He also asked that the Front's intention of forming an independent southern state be broadcast by an international radio station. The guerrillas were fighting to free black, Christian southern Sudan from the domination of Arab Muslims in the north. Getting an international broadcaster to state that simple truth was the easy part. Voice of America and BBC World Service swiftly complied. Negotiators seeking the release of the remaining prisoners began talking to the rebels by short-wave radio. There were now just five hostages: Haspels; a 29-year-old missionary pilot, Ron Pontier, from Clermont, Florida; a Canadian missionary pilot, 32-year-old Martin Overduin, from London, Ontario; Willem Noort, the missionary's Dutch nurse; and Alois Pscheidt, a West German mechanic working on the national park.

For two weeks, there were regular short-wave conversations between the negotiators in Juba and the garrulous kidnappers, who seemed totally unaware that repeating their long lists of demands was extending their time on the air and allowing the Sudanese security forces to home in on their position. A team from the Activity comprising signals and imagery intelligence specialists was providing the intelligence for a rescue mission. Delta hostage rescue operators, who only months earlier had helped to set up their Sudanese equivalent, spent hours taking them through the rescue mission time and time again, carefully drumming into them what they must do, how they must act, the need to avoid killing the hostages but to make sure that any rebels they sighted weren't going to be in a position to get up and return fire, not now, not ever.

Meanwhile the Activity intel team set about finding the rebels' precise location and working out what the opposition was. Pinpointing the rebel hide-out was easy. The way the rebels couldn't stop listing all their demands every time the negotiators made contact meant the Activity knob-turners had no problems getting a fix on the transmitter. Meanwhile, the imagery analysts directed the Keyhole satellite that was homing in on the rebel hide-out and, using sophisticated satellite communications equipment, downloaded the images so they could work out what the problems were on the ground. Both the Activity and Delta also took advice from the national park's head warden Phil Snyder, who had been in Khartoum when the rebels attacked and knew every inch of the area where they were holding their hostages. There was general agreement that the swamps in which the rebels were hiding meant a straightforward ground assault would not work. The rescue team's movement through the swamps would be slow and there would be no element of surprise while the guerrillas could lose the Sudanese troops easily among the tall elephant grass. They would have to mount a heliborne attack.

Two weeks after the hostages were taken prisoner, the Sudanese were ready to carry out the rescue mission. During one of the daily radio conversations, the negotiators asked to talk to Haspels so they could reassure him that his wife and children were safe in Nairobi. Three times they spelt out the word Kenya. Three times they used Khaki as the phonetic word for K rather than the normal Kilo. The five hostages recognised the coded message – soldiers were on their way – but to the illiterate rebels it was meaningless. 'Communications were difficult,' Haspels said. 'We had our captors holding us right there with hand grenades in their hands during radio calls. By using Khaki we knew that the army was planning something. We thought the very next day, the Sudanese Army would come and get us.' After passing on their message, the negotiators broke off contact, saying that atmospheric conditions were making it impossible to hear what the rebels were saying.

That night the Dutch missionary nurse doctored the rebels' dinner with a cocktail of Phenobarbital and herbs designed to knock them out and make them easy meat for the rescue team. The five hostages then fled to avoid the impending attack. 'Our guards fell asleep and by 9 o'clock that evening we were able to escape without carrying any supplies,' Haspels said. 'We only went a short distance and we sat in the rocks waiting for the army to come. But by 6.45 in the morning, it was obvious the army was not coming that day so we started heading for the Ethiopian border. All of a sudden the abductors appeared and took us back. They were angry and threatened to kill us and each of us got four to five lashes over the head and the back.'

The Sudanese forces had been unable to mount the assault because torrential monsoon rainstorms had swept in from the Indian Ocean and across the southern Sudanese marshes. The next day, the break in the weather the rescue mission was waiting for arrived. Both the hostages and the rebels heard the whack–whack–whack of helicopter rotor blades several miles off and knew that the rescue mission would soon be there. Haspels's stomach started churning. A few minutes later, the Sudanese Air Force Hind helicopter gunships came in from different directions across the swamps, where the rebels were holding their hostages, their two–pronged attack spewing missile and machine-gun fire that cut through the elephant grass the rebels were hiding behind like a scythe through a cornfield. Most of the kidnappers got up and began to run the minute they heard the rotor blades. But the men guarding the hostages remained frozen where they were for the first few minutes of the assault. Should they run for cover and lose the precious hostages, or risk staying in the open and have both themselves and the hostages killed, mown down by the gunships' heavy machine guns? 'Finally one of the leaders came and said, "Come on, run for the rocks," and that was what we did,' Haspels said. They waited until the shooting had stopped and came out from behind the rocks. By that stage, the Sudanese troops had killed eighteen rebels for the loss of only one of their own men and were hunting down the remaining few guerrillas in the bush. Two Americans and three other hostages had been saved. No one in Washington was claiming victory. President Reagan congratulated his opposite number, Sudanese President Gaafar Numeiry on the successful operation. US officials insisted they had not known it was about to take place. The truth was somewhat different. For the Activity and for Delta, Lado's death represented a small piece of payback for the Iran hostages. This time five Western hostages, including two Americans, had been successfully rescued and the kidnappers would not be able to try the same trick again. But as with the Dozier rescue, the role played by the Activity was to remain secret.[19]

Despite the continued opposition elsewhere within the army to their very existence, Cal Sasai, Bill Cowan, and the other members of the Activity team sent to the Lebanon had at least expected that when they came back from Beirut their report would be acted on. They were wrong. 'Well, nothing was done,' said Bill Cowan. 'We ran into bureaucratic stonewalling about making any changes.' Noel Koch put his finger on why a report written by special operations intelligence specialists working in their precise area of expertise would be ignored. Just like Jerry King, their unit commander, and Koch himself, Sasai and his team were treading on too many toes. The military wasn't used to direct criticism. Complaints of failure were normally passed slowly up the command chain and modified at every turn by subordinates anxious not to upset superiors who might have the power to destroy their careers. But the report written by the Activity team went straight to the top and was handed on back down. 'Their report reflected adversely on people who outranked them and had been submitted with no opportunity for the military system to sanitize their findings,' Koch said. 'This led to denials, ass-covering and all round outrage that the survey had been done at all. Thus it was decided that there were no problems and if there were they had been fixed.' The European Command's sole response to the report was to assign just one single intelligence officer to the US Office of Military Cooperation in Beirut, which ran American military operations on the ground.[20]

Koch's anger stemmed from the fact that he had been trying to brief the Joint Chiefs on the growth of radical Islamist terrorism in Lebanon for months. He was repeatedly stalled even after the embassy bombing in April. 'In August the answer came back,' Koch said. 'It was indeed critical that I brief the Chiefs but there was one slight problem. There had been personnel changes and we had a new Director of Joint Staff and two new Operations Deputies and it would be first necessary to brief them. August passed, as did September.'[21]

BY NOW, THERE WERE growing indications that Islamist terrorists were planning a 'spectacular' attack on the foreign troops who had arrived in Beirut as peacekeepers. 'We began to receive credible intelligence reports of possible car bomb attacks, sometimes even giving the make and the colour of the car,' Carl Stiner said. During the six months following the embassy bombing, US forces in Beirut received more than 100 warnings of car bombs, of which only a very few materialised. But on 26 September, the NSA reported a piece of intelligence that was to prove much more serious. It was an intercept of a message from the Iranian intelligence service in Tehran, telling Ali Akbar Mohtashemi, the Iranian ambassador to Syria, to contact Hussein Musawi and order him 'to take a spectacular action that would make the ground shake underneath the foreign forces'.[22]

The 'spectacular ground-shaking action' ordered by Tehran occurred at 6.30 a.m. on the morning of 23 October 1983. Carl Stiner was sitting in the office of General Ibrahim Tannous, the Chief of Staff of the Lebanese Army, discussing US training for the Lebanese troops. 'We heard a tremendous explosion,' Stiner said. 'Shortly after, the shock wave rocked the building. A huge black column of smoke topped by a white, rapidly spinning smoke ring – like an atomic explosion – was rapidly rising from an area approximately two miles away, near the airport.' He and General Tannous set off for the airport by car. On their way, they heard a second explosion as the French barracks was hit by a second suicide bomb, killing fifty-nine French troops. 'The Marines compound had been truck bombed,' Stiner said. 'When we arrived, there was almost indescribable devastation. I have never seen anything like it. Fires were burning everywhere, people were torn apart, and the building had just collapsed on top of itself. The scene was utter devastation. All four of the reinforced concrete floors had pancaked to one level. The surrounding area was covered with every kind of imaginable litter – wrecked jeeps, guns, bits of torn clothing, helmets, cooking utensils.' Staff Sergeant Cal Openshaw, a 34-year-old career Marine from Jacksonville, North Carolina, ran to the pile of rubble to help in the rescue. He was shocked by the sight of the bodies lying among the wreckage. Deprived of their normal flesh-like colour by the sudden loss of blood, they had turned to a pale grey-white that merged into the broken concrete blocks. 'I went into shock for about five minutes,' Openshaw said. 'It was really hard to look at the bodies at first. You stumbled across them before you knew they were there.' In the middle of the devastation, on top of the tangled mass of Marines' personal belongings, lay a copy of *The Dogs of War*, its pages fluttering over in the breeze coming in off the sea.[23]

'One of the strongest buildings in Beirut was now reduced to a pile of pancaked rubble,' Carl Stiner said. 'The heavy reinforcing steel rods in the concrete had all been sheared like straws. Within minutes, the intelligence community intercepted this unattributed message: "We were able to perform the spectacular act, making the ground shake underneath the feet of the infidels. We also got the army brigadier-general and the CIA Station Chief in the process." It was not so, thank God. But it was the first indication that Buckley and I were on the hit list.'[24]

The Activity's frustration was heightened by the fact that during their earlier recce they had come across the preparations for at least one of the attacks, but had been prevented from taking pre-emptive action by the Pentagon. 'We believed we knew the location of a garage in which a car bomb was being assembled,' one former Activity officer said. 'We proposed that we sabotage the car bomb, let it explode in the garage, making it look like ineptitude on the part of the bomb makers. But it was in a residential neighbourhood and the proposal was turned down because it would have caused too many civilian casualties. I thought it might encourage other neighbourhoods to try preventing such activities in their areas. The car bomb, so we believed, was the one used against the French.'[25]

Koch was left utterly exasperated by the refusal of the service commanders to comprehend the urgency of acting to deal with the Islamic terrorist threat. 'I never met the Joint Chiefs,' he said. 'I attempted to clear the air with the Director of Joint Staff after the fact, so that we might have our disagreements over special operations forces but do what needed to be done with regard to terrorism. I asked him how it could be possible that in the greater part of a year, no time could be found on the Chief's agenda to discuss the subject. I vividly remember his response in the aftermath of 241 deaths. He said: "Well you know, terrorism is an easy thing to ignore".'[26]

The commission set up under retired US Navy Admiral Robert L J Long to look into the bombing specifically pointed to the failure by the commander of Eucom and others to share intelligence properly, and the lack of efficient security measures around the Marines' barracks, as the prime reasons for the awful success of the terrorist attack. Colonel Tim Geraghty, the Marine commander in Beirut 'was not provided with timely intelligence, tailored to his specific opera-tional needs' and the defences at the airport barracks were 'not adequate to prevent continuing significant attrition of the force'. The Long Commission referred briefly to the Activity mission to Beirut in its unclassified report. The classified version quoted from Sasai's report and concurred with his conclusions that there was abundant intelligence but it was poorly sorted and evaluated. The commission's unclassified recommendations repeated the Activity call for the creation of a central 'all-source fusion centre' to process intelligence and to ensure that field commanders threatened by terrorism were kept properly informed.[27]

President Reagan said that as commander-in-chief he was respon-sible for the deployment and also therefore for any decisions that led to the loss of life. No officers were to be blamed, even though they had been warned of the dangers by the Activity's report and simply ignored them. Geraghty and another senior Marine based in Beirut were issued with 'non-punitive letters of caution', effectively ending their careers.

But that was it. Until the bombing of the Marines' barracks, with its staggering loss of life, the military hierarchy was simply not interested in doing anything differently, in even acknowledging that the rules of the game had changed, that Islamist terrorism was a new and potent threat, far more ruthless than its predecessors in organisations like the Red Brigades or even the PLO. It required a completely different mindset to that which had been built up over thirty-five years of Cold War if the military were ever going to find ways of defeating it. Cal Sasai's report had been ignored, filed away on a Pentagon shelf to gather dust. The commission had now agreed with virtually everything it said. 'No changes whatsoever from our recommendations were implemented until after the bombing of the Marine compound,' Bill Cowan said. 'At that point, every recommendation was implemented. But it cost 241 servicemen to get there.'[28]

Michael Ledeen, then a Pentagon consultant, said the failure to share intelligence 'drove a change in the structure of the intelligence community, because what they found was that we should have seen it coming, we had enough information so that we should have seen it coming. We didn't because of the compartmentalization of the various pieces of the intelligence community. So the people who listen to things weren't talking to the people who looked at things who weren't talking to people who analyzed things and so on.'[29]

But that didn't mean that the people who had got it so wrong in Beirut were suddenly going to listen to the Activity. Even within the special operations community, there were senior officers with little regard for Jerry King's unit, and that attitude was once again going to get US servicemen killed. Ever since coming to office, the Reagan administration had railed against the left-wing government of the small Caribbean island of Grenada, complaining that the Prime Minister Maurice Bishop was too closely aligned to the Soviet Union and Cuba. Then on 13 October 1983, Bishop was overthrown by the newly formed People's Revolutionary Army, which was led by a former political colleague who believed the popular Prime Minister had become too moderate. Six days later Bishop was freed by thousands of his supporters. But he was then taken away by the army and summarily executed. There were already fears in Washington for the safety of the US students on the island. On 25 October, Reagan sent in the Marines, the 82nd Airborne and the US Rangers, together with Delta and SEAL special operations forces. It took around 7,000 US troops eight days to overcome less than 3,000 Cuban and Grenadian troops.

It was a full three days before the Marines managed to find all of the American students, who were not in one place as originally thought but were at several different sites. None of the special operations missions went well and around eight SEALs and Delta operators were among the twenty-nine believed to have died (the precise figures for special operations dead remain classified). Anxious for a military victory to soften the blow of the 241 Marines killed in Beirut, President Reagan described it as 'a textbook success'. The views of those in the special operations community who were involved were largely unprintable but the word success didn't feature in any of them.[30]

One former ISA officer said that 'if lives had not been lost, the CIA's Grenada effort would have been laughable.' The Agency had closed down its station on Grenada during the Carter cutbacks. Its only agent on the island, a wealthy landowner, was away on Barbados and refused to return. But the ISA, which was set up to provide close-in intelligence support for special operations forces, was banned from taking part. General Richard Scholtes, the JSOC commander, said he didn't want it involved, dismissing it as 'a bunch of Delta rejects'. That reaction was seen within the Activity as a result of the Gritz fiasco.[31]

'Gritz damaged our relationship with JSOC, who thought that we were trying to take a mission, that was rightfully theirs, away,' one former ISA officer said. 'This situation really impacted during the Grenada operation. We had just finished a lengthy command post exercise, using the latest intelligence on that very country.' Jerry King was called to the Atlantic Command headquarters at Norfolk, Virginia to discuss planning for the operation. He was working with the staff to put options together when he was called by the command's operations officer and told the Activity's services were not required. 'We were later informed that the JSOC commander objected to our involvement,' one former Activity member said. 'Hell, if they had at least let us show up, we could have told them the medical students were at different sites.'[32]

The failure to bring in the Activity, and the resultant lack of actionable intelligence, caused immense problems for the invading US troops. Eric Haney was one of the Delta operators tasked to take the Richmond Hill prison where political prisoners were believed to be held. Because of disagreements between the commanders over when the invasion should begin, their Black Hawk helicopters arrived over the prison in broad daylight and encountered heavy fire from the ground driving them back. 'We had absolutely no intelligence about what to expect or where to expect it,' Haney said. 'We had no idea if there were any prisoners in Richmond Hill. We didn't know if the place was guarded – and if it was we didn't have any idea about the size and composition of the guard force. We didn't know how the Grenadians were organized, what kind of Cuban forces were on the island, or what type of weaponry they had. We didn't even have a rumour of decent maps. We were able to get our hands on a Michelin guide to the Windward Islands with a somewhat usable chart of Grenada.' In the event, they eventually discovered that there were not even any prisoners in the jail.[33]

Ironically, the Activity had wanted to put an intel team onto the island some months earlier but were prevented from doing so by the Pentagon. 'ISA had tried to get a few folks planted in Grenada the summer before the invasion,' said Bill Cowan. 'Intel on Grenada was virtually non-existent. ISA intel folks had deduced it to be a good place to have "eyes on the ground", but the Pentagon had nixed the idea.'[34]

John Carney, one of the Special Tactics combat controllers taking part in the invasion, was scathing about the lack of any intelligence on the island. 'Myriad explanations and excuses have been made for the lack of human intelligence about Grenada, a situation General Vessey later called "inexcusable",' he said. 'The CIA, the Defense Intelligence Agency, the National Security Agency and the State Department provided nothing. No one had a clue about the size and disposition of Grenadian and Cuban forces – even though the State Department had a White House approved plan for seizing the island. Urgent Fury was so FUBAR'd that almost every story told about it seemed plausible, and virtually every version of every story made print.' FUBAR'd, Carney added, is service terminology for 'fouled up beyond all recognition – or words to that effect'.[35]

5 'THOSE PEOPLE IN WASHINGTON'

CLINT ROLLED DOWN the window of the battered Toyota hire car and hoped it was going to be his lucky day. It was his second trip to the Lebanon with an ISA reconnaissance team and for the first time his instincts had failed him. The Lebanese roads were full of road-blocks. Some of them, just a few, were friendly to the team from the Activity. They had already developed a number of good contacts among the Lebanese Christian militias who could be relied on to be helpful. But most of the roadblocks were manned by Muslims of one sort or another and they were hostile to Americans – extremely hostile. Now he had stumbled on a Syrian Army checkpoint. It could have been worse. It could have been an Islamic Amal roadblock. He wouldn't have been the first American to be kidnapped, held for ransom and then shot by the Iranian-backed Islamic fundamentalists. But still, it was bad enough. If the Syrian occupation forces realised who he was, he would be arrested as an American spy. It was, after all, precisely what he was.

Stung by the bombing of the US embassy in Beirut, the murder of so many US Marines, and the blow to American prestige it represented, the Reagan administration was determined to retaliate. US officials knew Iran was bankrolling the Shi'ite terrorists and that if Syria couldn't be shown for sure to be doing the same, it was certainly turning a blind eye to the Hezbollah operations. But overt retaliation was out of the question. So the administration opted for covert intelligence operations, the speciality of the Activity. Clint and five other members of the Activity were sent back into Beirut to carry out a preparatory reconnaissance and to work out a plan for special operations attacks on the terrorist and Syrian military positions.

They had made a lot of good friends among the pro-Christian militias, who had promised any help the Americans needed. Those contacts were eased by the skills of Becky, a personable and highly attractive former model who was added to the team at the last moment because of her superlative skills as an analyst and agent-runner. Taking a woman, particularly such a strikingly beautiful one, on a Middle East mission was always going to be a risk. 'She was beautiful and still is in an "aged" way,' one former colleague said. But despite Jerry King's earlier ruling against using beautiful women, in Becky's case, the obvious advantages outweighed the disadvantages. There were very few men that she couldn't wrap round her little finger and few would suspect her of being part of a top secret undercover intelligence team. 'She was a great intel person, and her beauty drew the men quickly. She was absolutely out of the movies, was a great entertainer, a great conversationalist, and an all around super person. No way anyone would ever think she was working undercover ops. When she walked into a room, everyone stopped and looked! She knew how to flirt and keep their attention, but she was 100 per cent professional, no matter how many drinks, no matter how many times she was out with someone. I always admired this about her. She knew where the lines were and she never crossed them.'[1]

The five-person group had located landing sites for US Navy SEALs on the Lebanese coast, drop zones for Delta to parachute themselves and equipment in, and safe houses where they could rest up until they were ready to attack. They had located the terrorist hideouts and the key Syrian anti-aircraft sites that would need to be hit. They had even drawn up a number of plans for the attacks, one of which involved dropping in expensive Mercedes and Rolls-Royce saloons by parachute. The team obtained a number of Lebanese number plates that could be fitted to the cars. They would then look like they belonged to one of the wealthy Arabs who still lived in Beirut, providing ideal camouflage for any operation.[2]

But right now all that was at risk. The dust from the Toyota's tyres was still swirling around the car as the window rolled down; the sunlight shining through it was making the Syrian conscript blink as he bent down to check Clint out. He took his hand off the window handle and felt for the pistol under his seat. He slipped off the safety as his mind raced through the options. The Syrian soldier was clearly nervous, too nervous to come really close. He gestured with his rifle in his right hand as he thrust out his other hand, asking in Arabic for their papers. Clint, a major in Army Special Forces before he joined the Activity, had spent three years with the Studies and Observations Group in Vietnam and according to one former colleague was 'easy-going, unflappable, and very quick thinking'. They were qualities he needed now in spades. Wracking his brain for something from the old SOG days that might help him get out of this fix, he could think of nothing better than to babble incoherently in Vietnamese at the startled guard. Uncertain of what to do next, the Syrian soldier started shouting louder in an attempt to get his message across. The American looked at him as if he had no idea what he wanted and responded just as loudly in Vietnamese. Clearly phased by this response and too nervous to force him out of the car, the Syrian soldier chose the easiest option, waving him on through the checkpoint, to Clint's considerable relief.[3]

The deaths of 241 Marines, the worst loss of US troops since the Vietnam War, had left Washington uncertain over what to do next.

With political pressure beginning to build for the withdrawal of the remaining Marines, the Reagan administration seemed unable to make up its mind on the way forward. In the immediate aftermath of the bombing of the Marine barracks, the Joint Chiefs ordered the Activity to send a team into Beirut to look at ways of retaliating against the Islamic terrorists who were responsible, or their backers, Iran and Syria. The CIA had candidly admitted it did not have the expertise to work out how America could retaliate. It had no experts with the specialised knowledge that would allow them to select and reconnoitre potential targets for the military. Bill Cowan was the team's senior operator. Along with the team leader, an army colonel, he stayed up all night working out a plan of action, which was then signed off without problems by Caspar Weinberger. Each team member was carefully chosen, each had specific capabilities and experience that would be invaluable on the ground in Beirut. They were all warned that this was going to be a highly dangerous mission. They would need to get out among the people on the street but that made them extremely vulnerable to kidnapping or worse. They said goodbye to their families and then waited for the order to leave. They waited and waited, Cowan said, 'while ranking military and civilian leaders in the Pentagon debated whether we should go and then, following their approval, while the bureaucracy worked through an agonizingly slow coordination and approval process. It took five weeks for the coordination process and the Pentagon to finally allow us to get on airplanes to go. Every day I left home with my bags, said goodbye to my family, got ready on a plane, every night I was home again.' While they were waiting, the French retaliated for the death of their fifty-nine troops, sending in ground attack aircraft to attack the terrorist bases in the Beka'a Valley. But neither the Pentagon nor the State Department seemed prepared to do likewise.[4]

The Activity team arrived in Beirut in early December 1983, flying in via Cyprus and then by helicopter, first to an aircraft carrier anchored off the Lebanese coast and then into Beirut. The Lebanese capital was in a mess with sporadic outbreaks of fighting going on all over the city. That day, two dozen US Navy ground attack aircraft had taken off from the aircraft carriers USS *Independence* and USS *John F. Kennedy*, on a bombing raid supposedly targeted at the Iranian terrorist training base in the Sheikh Abdullah barracks at Baalbek, although they in fact attacked Syrian gun positions. The Syrian gunners fired up at them with Soviet-made ZSU-23 anti-aircraft guns, dotting the sunny sky with small balls of white smoke, while the US aircraft released red heat balloons to deflect heat-seeking surface-to-air missiles. Two aircraft, a single-seater A7E Corsair and a twin-seater A6E Intruder, were hit by SAM7 shoulder-launched surface-to-air missiles fired by Syrian troops. The Corsair crashed in flames into the Christian-held port of Junieh, north of Beirut. The pilot parachuted to safety, landing in the Mediterranean where he was picked up by the Lebanese Army and handed over to the US Navy. The Intruder crashed into the middle of a group of camouflaged Syrian anti-aircraft artillery positions near Kfar Salwan, in the Chouf Mountains, 15 miles east of Beirut. The pilot, Lieutenant Robert Goodman, died and his co-pilot was taken prisoner. The raids were the first by American warplanes against targets inside Lebanon since the Marines were deployed sixteen months earlier. It was also the first time any US ground attack aircraft had been lost in combat since the Vietnam War. The Druze militias responded to the attacks with heavy shelling of the US airport barracks, killing eight Marines, and the warships of the Sixth Fleet anchored off the coast replied in kind. The loud booms of the US Navy heavy guns could be heard across the capital as the Activity team settled in to its mission.[5]

The first job the Activity team had to do was orientate themselves, get to know the ground they were operating on. Then they had to drive up into the mountains above Beirut to find the Syrian anti-aircraft batteries that had shot down the US Navy aircraft and work out ways of retaliating effectively against the Syrians. 'Clint and I stopped at a small restaurant overlooking Beirut,' Cowan recalled. 'It was between the Christian and Muslim sectors, and it turned out this restaurant was Muslim-owned. We made friends with the owner and sat around a while drinking beer and chatting. Typically, the Lebanese would think back to the days of Beirut's beauty and talk about how grand it was. Within a short while, he was giving us specific directions to the Syrian AA site which had shot down Navy Lieutenant Robert Goodman's plane. We could have found it by map, but he was eager to help us after we were all comfortable with each other. Later, as we were leaving, he looked down at my boots, which were brand new Danners (before Danner became the major supplier of military boots) and he said: "You know, if the Syrians see you in those boots they'll kill you just to take them from you." I paid no attention to what he said until a week later when a Christian local told me the exact same thing.'[6]

It wasn't just their boots that the two Activity operators were likely to lose. Any trip into the Syrian-controlled areas was extremely difficult. They carried out a reconnaissance of the two Syrian anti-aircraft positions around the villages of Arbaniyeh and Ain Soha, seven miles north-east of Beirut. The villages were under the most obvious flight path of any aircraft attacking Syrian positions from the sea, as the US Navy aircraft did, and were packed with ZSU-23 four-barrelled anti-aircraft guns and radar installations. They had to get in close up to the Syrian positions and plant laser-guidance beacons that would allow the air-to-ground missiles fired by US aircraft to home in on the target. But all the various militias and armies occupying Lebanon had check-points everywhere. There was likely to be another roadblock with trigger-happy guards around any bend in any road and the Syrian posts were among the most difficult for the undercover Americans to get through. Clint's successful attempt to bluff his way past a Syrian check-point by babbling in Vietnamese was not the first time that any of the Activity team had found themselves in that position. A couple of days earlier, Cowan and a colleague were driving their rental car along one of the mountain roads leading up to the anti-aircraft positions. As they came round a curve in the road, they saw a Syrian checkpoint straight ahead of them and, thinking quickly, pulled into a petrol station, where they asked the attendant to fill the car's tank. Given that it was already pretty full, this was always going to be difficult. But a confused pump attendant was easier to handle than an aggressive Syrian soldier and after paying for the little petrol that could be squeezed into the tank, the two Americans turned round and headed back down the road away from the checkpoint.[7]

The other main targets were the Iranian-backed terrorists, chief among them Hussein Musawi and the other radicals who were creating groups that were then in their infancy but would later become synonymous with Islamic fundamentalist extremism, chief among them Hezbollah and Islamic Jihad. The Activity team was given a hit list of people that the Reagan administration would like to see taken out. Assassination per se was banned but the sort of people they were hunting down were unlikely to come quietly if Delta or the Activity itself came looking for them and the minute the terrorists went for their guns, the US troops would have been entitled to shoot to kill. But all that was for later; right now the Activity team was just gathering information, preparing for the retaliatory attacks and 'snatch' operations designed to take terrorists back to America to face US justice, not carrying them out. That didn't stop the mission from being highly dangerous and difficult. They were operating in an intensely hostile environment.

'We were receiving information from Washington DC about who might be targets and where the targets might be located,' said Cowan. He and Clint led the operations on the ground while the team commander liaised with the embassy. 'The senior guy was an Army type, senior to me. He acted as liaison to the Embassy and sounding board for Clint and I, who were the 'get about town' operators. Clint and I were all over Beirut and the country. We took the information we had been given and we got out on the ground and tried to verify what we could. The senior guy rarely ventured from the hotel or the Embassy. Great, great guy, but danger wasn't his thing. We had a number of targets that we had no problem identifying. We had a list provided by the CIA. That's because the CIA had good information on people that were involved in the bombing. We were not looking specifically for those people inasmuch as we were looking for where they were located. What houses were they living in? What buildings were they frequenting? So we were looking for places more than the individuals that were in them. The CIA really had a handle on the folks; we were looking to have a handle on the locations.'[8]

The Activity team developed a number of schemes to infiltrate agents into the terrorist organisations or into the areas around them. They coordinated their efforts daily with Bill Buckley, the CIA station chief, who provided them with details of a garage used by the terrorists to prepare the truck bomb used against the Marines' barracks. The man who built the bomb had been identified by the CIA as a member of an Iranian-trained Islamic fundamentalist group, said Robert Baer, one of the Agency's Lebanon specialists. 'His name was Ibrahim Safa,' Baer said. 'He was working with the Pasdaran – the Iranian Revolutionary Guards – out of the southern suburbs of Beirut. In the hierarchy of things, he was just a thug who'd found God. He'd been a bang-bang man in the civil war in the 1970s who knew explosives.'[9] The Activity team had carried out a reconnaissance of the garage, which was in a dangerous Shi'ite area of southern Beirut. But getting close in was going to be difficult. Then one of the team met an American businessman for the company that had the contract to repair telephone lines in the district in which the garage was located. He devised a plan, which envisaged inserting a French-speaking under-cover specialist, a member of the ISA who had been picked out in the trawls of the army personnel computer, into the area. His cover would be as a telephone repairman. This would not just allow him to get in close, he would also be able either to bug the terrorists' telephones and/or cut the lines to hamper their communications.[10]

The location of every terrorist leader the Americans were looking for, including the home of Sheikh Muhammad Hussein Fadlallah, the spiritual leader of Hezbollah, was mapped out by the team. They also cultivated a number of useful agents inside the Christian militia – people who would be able to provide assistance on the ground to any special operations missions the Americans decided to carry out – and they surveyed possible beaches that could be used to insert Delta or SEAL commandos, knowing it was likely that if a mission went ahead they themselves would be going in ahead of it. The team leased safe houses and set up sources of rental and stolen cars and trucks. By the end of their reconnaissance mission, the Activity team felt they had covered every angle, and virtually every part of Beirut, providing their bosses with a comprehensive list of military options. These were always designed to ensure that the risk to non-terrorists would be kept to a minimum. 'Some involved highly sensitive intelligence operations to penetrate the terrorists' sanctuaries,' Cowan said. 'Others involved the precise use of military force against selected targets. None, however, included specific recommendations that could have caused casualties to innocent civilians.' Any target that might lead to collateral damage, the military jargon for civilian deaths, was ruled out.[11]

Cowan and the team leader flew out shortly after New Year, leaving the others behind to develop intelligence sources. They went via Stuttgart to brief Eucom commanders, who this time knew they had been in Beirut, and met General Richard L Lawson, Eucom deputy commander-in-chief. A tough air force general who had earned the nickname 'The Shark', it was Lawson who had reacted furiously to the fact that they had been sent to Beirut after the embassy bombing. 'I didn't even know ISA was there until I found out accidentally during a walk through a building after the bombing,' he complained. 'I threw them out, just three more Americans that could be captured.' This time he listened quietly for nearly an hour as the team outlined the series of options they had put together. 'We briefed him on our mission and our recommendations,' Cowan said. 'At the conclusions, he leaned forward, slammed his fist down on his desk and said: "Goddamn it. I hope those people back in Washington will listen to what you're saying." So did we.'[12]

They returned to Washington full of enthusiasm for the potential of the operations they had put in place, Cowan said. 'We came back to the Pentagon with a rather substantial report that talked about the options we could do – not just in terms of striking back, but other rather good intelligence operations that we could have activated.' They had no doubt that some at least of the operations would go ahead. They were not alone. Delta was poised to carry out attacks in Beirut. 'We knew just where to strike,' said Eric Haney. 'For months now we'd been tracking several of the most active terrorist cells in Beirut and we were ready to make a clean sweep of them. It wouldn't put an end to the terrorist activity in the region, but it sure would put them out of action for a while. I fully expected a return engagement in Beirut.'[13] But by mid-February nothing had happened and the demands from Congress for the Marines to be withdrawn were increasing. 'Our enthusiasm quickly turned to dismay,' Cowan said. 'Response to our efforts was, at best, bureaucratic, and at worst, almost antagonistic. We had senior people in the Pentagon who absolutely berated us for even suggesting that we retaliate. We were surprised to say the least. There was absolutely no follow up to anything we recommended.'[14]

Cowan and the team leader went to see Ed Hickey, director of the White House Military Office and a deputy assistant to President Reagan in the White House East Wing. He and a senior military assistant listened intently to what the two ISA officers had to say and asked sensible questions about their proposals, encouraging them briefly to imagine that something might come of their mission after all. But when the briefing was over, Hickey leaned back in his seat, thought for a moment and then told them: 'Gentlemen. You know, if the president could hear what you have to say, he would order them to be done immediately. The president is not afraid to take action. Unfortunately, they'll never make it to his office.' He then pointed over his shoulder towards the Pentagon and said: 'They will never let him see it. They will never let it get through the bureaucracy.'[15] Hickey was right. Nothing was done.

THE SITUATION IN BEIRUT was already spiralling out of control. On 18 January 1984, Malcolm Kerr, the 52-year-old president of the American University of Beirut, was shot dead by gunmen claiming to be from Islamic Jihad. The two gunmen had entered the university unchallenged and made their way to the third floor where Kerr had his office. As he walked out of the elevator they were waiting for him, shooting him twice in the head with a silenced pistol. Just over three weeks later, Islamic Jihad kidnapped Frank Regier, an engineering professor at the university, pushing him into a car as he walked out of the campus gates. Regier was lucky. Two months later, the Shi'ite Amal militia rescued him and a French hostage. But his kidnapping led the US embassy to begin evacuating all non-essential staff and momentum was building up in Congress for the withdrawal of the US Marines. A few days later, President Reagan finally agreed to withdraw the Marines. The last left on 26 February. The Syrians, the Iranians and every Islamic terrorist in the Middle East knew they could do what they liked to the United States with impunity.[16]

Over the next few weeks, Islamic terrorists kidnapped first Jeremy Levin, the CNN bureau chief in Beirut, and then Bill Buckley, the CIA station chief, who was grabbed in the apartment building where he lived as he was about to leave for work. None of the accounts of his kidnapping mentioned he was a CIA officer, describing him as a first secretary in the political department. But it cannot have been long before the terrorists knew the identity of their new hostage. 'Not long after his capture, his agents either vanished or were killed,' Carl Stiner said. 'It was clear that his captors had tortured him into revealing the network of agents he had established – the source of most of our intelligence in Beirut. The United States had once again lost its primary intelligence sources in Beirut, making it even more dangerous for the Americans remaining behind.'[17]

As head of the Activity, Jerry King had enjoyed a tempestuous relationship with those around him, vigorously defending his unit and personnel against its numerous critics inside the army. His hard-edged attitude had won him few friends among the traditionalist opponents of special operations forces and even within the closed world of the special operations community he had managed to make a few enemies. Never afraid to say what he thought, he had clashed on a number of occasions with Bill Odom, his immediate superior, who he regarded as too political and not someone who was 'ever likely to stick his neck out'. Odom swung from instructing the Activity to 'set the Middle East on fire' to worrying about the most basic principles of agent-running, King said. Another former ISA officer said Odom told King to infiltrate operatives into terrorist organisations in the Middle East. 'When it was pointed out the rite of passage in a couple of the ones he identified was to kill, he wasn't so enthusiastic,' the officer said. 'He then agreed to our strategy of recruiting locals that had or could gain access to the various gangs engaged in terrorism. We concluded that this approach might prove beneficial and, more importantly, allow us time to recruit and train our operatives to the desired level of proficiency.' King took to requesting all orders from Odom in writing after instances where the general appeared to forget what he had told the ISA commander to do.[18]

King knew that Odom was not his biggest fan and it was no surprise that the tough-talking colonel found himself elbowed aside. In March 1984, he was assigned a post in the 82nd Airborne Division, which although based at Fort Bragg, was not a special operations unit. King's no-nonsense approach, and his refusal to kiss arse and to play the politics that was so often needed in the upper echelons of the Pentagon, had not done either his own career or the unit too many favours. But his professional ability and experience, honed in the Special Forces operations in Vietnam, had proved invaluable in the unit's formation. The teams and structures he put in place, his operatives' careful attention to detail, the emphasis on continuous tradecraft and linguistic training and the refusal to accept failure, even on the most difficult of missions, were fundamental to the Activity's success. King's carefully worked out plans that any commander should be succeeded by his deputy in order to maintain continuity were ignored and although Cal Sasai took charge for a few months, he was passed over for the permanent role of commanding officer in favour of an outsider.[19]

Colonel Howard J Floyd had begun his career with the 101st Airborne Division before moving into conventional military intelligence assignments. He reorganised the ISA to emphasise the intelligence role. Under King, the command group of around eight people oversaw all activities. There was a Directorate of Personnel and Administration; a Directorate of Support, which provided supplies and funding; and a single Directorate of Operations and Intelligence. There were also three mission squadrons, Sigint; Communications; and Operations, which contained the former Delta and Special Forces soldiers who provided the shooters. Each squadron was made up of a number of troops, which provided personnel for the actual missions and contained between a dozen and fifteen personnel per troop. Shortly before he left, King had added a technical section to the Directorate of Support, to procure and develop special equipment, provide forged documents and develop operative disguises, much in the manner of James Bond's 'Q'.[20]

Three months after taking over, Floyd split the Directorate of Operations and Intelligence in two, making it the Directorate of Operations and hiving off the old directorate's Research and Analysis

Division to form a separate Directorate of Intelligence. This had three separate divisions. A Research and Analysis Division, which had three separate branches, one covering Latin America, one Middle East and Africa, and one Exploitation, provided all-source intelligence to assist in the planning and support of intelligence-gathering missions. The Management and Threat Division acted as a clearing-house for intelligence from national agencies such as the CIA, the NSA, the NRO and the DIA. This did not just include intelligence related to the mission requirement. Management and Threat also provided 'estimate and current research to minimize the threat from foreign counter-intelligence services and terrorist activities'. The third division was Administration.[21]

Floyd soon found himself up against the same difficulties that King had faced in getting approval for missions, complaining that at times he had to deal with seven different general counsels to get any operational plans passed, in contrast to colleagues in the British SAS who could get orders signed off swiftly by a government minister. One mission where obtaining authorisation from every quarter proved particularly difficult occurred in November 1984. Amid fears of a Soviet takeover of the Seychelles, a small group of islands on the main shipping route between the Cape of Good Hope and the Persian Gulf, the Activity was ordered to draw up plans for an evacuation of US personnel from the main island of Mahé. The US ambassador was getting edgy but it wasn't just the embassy staff who were at risk. There was also a US Air Force space tracking station on the island. President Albert F Rene, a left-wing dictator who had taken over the country seven years earlier in a coup, had reinforced his position with elections that only allowed one result and was moving increasingly closer to Moscow. Russian, East German, North Korean, Cuban and Libyan military advisers were all over the islands and the US embassy was getting increasingly nervous. The East Germans had set up radar installations aimed at monitoring the top secret US naval base on Diego

Garcia, 600 miles to the east, from which US Navy Trident submarines patrolled the Indian Ocean, while the Russians were conducting a survey of the islands' continental shelf that the Pentagon believed might be in preparation for the construction of a Soviet naval base.[22]

Floyd and his commanders made contact with the personnel on the USAF tracking base, who were unable to help in providing any intelligence. So the Activity mission planners sketched out a plan to send a pathfinder team to the Seychelles. Operating under cover, the small team was to draw up evacuation plans and prepare infiltration and exfiltration routes for US Special Operations Forces, including surveys of landing sites on Mahé's beaches, in the event that US citizens needed to be extracted under fire. The tasks included complete surveys of the US embassy and USAF tracking base, including precise details of all exit and entry points together with any obstacles that might hamper a rescue mission, and estimates of the likely opposition, from the tiny, 1,000-strong national security force to the North Koreans and Cubans who were training them.

The Pentagon put the Activity's plans to the State Department, which needed to give the go-ahead for the covert deployment. But there was no reply. So Colonel William Garrison, Floyd's deputy, and Bill Cowan went to the State Department to gee them up. Garrison, a tall, lean Texan, who seemed perpetually to have half a cigar hanging from his mouth, told a group of senior State Department officials that he and his colleague needed some help. 'Gentlemen,' he said in a Texan drawl. 'We've come over to brief you on something of importance. We're here to save your colleagues. We're here because we need something from you.' He then paused slightly for effect, before adding: 'We need a decision.'[23]

A few days later, the State Department gave the go-ahead for the mission but the whole process typified the way in which the Activity's every move seemed to be blocked at every turn. Bill Cowan would later write that Activity personnel were repeatedly hindered in their efforts to carry out 'priority missions... by lack of confidence in their capabilities, misunderstanding of their roles and missions, and too often general mistrust of elite units by more conventionally minded military and civilian leadership'.[24]

That mistrust had been made even worse by a long-running and damaging investigation into allegations of fraud that was about to reach its climax in a series of court cases that saw a number of members of the US special operations forces jailed. It had begun with Jim Longhofer's Army Special Operations Division before extending right across the special operations community. The financial improprieties were in part a result of Ed Meyer's conviction that everything possible had to be done to protect the secrecy of the various special operations units. 'We had a tremendous concern in the operational security area,' he said. 'We would have used every means to keep the people involved from being known.' The need for secrecy was not in doubt but it had all sorts of consequences that Meyer would never have wanted. The blanket secrecy allowed illegal activities to go unchecked, while the investigation and court cases that followed, led to information that should have been kept secret, including the existence of the Activity itself, being widely reported in the media.

In an operation codenamed Foreshadow, authorised by General Jack Vessey, the then vice-Chief of Staff, all mention of the Special Operations Division had been removed from the army records. Jim Longhofer set up a number of secret operations around the world. Money was channelled through secret accounts and bogus front companies that existed in name only. The secret units included a counter-espionage and security team codenamed Yellow Fruit. Set up in June 1982 under the command of Lieutenant-Colonel Dale Duncan, its role had been to provide 'operational security and counterintelligence support to classified, sensitive special operations and intelligence elements', including the Activity. Duncan 'retired' from the army to set up a private security consultancy firm called Business Security

International, which was based just a few miles from the Pentagon at 4306 Evergreen Lane, Annandale, Virginia. In fact Duncan was still in the army and Business Security International was a bogus front company, a cover for Yellow Fruit, but an illegal cover.[25]

'Establishing these organizations was in direct violation of existing Federal Law,' one former ISA officer said. 'We had formed a bogus front company and quickly had to close it because of the same law. The CIA was the only Federal Agency allowed to form such front organizations. In our case, the biggest problem was the one we had formed was on the brink, pending contracts, of making considerable profits. We continued to work with the agency to develop a means – joint operations – to enable us to legally form and maintain front organizations.'[26]

YELLOW FRUIT BEGAN to spy on the special operations units, including both Delta and the Activity. 'We were unaware that Yellow Fruit existed until we received reports that ISA operatives were being trailed during an exercise,' a former member of the Activity said. 'We called the Pentagon and asked if they had counter-intelligence agents working the exercise. Our concern was to determine if these were good guys or bad guys. Unable to get any answer, we assumed they might be bad guys and set out to ascertain who was watching us. We trapped one of the watchers in a bathroom and recognized him as an army intelligence type who worked for Longhofer. We also identified individuals trying to observe JSOC, Delta and us in the exercise area. We actually pinpointed their location. In short, we compromised their operation. When one of them was confronted he said what they were doing and identified Longhofer as his contact in the Pentagon.'[27]

Jerry King had repeatedly clashed with Longhofer over the latter's ambitious attempts to extend the remit of the Army Special Operations Division. Longhofer even expanded his operations to Korea when one of his officers was posted there. One member of the Activity recalled how the officer concerned fabricated a mission in Korea for the ISA in order to use its expertise in satellite communications. The officer wanted to test out a plan that he had put forward to use helicopters to monitor North Korean spies trying to infiltrate the south. 'The Activity was tasked by the Department of the Army – later turned out it was Longhofer's crowd – to provide communication support for a presidential trip to Korea,' the former ISA officer said. 'After arriving in Korea, the team leader reported that he had been contacted by an officer who had worked with Longhofer in Army Special Operations Division prior to being assigned to Korea and told he was to support a test devised by that officer. Recognizing a skunk in the wood pile, the team was ordered to report to the American embassy and if they were not needed to support the President's trip, return to base. They returned to home station. It seemed that this officer had come up with an idea and asked Longhofer to acquire satcom support to help prove his theory. When I later learned the details, it struck me as a crack-pot idea with little if any benefits. However, conducting the test would have made the officer concerned look good to his superiors.'[28]

Five months after Yellow Fruit was set up, Longhofer was head-hunted by Bill Casey, who saw the Army Special Operations Division as a useful tool in the Agency's attempts to provide arms and funds to the Contras. Congress was closing in on the operations to support the Nicaraguan rebel forces and Longhofer, with his ability to mount covert operations that Congress didn't know about, was a useful ally. He was assigned to the CIA as chief military assistant to the Agency's operations directorate and began to use some of his secret operations, Yellow Fruit included, to channel arms to the Contras. But Casey's plan would only work so long as Longhofer continued to control the Army Special Operations Division as well. The new commander of the SOD was Colonel Robert Kvederas, but it was soon clear to superior officers that Longhofer was still calling the shots. When Major-General Homer Long, the Assistant Deputy Chief of Staff Operations, was given overall charge of the Army Special Operations Division, he told

Longhofer to butt out. 'Longhofer was trying to run the show at the same time while over at CIA,' Long said. 'One of the unpleasant experiences I had with Longhofer was to call him into my office and tell him he was to have nothing to do with that outfit.' Long told him he wasn't in charge of anything related to Army Special Operations Division. 'Now that infuriated him. I think if he had a knife he would have cut my throat.' Long told army investigators that he believed that Longhofer was getting special protection from Ed Meyer and that after being bawled out by Long he had gone to the Army Chief of Staff and got the OK to continue doing what he was doing, albeit in a more covert way. 'My belief is he then went to the chief,' Long said. 'By notes and personal contacts he kept his contacts going, pulling strings. He was a real operator.'[29]

Then in June 1983, Ed Meyer retired. Suddenly the Army Special Operations Division's main defender at the top of the army hierarchy had disappeared. General John Wickham, the new Chief of Staff, and John Marsh, the Army Secretary, found out that there were tens of army secret operations that they didn't know anything about and ordered an investigation. It was going nowhere until August when two separate members of Yellow Fruit made complaints against Dale Duncan. The first was Tom Golden, a long-term army intelligence officer who had met Duncan by chance while on a fishing trip to the Bahamas and had been offered a post with Yellow Fruit. 'I worked directly for Colonel Duncan,' he later told a congressional inquiry. 'One of the first jobs that I was given was to establish accountability for covert funds that had been advanced to individuals and had been expended by the organization,' Golden said. He pretty soon became concerned that fraud was taking place on a massive scale. Duncan had submitted receipts for $89,000 in expenses, Golden told the inquiry. The only problem was 'the receipts were bogus'. He also told the inquiry about a top secret document containing plans to get round the congressional bans on military aid to the Contras by using the Army

Special Operations Division and Yellow Fruit, organisations that as far as army records were concerned did not exist, to deliver weapons and money to the rebels fighting the Sandinista government. Congress was building up to a ban on all military aid to the Contras and it was a matter of deep concern within Yellow Fruit. 'Everybody was worried,' Golden said. 'What was talked about in the office was the Boland Amendment. It was going to cut off aid to the Contras and we would all be out of a job and how are we going to get round this thing?'[30]

The suspicions of fraud and the plans to get round Congressional bans on aid to the Contras were not the only potentially illegal actions causing Golden concern. Shortly afterwards he and another member of Yellow Fruit were told by Duncan about plans for a major counter-espionage and security operation. An annual convention of armed forces special operations officers and CIA special activities officers was to take place at the Twin Bridges Marriot Hotel, in Arlington, Virginia, in September. There would be 150 former special operators there and Yellow Fruit was going to bug the bars, restaurants, bathrooms and all their rooms to try to catch out anyone who was talking about secret operations. 'Everyone was going to get drunk and start talking about classified operations and this was going to be an opportunity to get a handle on them,' one army official alleged. Female army intelligence officers would be wired up to pick up drunken conversations and Duncan was even talking about hiring a prostitute – some even suggested a transvestite prostitute – to try to seduce Jerry King. As far as Duncan and Longhofer were concerned, Jerry King was 'the enemy', one former member of Yellow Fruit said. 'The dining-in was going to provide an opportunity to nail him.'[31]

Both Golden and the other officer, a former Army Special Forces intelligence expert called Mike Belcher, were concerned that the wiretaps were illegal and refused to cooperate. The operation was sub-sequently called off. Apart from anything else, King had never intended to attend the reunion. But Golden had decided that the financial arrangements at Yellow Fruit were illegal and reported them to a superior, who passed it on to Jim Longhofer. A week later, Longhofer rang Golden and told him to go home and never come back to the Business Security International offices again. 'We'll call you. Don't call us,' Longhofer said. A few weeks later, Golden was ordered into the office to see Duncan who told him that Longhofer had investigated the charges Golden had made against him and absolved him of any wrongdoing. Golden was being transferred out to a punishment posting.[32]

But the affair refused to go away. Mike Belcher had reported the lax security at Business Security International to Jerry King, who had been his commanding officer in Vietnam. He called King at home late one evening and asked him for advice. He was cagey about the details of the organisation he was working for and what it did but said he believed that it had been involved in 'a major security violation'. He had found a top secret document lying in an unlocked drawer at a time when there were civilian painters working in the offices. When he reported this to the unit security officer, he was told to forget it, he said. Jerry King told him he should report it to Longhofer. But Belcher said he thought that if he did that, he would just end up getting fired. King offered to arrange an interview with the army inspector-general, but Belcher was again hesitant so King said he should talk to the Activity's own military lawyer who could advise him on what to do. The lawyer reported his conversation with Belcher to Major-General Albert Stubblebine, the commander of the army's Intelligence and Security Command, who ordered an immediate investigation. It turned out that the top secret document left lying around for the decorators to read was a file on the Activity. Longhofer now submitted a report on his preliminary inquiry into the allegations against Duncan in which he accused Golden, Belcher and other complainants of pursuing 'a personal vendetta' against the Yellow Fruit commander. But it was too late to stop the investigation ordered by Stubblebine, which recommended that the

Justice Department be called in and that Longhofer, Duncan and other members of Yellow Fruit be suspended.[33]

The investigation widened out to include every special operations unit, including Delta, SEAL Team Six and the Activity. More than eighty members of Delta were investigated for suspected fraudulent expenses claims. Two ISA officers, one of whom had already been posted out as a result of a personal conduct violation, were found to have been involved in fraudulent claims. 'Have you ever had a feeling that something is wrong but you can't identify what?' one former ISA officer said. 'I used to describe the feelings as "smelling smoke, but unable to find the fire". Accounting for funds and supplies was always a major issue for the CO who was concerned about the accountability of funds. The unit was organized into Directorates. Funds and supplies were under the Support Directorate. It was discovered that two individuals had been misusing funds for personal benefit. Both went to jail. They had, through various means, secured real receipts with dummy dollar figures.'

But although two ISA officers were involved in fraud, one of their former colleagues dismissed any suggestion that this was a widespread practice. The Activity's missions gave them access to large sums of money, he said. Senior officers could have made a fortune out of some of the transactions in which it was involved. They chose not to and continued serving their country loyally. 'As was pointed out to higher headquarters, because of the financing mechanism the unit established, the billions of dollars deposited by the Iraqis [to buy the American self-propelled howitzers] could have been ripped off. We had all the necessary documents to legally, from the banks perspective, empty the account. But we didn't.'[34]

Longhofer subsequently denied allegations that the Army Special Operations Division was 'out of control' and accountable to no one. The charges against him were 'trumped up to destroy the Army's special operations capability,' he said. 'Our operations were directed and approved by the President and officials of the CIA, DOD and the Department of the Army. Additionally, representatives of appropriate congressional committees were briefed on our programmes and operations. Allegations that we did not observe laws and had the attitude that we did not have to follow the rules are false. We operated under special covert rules. All of us viewed our activities as a scalpel that had to be firmly guided and controlled.'[35]

But one former ISA officer derided Colonel Longhofer's claims to have operated under 'special covert rules' that allowed the Army Special Operations Division a licence to operate in the way it did. 'To my knowledge "special covert rules" do not exist,' the officer said. 'Sounds like some bullshit he and others in his office frequently used to overwhelm opposition. Longhofer and his crew had what I would describe as a "cowboy" mentality. They were bright, articulate and imaginative. Unfortunately, not all their ideas were well thought out.'[36]

Another dismissed Longhofer's insistence that Congress was kept fully informed of what he and his colleagues in the Army Special Operations Division were doing. 'I don't believe that they actually briefed Congress,' he told investigators. 'I thought that their maintaining that they had actually briefed Congress was a gross overstatement of fact. I did not have too much confidence in the information relayed. They were too footloose and had too many easy answers. I had many doubts about how the monies were controlled. It was not a good situation. There was some hanky-panky going on.'[37]

Dale Duncan was eventually jailed for ten years by a court martial for submitting a fraudulent expenses claim. His sentence was subsequently commuted to seven years and he was released after serving only two years at Fort Leavenworth military prison in Kansas. Longhofer was jailed for two years for dereliction of duty and conduct unbecoming an officer. His commanding officer subsequently cut that sentence in half. He was released after sixty-three days at Fort Leavenworth when a US Army Court of Military Review overturned his conviction on the grounds that his trial had not begun within 120 days of his being charged. His sentence was subsequently commuted and he was freed. The whole affair did immense damage to the reputation of the Special Operations Forces and because the Activity was the most secret of all the units involved, the media tended to focus on it, giving the false impression that it was at the heart of the wrongdoing. Ed Meyer subsequently admitted that he should have paid closer attention to what Longhofer was doing. 'I think the lesson is that whatever kind of operation we conduct needs to have oversight,' he said. 'And somehow there has to be an accommodation between the oversight side and the operations side, because these are the wars of today and tomorrow.'[38]

6 THE FELIX NETWORK

MICHEL WAS A Lebanese exile living in Washington and keen to hear the latest gossip from the Christian community in East Beirut and Junieh. It was October 1985. There was no shortage of news from Lebanon on the television and in the newspapers. But it always seemed to focus on the fighting in Beirut, or on the missing American hostages. The telephone call had promised more, much more. The real story from back home, and particularly what was going on inside the Phalangist militia, the Lebanese Forces. The guy on the phone had said his name was Paul, Paul Dunbar. The name meant nothing to Michel but Dunbar mentioned a mutual friend in Christian east Beirut, a prominent member of the Lebanese Forces, who he said had told him to look Michel up and give him his best. Could they meet up for a drink? No problem, said Michel. It would be good to hear from someone who really knew what was happening back home. They arranged to meet in a bar in Crystal City, close to the Pentagon, the next afternoon. Dunbar arrived within minutes of Michel. He bought them both a beer and they sat down in a corner, away from the TV screens replaying back-to-back football games. Dunbar wasn't what

Michel had expected. He had seemed friendly and open on the phone, someone you could spend an enjoyable evening with. But here in the flesh, he was stiff and formal and when Michel tried to ask him about their mutual friend, he just shrugged off the question, as if he didn't want to talk about it at all.

Michel was already trying to work out a way of ducking out of the meeting when Dunbar dropped the bombshell. He was an official representative of the US government. There was something Michel could do for them. He wanted to meet another friend of Michel's. He wanted to meet Shamon. There was a highly sensitive matter of mutual benefit to both the United States and the Lebanese Forces that he needed to discuss with him. Shamon was the Lebanese Forces' main conduit to the outside world. Although his parents were Lebanese Christians and he was born in Beirut, he had been brought up in France. But when the civil war broke out in the mid-1970s, he went home and volunteered to join the Lebanese Forces militia, swiftly rising through the ranks to the top of its intelligence organisation. His international contacts led the senior Phalangist officials to select him for a special overseas mission, developing the Lebanese Forces' ties with intelligence agencies that would be interested in mutual cooperation, like Israel's Mossad and the French DGSE. He had effectively become a roving ambassador for the Phalangists. But it was his contacts inside Lebanon that Dunbar was after. Dunbar was a senior member of the Activity. It had been tasked to carry out a mission that few inside the US military, and indeed the CIA, believed possible, to rescue the US hostages held by the Islamic fundamentalist Hezbollah in Beirut. It was a formidable task and Shamon was the only man with the kind of contacts that might just make it possible. He had a widespread network of agents inside Lebanon's Shi'ite community, some personal friends, some simply contacts. It was a network that extended right into the heart of Hezbollah itself.

Michel was understandably suspicious. If this guy Dunbar was from the US government and he wanted to meet Shamon, he had to be some kind of spook. That was what Shamon did. That was all he did. But he was really tight with both the CIA and the DIA. If a US spook wanted to get in touch with Shamon, he could do it easily. He certainly wouldn't need to go through Michel. But despite his concerns, he contacted Shamon, who was as puzzled as Michel over who these 'official US government representatives' might really be and told him to set up another meeting and this time find out what this Dunbar guy really wanted. Shamon wasn't about to fly all the way to America unless it was worth his while.

Two weeks later, Michel met Dunbar again, still close to the Pentagon but this time in an Irish bar in Alexandria. He arrived to find the man from the Activity sitting at the back next to a large muscular looking character who in Michel's words was 'every bit an infantry soldier'. Dunbar seemed much more relaxed than when they first met. He asked Michel what it was like for a Lebanese citizen living in Washington, how he was enjoying his time in the States, what did he miss most about the Lebanon? It was the kind of conversation that Michel had been looking for during their first meeting. Now it was not what he was looking for at all. Meanwhile, the other guy was playing the strong silent type. He just kept scanning the bar, watching the door, clocking who came in and out, saying nothing, just watching. Michel and Dunbar danced around the subject for half an hour or so before Paul finally told Michel that they were looking for information about the Lebanon. When Michel asked who was looking, Dunbar would only say that he and his friends were involved in 'anti-terrorist activities' and were 'operating under an inter-agency mandate'. They needed to know as much as possible about the various terrorist groups based in Lebanon, Dunbar said. Then almost as an aside, he added that it might also be useful to have any information that Shamon had about the US hostages. If Shamon was prepared to come to America to meet him, he would introduce him to his superiors who would be able to reassure him that they were on the level and that it was a genuine US government operation.

It was now clear to both Michel and Shamon that what Dunbar really wanted to know about was the hostages. But why couldn't he just go through the normal channels? Nevertheless, Shamon agreed to come to Washington to meet him. Dunbar and his burly colleague picked Michel up and drove him to the National Airport to meet Shamon. What followed appeared even to Shamon to be excessive security measures. 'We changed cars three times, drove in circles and took other evasive action,' he recalled. 'In the end, I was not sure that they even knew where they were heading.' After nearly an hour, they pulled into the car park of a hotel only a few minutes from the airport. They went upstairs to a large suite where Paul's 'superiors' were waiting. Shamon was going to need a lot of persuading before he agreed to give these guys anything. Eventually, it would get to the point where the guys from the Activity were just about the only people in US intelligence he did trust. But right now he didn't have the faintest idea who they were. He was not about to tell them anything of any real value.

But the Activity operators were if anything even more unsure of whether or not Shamon was their man. He certainly had a better handle on what was happening in Beirut than anyone else they had access to but they were as concerned to know how much they could trust him as he was with them. The atmosphere was tense, both sides probing the other, trying to build the relationship of trust that is the main building block of any connection in the world of espionage. The Activity men were sizing Shamon up, working out how to handle him, what would get his cooperation, and most important of all, was he still on top of the scene inside Lebanon. They ask about Middle East terrorist groups and their influence in Lebanon, about the Syrians, about the Soviets. Shamon was reticent, his answers curt and brief. Eventually they worked their way round to the Lebanese Forces themselves, checking out the complete wiring diagram, who does this; who does that; who's in charge of this, who's in charge of that; who's in; who's out. The questions were becoming much more probing, yet paradoxically Shamon was beginning to feel better about the whole meeting. The questions they were asking clearly showed that these guys knew Beirut. The elaborate security measures, the need to set up their own channels, all pointed to a highly secretive special operations unit, Delta, or something like that. Something *like* that was right. The first steps in creating the relationship of trust had been taken and Shamon was soon told precisely what they were looking for and why. The CIA looked down on Shamon and his network. But in the hands of the expert agent-handlers in the Activity's intelligence squadron, he would prove to be an invaluable asset, the central figure in an ISA spy network codenamed Felix. This collection of agents and sub-agents inside the Lebanese Forces, the Shi'ite Amal and right inside Hezbollah would ultimately pinpoint the location of every one of the US hostages as part of plans for a rescue mission by a joint force of Delta and SEALs that would be guided into location by the Activity.[1]

THE MUSLIM AREAS of Lebanon had become virtual satellites of the vehemently anti-American regime in Iran. Three months before the meetings in Crystal City, Hezbollah's spiritual leader, Sheikh Muhammad Hussein Fadlallah, had accused America of trying to assassinate him, killing large numbers of innocent Lebanese in the process. The attack had taken place on 8 March 1985. It was Friday, the Muslim holy day. There were crowds of fervent Shi'ite Muslims leaving the mosque in Beirut's Bir al-Abed district. The population of the predominantly Muslim district had been swept up in the anti-American fervour that had spread from Iran to Lebanon in the wake of Washington's tacit support for the Christian Phalangist militia. The Bir al-Abed mosque was now the de facto headquarters for the Hezbollah fundamentalists, largely because it was close to the home of Sheikh Muhammad Hussein Fadlallah. The guards were quick to tell the young man who parked his pick-up truck on Snoubra Street outside Fadlallah's home that he had to move it. But there was a mass of traffic and the driver of the pick-up truck rushed off, saying he just had to get his spare tyre fixed. There seemed little the guards could do and anyway, Sheikh Fadlallah's armoured Range Rover was just arriving. As it parked outside his house, the pick-up truck exploded. The seven-storey apartment block opposite Fadlallah's home collapsed and the whole of the street seemed to be engulfed in flames. Sheikh Fadlallah 'miraculously' survived the explosion, his followers announced. But few of the drivers attempting to make their way home from Friday prayers were so lucky. They were burned to death in their cars together with their passengers. The blast was the third car bomb explosion in Muslim West Beirut in as many weeks. No one claimed responsibility. As the last of the flames were dampened down, people were already on the street, burning the Stars and Stripes and chanting that America was 'the Great Satan', the same slogan used by supporters of Ayatollah Khomeini in Iran. But most people, including Sheikh Fadlallah, seemed to blame the Israelis. Selim al-Huss, the Labour and Education Minister, said he 'had no doubt that Israel was behind this ugly crime'. The following day, suicide bombers drove a Mercedes limousine packed with 100lbs of high-explosive into an Israeli army vehicle, killing seven Israeli soldiers. The Israelis vehemently denied they were responsible for the blast outside Fadlallah's home and it subsequently emerged that Christian militiamen linked to the CIA had carried out the attack, which was supposedly financed by the Saudi government.[2]

'There were allegations that we were involved with Lebanese intelligence and the bomb that tried to blow up Sheikh Fadlallah's house,' one former ISA officer said. 'In fact, the CIA had been working with a group of Lebanese military people. But the intent was not to take out a target or to go back and blow up Sheikh Fadlallah's house or his headquarters. The real point of that work at that time was to try to develop an effective counter-terrorist unit. My understanding is that it was a group of rogues within that who thought they would go ahead and blow that up because it would make us happy. But I had good associations with the agency throughout that period. I've been told by numerous people that it was not an operation intended to do that. I believe it, because it was poorly executed. I believe had the CIA been involved it would have been a better job. The reaction obviously was that we create more hate and discontent towards us; people clearly rose up against us. Hezbollah then grows by numbers, we create more terrorists than we had before we started, we get a black eye throughout the Middle East, it hits the front page of the newspaper, and it's an enduring problem. Any time you conduct an operation that causes civilian casualties, you lessen your ability to work effectively in and among those people who you are trying to target. Our only success in dealing with terrorists – whether they be in Lebanon or wherever throughout the world, is our ability to find Muslims who will support us, who will do things for us. When we intentionally or otherwise kill civilians, create collateral damage, we're less likely to find people who will do things for us.'[3]

THE ACTIVITY, NOW 283-strong, had agents in Nigeria, Somalia, Morocco and ten countries in Latin America, a region where the advance of Moscow-backed guerrillas and political parties were seen in the Reagan administration as a particularly serious threat to America.[4] Caspar Weinberger, the US Defense Secretary, told Congress in his 1985 annual report that 'the Soviets have undertaken, both directly and through surrogates, a global campaign of destabilization, focused on the third world, that seeks to obtain objectives without direct confrontation with the United States.' This represented the most prominent direct threat to US security, Weinberger said. 'US special operations forces are being employed to counter these destabilization efforts,' he added. 'By assisting others to prepare their own defences, we enhance the free world's ability to cope with Soviet expansionism, reduce the likelihood that US forces will become involved in combat, and demonstrate our determination not to default on our commitments.'

US special operations forces, largely Army Special Forces but also Delta, SEAL and ISA operators, were deployed across Central America as part of Task Force Bayonet. Most were only involved in training, as in El Salvador. This work, known as security assistance or Foreign Internal Defense, was, as Weinberger said, designed to ensure that they could defend themselves against the communist-backed insurgents and to prevent US troops from becoming actively involved in the conflicts themselves. They carried out training in small unit counter-insurgency tactics, strategic reconnaissance and rapid-reaction operations. But a small number of troops were directly involved in the operations themselves. These almost invariably included members of the Activity, always operating in small teams, sometimes on the ground collecting human intelligence, sometimes in the air, monitoring the insurgents' communications.[5]

The capture in April 1985 of seven members of the Nicaraguan security services inside Honduras and a tour of Warsaw Pact capitals by the Sandinista President Daniel Ortega, persuaded the Reagan administration that it needed to be ready to invade Nicaragua to stop the spread of pro-Soviet states in Latin America. Ortega's visit to Moscow for talks with Soviet President Mikhail Gorbachev, during which he signed a deal including substantial Soviet assistance for his government, was denounced in Washington as part of 'a strong and well-planned strategy of the Sandinista government to strengthen its ties with the Soviet Bloc.'[6] In an operation codenamed Grazing Lawn, a team of signals intelligence operators from the Activity was sent to Honduras to collect intelligence on the Sandinista troops that any invasion force would have to overcome. The team operated one signals intelligence aircraft out of Tegucigalpa airport. By now the controversy surrounding the Army Special Operations Division had led to its Sea Spray air operations being assigned to the ISA under the codename Quasar Talent. The Grazing Lawn team, which would remain in Honduras until January 1986, when it was withdrawn 'for security reasons', also maintained a fixed communications monitoring, analysis and reporting site on a nearby mountain. The intelligence, or 'take', the team produced was flagged Secret Quiet Falcon. Security was provided by four members of the ISA's own operational security branch as well as three Special Forces-trained NCOs, two from the US Army's 1st Special Forces Group, based at Fort Lewis, Washington, and one from Delta. It is unlikely that any of the Quiet Falcon 'take' was provided to the Contras directly, which would have been illegal under the terms of the Boland Amendment. But it would almost certainly have been passed to the National Security Council, where Lieutenant-Colonel Oliver North was already playing a key role in coordinating support for the Contras.

Grazing Lawn was part of what US officials claimed was 'an elaborate intelligence network' preparing for a possible invasion. *The New York Times* quoted intelligence officials as saying that major Nicaraguan installations were lightly defended and that, with minimal risk, American pilots could destroy the small Nicaraguan Air Force, radar, artillery, tanks, supply depots and command centres. 'If proper tactics and proper ordnance were applied to those sites, they'd never know what hit them,' one said. Invading Nicaragua would be likely to provoke widespread criticism both at home and abroad but it would be as easy as 'falling off a log'. Despite the optimistic talk coming out of military intelligence and Southern Command – which believed it would take the United States two weeks to gain control of 60 per cent of the population – the Joint Chiefs were much more cautious, estimating that an invasion would require 125,000 US troops; that there would be as many as 4,000 casualties; and that the US would have to maintain a strong occupation force in Nicaragua for at least five years.[7]

BUT DESPITE ITS continuing involvement in Task Force Bayonet, the Activity's attention kept being drawn back to the Middle East. At 10 a.m. local time on Friday 14 June 1987 Trans-World Airlines flight 847 from Athens to Rome took off from the Greek capital with 153 passengers and crew on board, 135 of them Americans. Two of them were Lebanese Muslims, members of the radical Shi'ite Hezbollah terrorist group. They announced that they were hijacking the aircraft shortly after it finished its climb. The hijackers – who were demanding the release of 700 Lebanese Shi'ites held prisoner in Israel in return for the lives of the TWA847 passengers – initially told the American pilot to fly to Algiers. But there was not enough fuel on board so they ordered him to fly to Beirut. The aircraft then settled into a regular shuttle between Beirut and Algiers and back again while the US administration tried to work out what to do. When the Lebanese authorities refused to refuel the aircraft one of the passengers, Robert Stethem, a US Navy diver, was shot dead and dumped unceremoniously on the tarmac.

General Carl Stiner, who had now been appointed commander of JSOC, was ordered to prepare plans for a hostage rescue operation. Britain and Italy agreed to allow the Americans to use their bases at Akrotiri on Cyprus and Sigonella on Sicily. Delta, SEAL Team Six and the Activity were all put on alert to move at a moment's notice. But the mission was held up partly because the air force was unable to provide air transport quickly enough. The shocking shortage of dedicated special operations aircraft, like the MC130 Combat Talon transport aircraft and the long-range MH53 Pave Low helicopters, was part of a continuing problem that a number of the Congressional supporters of special operations had repeatedly raised. The lack of funding for the aircraft was the direct result of the continued prejudice against special operations among senior officers. Only a few weeks earlier, Senator Sam Nunn complained that 'our special operations forces are probably the most likely to be used in today's environment of any forces we have in the military and yet, several years after the Iranian hostage problem, we still do not have the airlift problems of those special operations forces worked out.'[8]

With Delta forced to wait a good 24 hours for the aircraft to move their men to Cyprus and Sicily, the Activity commander, Colonel Howard Floyd, ordered the shooters from his Operations Squadron to prepare to fly to Beirut and Algiers on scheduled civil aircraft as a contingency measure, in case Delta couldn't make it. Late on Saturday night, at a meeting in the Pentagon with senior officials from the DIA and the Joint Chiefs' planning staffs, Floyd was told to prepare two separate hostage rescue plans, one assuming the aircraft was stuck on the runway at Algiers airport, the second that it was in Beirut. By half past four on Sunday morning, Floyd's deputy Bill Garrison had the two plans ready. Pathfinders from the Activity's Operations Squadron were to be inserted covertly into both Algiers and Beirut to prepare secure landing zones for the Delta and SEAL commandos. Senior DIA officials approved the plans and, with TWA847 now in Beirut, teams from both the ISA Operations and Intelligence Squadrons, including pathfinders and signals intelligence operators, flew out of Washington's Dulles Airport. They were headed for the British base at RAF Akrotiri, in the south-west of Cyprus, where a large hangar was now full of several hundred US special operations forces. The Activity teams flew via Frankfurt, where some left the flight and waited in reserve, in case the hijacked aircraft returned to Algiers. One ISA special operator was secretly inserted into Beirut as part of a four-man team, which included a representative from Delta, US Navy SEALs and a Special Tactics combat controller, to call in air support. The Activity representative reported that the hostages had been removed from the TWA airliner and, according to local sources, were being held together in a central building close to the terrorists' headquarters in Bir al-Abed. The Activity planners put together a mission plan in which Delta and SEAL commandos would carry out an assault on the building to rescue the hostages while navy aircraft from a US carrier standing off Beirut dropped smart bombs on the terrorist base. The sizes of the bombs were carefully calculated to ensure that the blast did not affect the hostages themselves. But the plan was rendered redundant when the terrorists started distributing the hostages across various houses in the southern suburbs. That move led the JSOC team at Akrotiri to send an ISA team into Bir al-Abed to collect intelligence on where the hostages were now being held. They would then direct Delta and SEAL rescue teams to the target and act as guides for the exfiltration of the hostages and rescue teams. But by now the mission was becoming far too complex and it was decided it was not safe to go ahead.[9]

Eventually, on 30 June, more than two weeks after the aircraft was hijacked, the Israelis agreed to free the 700 Shi'ite prisoners. The remaining thirty-one hostages held by the hijackers were released and taken to Damascus where they were to be handed over to the American ambassador. The hostages survived but the failure of yet another special operations rescue mission led to a furious debate within the Pentagon. 'Watching the Red Cross vans carry the hostages out of Beirut towards Damascus was a bitter experience,' General Stiner recalled. 'We could not get out of our minds the certainty that we'd had the capability to do a rescue operation that would have been a piece of cake. But we failed to bring it off. As we flew back home I decided to speak straight in the debriefing I'd very soon be giving to the Chairman and Joint Chiefs of Staff. The next day in the Pentagon, I gave my debriefing. After going through the story in detail, I concluded with something like the following: "Gentlemen, we should all be embarrassed by the failure we have just struggled through. In my mind, the consequences of failure of this nature are just as devastating as losing a major battle, especially politically. We ought to be able to figure out that the terrorists understand better than we do the timing of the decision-making process here in Washington and the time required for launching and getting to where they have perpetrated their action. We are the most powerful nation in the world and if we cannot give this mission the adequate priority – with dedicated lift assets – then we ought to get out of this business and quit wasting the taxpayers' money".'[10]

But despite Stiner's criticism, the problems persuading senior officers of the need for special operations forces to be properly equipped, so they were capable of doing a timely and effective job, continued. Less than four months later, Palestinian terrorists hijacked the *Achille Lauro* cruise liner, murdering the 69-year-old wheelchair-bound American Leon Klinghofer. It was eighteen hours before the Air Force finally found an aircraft to take the Delta and SEAL commandos to the Sigonella air base ready for a planned rescue mission.[11] The attitude of the army chiefs in particular was a disgrace. The Army Chief of Staff, General John Wickham, and his vice-chief General Maxwell Thurman, were furious to discover that the Activity had been involved in the TWA847 operation. They insisted that they should have been informed of the involvement of an army unit and accused Floyd of not going through the proper channels to get permission to deploy, even though he had been ordered to move by senior officers in the DIA and on the Joint Chiefs' planning staff. In what must count as one of the stupidest orders ever given to a special operations unit, they told Floyd that none of his men were allowed to leave the military district of Washington unless they requested permission twenty-one days in advance. The move effectively neutered the Activity. It was designed to go into action to collect actionable intelligence and set up secure landing zones for rapid reaction special operations forces, Delta and SEAL commandos who had to be ready to move within hours. Yet it had to give notice of any mission three weeks in advance. The ludicrous order was just one of a series of actions imposed on ISA commanders by senior army officers that delayed operations for months and led Floyd to ask on several occasions to be relieved of his command. The approval process for operations was 'atrocious', Floyd later complained, recalling that at times the Activity had to brief as many as seven different army lawyers on the missions it wanted to undertake. At one point, Floyd wrote to the commander of the Intelligence and Security Command, which was now in charge of the ISA, saying it was 'in the best interests of this command to deactivate USAISA' and asking that this be done at the 'earliest possible' moment. INSCOM subsequently requested approval from the office of the Assistant Chief of Staff for Intelligence to close down the Activity. The request was bluntly rejected after one senior officer pointed out that – given the Activity's 'special relationship' with the Pentagon, the Joint Chiefs and national agencies like the CIA and NSA – 'a unilateral decision like this would ricochet throughout the system'. [12]

BY SEPTEMBER 1985, seven US citizens were thought to be held by Lebanese-based terrorist groups either in the southern suburbs of Beirut or the Beka'a Valley. In fact there were only six. Unbeknown to the outside world, Bill Buckley was already dead. Those who remained alive at that stage were the Reverend Benjamin Weir, a Presbyterian minister, who had been kidnapped on 8 May 1984; Peter Kilburn, a librarian at the American University of Beirut, taken hostage on 3 December 1984; Father Lawrence Jenco, a Catholic priest, kidnapped on 8 January 1985; Terry Anderson, the Chief Middle East Correspondent for the Associated Press, who disappeared on 16 March 1985; David Jacobsen, an administrator at the American University of Beirut Hospital, who was kidnapped on 28 May 1985; and Thomas Sutherland, Dean of Agriculture at the American University of Beirut, taken hostage on 9 June 1985.

Early in September, a Special Operations Task Force, commanded by Carl Stiner and almost certainly including members of the ISA, deployed to the British base at Akrotiri in Cyprus in readiness for a possible hostage rescue. 'We had intelligence information indicating that there might be a release of all the hostages,' Stiner later recalled. 'My orders were to set up a mechanism for their pick-up and covert return to the United States. We were also prepared for a rescue operation in case something went wrong.'[13]

There was no real intelligence. The information that the hostages might be released came from the National Security Council where Lieutenant-Colonel Oliver North was directing a complex scheme to supply arms to Iran in exchange for the release of the seven hostages held by Lebanese terrorist groups linked to the regime in Tehran. The idea of supplying arms to Iran in return for the hostages was originally suggested by the Israelis. For them, it offered an opportunity to assist Iran in its war against Saddam Hussein's Iraq, which Israel saw as a major threat to its security. For the Reagan administration, it removed its biggest problem – the seeming impotence in the face of the terrorists who had kidnapped the so-called 'forgotten seven' – while at the same time improving its poor relations with a country that was seen as vital in holding back Soviet expansionism. The Iranians agreed to secret talks, allegedly offering to release all seven hostages in exchange for TOW anti-tank wire-guided missiles. By the time the first 100 missiles were passed by Israel to Iran at the end of August 1985, Buckley had already died, although the Americans, and quite possibly the Iranian negotiators, were not yet aware of his death. The first 100 missiles were seen as a sign of good faith. A further 400 missiles were handed over in mid-September and these were certainly initially expected by North to result in the release of at least four, if not all, of the hostages. In the event, the Iranians said that only one hostage would be released. Buckley could not be freed as he was 'ill'. The Reverend Benjamin Weir was freed. General Stiner and his task force went home empty-handed. Just under three weeks later, almost certainly prompted to do so by Tehran, the Islamic Jihad announced that Buckley had been 'executed'.[14]

The death of Buckley sparked anger within the American covert operations community. 'We at one point were very close to running a rescue operation to get Bill Buckley back,' said Bill Cowan, then a member of the Activity. 'I was told by people who would know that we had a very good fix on where he was. We had somebody inside that building who was providing good, credible information. We in fact moved forces into Europe, maybe further, in preparation to rescue Bill Buckley and the operation was cancelled by the White House. Some say by Oliver North. It was cancelled shortly before it was going to happen. Those who I've spoken with who were in the know say it was cancelled because we had a very active programme going on, out of the White House, [exchanging] arms for hostages, and the rescue of Bill Buckley might have impacted negatively on that programme.'[15]

AT THE BEGINNING OF 1986, a task force led by US Vice-President George Bush produced a report on The National Program for Combating Terrorism. US policy on terrorism was 'unequivocal', the report said. It would not negotiate with terrorists. 'This policy is based upon the conviction that to accede to terrorist demands places more American citizens at risk.' A 'no-concessions policy' was the best way of ensuring US citizens were safe from terrorism. 'The US Government will pay no ransoms, nor permit releases of prisoners or agree to other conditions that could serve to encourage additional terrorism.' The report added that the US Government would encourage other governments to take 'similar strong stands' against terrorism. Quite how that policy statement fitted in even with the decision to persuade Israel to release Shi' ite prisoners in return for the hostages taken from TWA847, let alone the administration's willingness to trade arms for the hostages held in Lebanon, is far from clear.[16]

A secret history of the Activity's operations during 1986 records that there was a marked increase in the tempo both of operations and mission planning. The year began with the first signs of successes from the Lebanese Forces intelligence network, which was fully up and running by the beginning of February. All the Felix intelligence reports were faxed through to a Canadian telephone number, which automatically redirected them to the ISA offices in Arlington. They were also passed on to both the CIA and the NSA and were checked out by a dedicated spy satellite positioned above the region, which showed that the vast majority of the Felix product appeared to be accurate. The Lebanese Forces had well-placed sources among all the religious groups in Lebanon and provided evidence that the hostages were being kept at two separate locations. Some were at Britel, six miles south-west of Baalbek and 4,000 feet up in the mountains above the Beka'a Valley. Others were at the Sheikh Abdullah barracks in Baalbek. Felix also produced details of plans by Abu Nidal to attack the US consulate in Adana, Turkey, and identified a Paris safe house used by Ali Atwa, one of the Hezbollah terrorists involved in the TWA847 hijacking.[17]

On the morning of 17 May 1986, the fax in the Activity's Arlington office that was dedicated to receiving the Felix reports began to feed out a single sheet of paper describing the 'transfer of the hostages to the region of Hakrak'. It said: 'The source of Riad Tleis has verified that the prisoners and foreign hostages were transferred from the locality of Brital and the Sheikh Abdullah barracks in Ba'albek to a Hezbollah military camp located in the region of Hakrak in the heights of the northern Beka'a.'[18]

Robert McFarlane, Reagan's former National Security Advisor and a key figure in the so-called 'Concept', the arms for hostages programme, secretly visited Tehran with Oliver North for talks with Iranian officials. North's operations plan for the trip defined the objective as 'to secure the return of four American hostages who continue to be held by Hezbollah elements in Lebanon.' These were now Jenco, Anderson, Jacobsen and Sutherland, Kilburn having been executed in April in retaliation for US air attacks on Libya, which were themselves sparked by the bombing of a Berlin disco in which two American servicemen were killed. North defined the purpose of 'the Concept' as being to 'provide incentives for the Government of Iran to intervene with those who hold the American hostages and secure their safe release.' But the talks foundered on Iranian demands that more spare parts and missiles be produced before they release any more hostages. Although there was agreement to continue talking, Admiral John Poindexter, the new National Security Advisor, and other members of the NSC now believed that the arms–for–hostages negotiations had reached stalemate. On 31 May, Poindexter wrote a memo to North in which he said: 'I am beginning to think that we need to seriously think about a rescue effort for the hostages.' North wrote back saying that the Joint Chiefs had 'steadfastly refused to go beyond the initial thinking stage unless we can develop hard evidence on their whereabouts.' There was already an ISA officer in Beirut preparing the ground for a hostage rescue should it be ordered, North said, adding that Richard Secord, a former air force general who had been Vaught's deputy in the planning process for a second Iran hostage rescue mission, believed a successful special operations rescue mission was a distinct possibility. Secord was a former head of the US military mission to the Shah's armed forces and had been brought into the arms–for–hostages operation because of that expertise. 'Dick, who has been in Beirut, and who organized the second Iran mission, is convinced that such an operation could indeed be conducted,' North told Poindexter. The following day, President Reagan approved military planning for a special operations hostage rescue mission and revived the previous plans put together by the Activity.[19]

Over the next nine days, Delta, SEAL Team Six and the Activity carried out an extensive exercise, codenamed Quiz Icing, which practised what the secret history for 1986 described as 'a hostage rescue operation in a non–permissive environment'. The Activity provided both human and signals intelligence operations for the exercise, the secret history said. 'ISA was also tasked to receive, sustain and exfiltrate the counter-terrorist team. Receiving and exfiltration constitutes locating, surveying, reporting and operating landing zones and drop zones. ISA executed their mission primarily through tradecraft means. ISA's success was very impressive and well received.'[20]

Colonel Floyd made further changes to the ISA's organisation in June 1986, with the Directorate of Operations absorbing the newly formed six-man training cell, designed to teach tradecraft, explosives, weapons handling, special operations tactics, and communications. Floyd relied heavily on his deputy Bill Garrison, a dynamic, highly respected special operations expert who would go on to command both Delta and JSOC. They maintained the continuous training policy put in place by Jerry King, with the Activity carrying out a total of twenty-nine airborne exercises in 1986, 'the goal being to attain night combat equipment proficiency'. There was also intensive instruction in weapons training, demolitions, communications, languages, and in particular tradecraft, the expertise of the spy that concentrates on running secret intelligence operations while merging into the background and remaining undetected. 'Tradecraft is a part of life in ISA and training in tradecraft was extensive throughout the year,' the secret history for 1986 said. But the training did not all go to plan. There was 'a major problem' on Exercise Powerful Gaze, a joint special operations exercise carried out in the second half of March 1986 in the Jacksonville area of North Carolina. The Activity's role in the exercise was to 'provide sub-unit and headquarters level Humint and Sigint intelligence,' the annual unit report said. 'ISA was also tasked to receive, sustain and exfiltrate the counter-terrorist team.' But eight members of the unit were arrested by state bureau of investigation agents who saw them preparing beach landing zones and assumed they were drugs smugglers. A few weeks later, one member of the unit was killed during an exercise at the Keesler air force base, in Biloxi, Mississippi.[21]

Meanwhile Felix reported that the hostages were being continuously moved. 'On 12 June, the American hostages were transferred from the "Miqraq" fort in the Baalbek area to the headquarters of the Iranian Revolutionary Guard located at Britel town; and they are still there,' the Activity's Lebanese sources said. The spy satellite was now moved to concentrate full time on Britel. That was followed by another message, giving more details:

'Please note the positioning of the hostages:

1) CR [Cable Reference] 46 where the hostages are probably 70 per cent being detained at the moment.

2) Concerning Britel village, specific sources identify the detention area of the hostages in the 'al-Husayniya' building or barracks situated at the Britel village with map coordinates: 221440/189200. Coordinates from the Sheikh Abdullah barracks in the Britel area with the deployment of the DCA. 194480/227980 193980/227980 194420/ 227620 PS Coordinates of the Mosque of Britel are 188700/221500'

BY NOW, FELIX WAS providing a wealth of intelligence – hundreds of pages of intelligence reports were produced every week. They were all passed on to the CIA, the NSA, the NSC, and indirectly the State Department, all of whom bombarded the ISA with follow-up questions. 'We did not bargain over the intel,' Shanon said. 'The traditional way the Lebanese Forces and the Lebanese Government handled intel of this kind was to send ninety per cent and bargain for the rest. We gave ISA everything we got – everything on the Palestinians, Shi'ites, Libyan agents, Iranian agents, Syrian activities.' Perhaps predictably, many of the people back in Washington were reluctant to accept that the intelligence the Activity was producing was entirely genuine. They repeatedly asked for the sources, something no one was likely to give, and queried how these guys in the Christian militia could know what Hezbollah, the Phalangists' sworn enemy, were doing with the hostages. But time after time, the spy satellite provided collateral evidence that showed that 'Source Felix' was producing high-grade intelligence. 'Everyone wondered where we were getting this unusual and accurate information,' one former member of the Activity said. 'They [the Christian militia] provided us with the exact location of every hostage.

They told us where they were being moved to, each new location. We were able to verify this by other means. We could have launched the operation and freed the hostages.'[22]

At the end of June, an ISA colonel was spirited into Junieh from Cyprus by the Lebanese Forces. Using the codename Gaby, he checked all the preparations the Christian militia had made for a possible hostage rescue, reconnoitring the staging areas they had set up and going in as close as possible to look at the sites where the hostages were now being held, which was in a house at Aarsal, seventeen miles north-east of Baalbek and just eight miles from the Syrian border. 'Gaby' spent ten days in the country, guarded by members of the Lebanese Forces. He met their sub-agents and assessed the reliability of the Felix network and its assets, meeting a number of the sub-agents who had been reporting on the activities of the hostage-takers. Among the potential obstacles for a hostage rescue that he noted down were a high-voltage cable, which ran over the site and would limit the ability of helicopters to get close in, and a Syrian radar installation four miles to the east of Aarsal that might detect helicopters flying at altitude. Gaby then returned to Arlington to give the go-ahead for the mission and the Activity began drawing up the plans, working out who would do what and how.[23] 'We ran several missions into Lebanon and spent considerable time on developing contingency plans,' one former officer said. 'Some were self-generated and others directed from on high. It became a common joke in the unit that when the rest of the army had a holiday and especially a three-day weekend, we would be called to deal with some type of a crisis, real or perceived.'[24]

Throughout June and the first few weeks of July, the secret talks with Iran appeared to be in stalemate but after a number of false dawns, on 21 July the Americans received indications from the Iranians that another American was about to be released. Three days later, Father Jenco was separated from other US hostages, who were now in Beirut's southern suburbs, and taken to the Beka'a. He was released on 26 July and was debriefed by North. Jenco told him that Buckley had not in fact been executed. He had died from some sort of illness. Briefing Poindexter on his conversations with the American priest, North said that 'although Iranian influence over the hostage holders is still considerable' the captors themselves appeared to be increasingly disenchanted with the Iranian relationship. 'The continued reluctance of the Hezbollah itself to follow precise Iranian instructions on how to release the hostages is seen as an indication of efforts by Hezbollah to demonstrate at least partial independence.'[25]

August saw a further change of command at the Activity with Floyd, fed up with the way his unit was being messed around and hampered from doing its job, demanding a fresh assignment. He was replaced by Colonel John G Lackey III, a 46-year-old Special Forces intelligence specialist from Statesville, North Carolina, who had useful experience in the office of Assistant Chief of Staff for Intelligence, and the unit completed its move to a new location at Fort Belvoir. Plans to move the Activity from Arlington had in fact been in place since Jerry King's time in charge. A total of $25 million was set aside to provide a new custom-built facility for the Activity, with everything it needed, all in one single location. But with the continued hostility to the Activity from on high leading Floyd to question whether it was worth maintaining the unit at all, he had agreed to allow the $25 million to be used to improve Delta's facilities at the Pope air force base next to Fort Bragg.[26]

By now, plans for Project Round Bottle, an operation to rescue the hostages, were in place and throughout August and September the American special operations commandos expected to take part in the operation ran through them again and again, honing their skills, ensuring that each man knew precisely what his role was and what he should do at any given time, including what to do if one of any number of possible hitches occurred. Felix was reporting every available detail on the hostages and tracking their positions as Hezbollah moved them around. But Felix was far from being the only source of intelligence on what was going on in Beirut and the Beka'a. An American KH11 Crystal satellite was producing highly detailed imagery of the areas where the hostages were being held. The NSA was monitoring telephone and radio communications using a variety of means of collection – a Vortex satellite positioned over Africa; a joint NSA and CIA special collection facility based in the US embassy; and the British signals intelligence site at Ayios Nikolaos on the eastern side of Cyprus.[27]

The plan was to locate sixty Delta and SEAL Team Six commandos on board a US Navy ship north of Cyprus where they would be transferred to a Christian-operated cargo ship that made regular sailings between Beirut and the southern Cypriot port of Larnaca. The commandos would move between the two ships by dinghy while their equipment transferred on lines set up between the ships, an extremely risky operation. The rescue force and their equipment would then be hidden inside empty containers on the deck of the cargo ship. The team were to wear civilian clothing or non-US combat clothing with no markings. They would carry equipment that allowed them to monitor what was being said inside buildings by bouncing laser beams off the windows; satellite communications links that would provide them with real time intelligence from the NSA, the DIA and the CIA; and computerised communications systems. They also had explosives and equipment that would allow them to break into the strongest doors. They didn't need to take weapons with them. The Lebanese Forces had agreed to supply them with AK47 and M16 assault rifles and Uzi sub-machine guns that could be used in the operation and left behind. The ship would moor up at dock number five in a part of the port of Beirut that was completely under the control of the Lebanese Forces. The five containers, with their secret cargo, would be offloaded and taken to a remote part of the port. That night, the Lebanese Forces, under Activity direction, would pick them up and drive them in jeeps and trucks to east Beirut. There they were to split into three teams, one of which would go to West Beirut and rescue those hostages still hidden in Bir al-Abed, a second would make for the Sheikh Abdullah barracks in the Beka'a, where the other hostages were now being held. The third team would remain in reserve in case either of the other teams needed back-up. They would travel in 4x4 SUV cross-country vehicles bearing the insignia of the Amal militia or Hezbollah. Every member of each team had false identification provided by the Activity using genuine Lebanese documentation provided by the Lebanese Forces agents as templates. The Christian militiamen would set up diversions to draw the attention of any Amal and Hezbollah units in Bir al-Abed, and the Iranian Revolutionary Guards at the Sheikh Abdullah barracks, away from the hostages while the rescue teams went in. Each team would have Activity guides who had repeatedly gone over every inch of the routes, looking for any possible hitches that might occur. But despite their invaluable assistance in helping to set up the mission, the Lebanese Forces were to be kept at a distance during the actual rescue. One ISA operator said: 'The operation was "Made in the US of A". We could have used additional support but the idea was to carry out a clean, neat, quick operation. Every support activity would have complicated matters. This was supposed to be a quick and dirty operation. We did not rely heavily on the Lebanese Forces to fight or even to conduct operations that would have supported us. We were ready to do the operation alone, single-handed, and come home with the hostages.'

The assaults on Bir al-Abed and Baalbek were to be closely co-ordinated to ensure they hit at precisely the same time. Both Gaby's recce operation and Father Jenco's debriefing suggested that there were unlikely to be many guards around the hostages. The team that hit the house in Bir al-Abed would head for the coast, using one of several possible escape routes marked out by Gaby. It would rendezvous with a team from the Activity that would exfiltrate the hostages and their Delta rescuers by small boats or helicopters to US Navy vessels standing off the shore. The team that carried out the assault on the Sheikh Abdullah barracks in Baalbek would also make for the coast but there was a standby plan that allowed them to call in assistance from the Israelis who would send in a heliborne team to extract them and the hostages.[28]

Meanwhile, the deep flaws in the whole arms-for-hostages operation were being exposed. Having handed over two American hostages, Hezbollah simply kidnapped two more. On 9 September, Frank Reed, director of the private Lebanese International School in West Beirut's Sanayeh district and convert to Islam, was kidnapped. The terrorists intercepted Reed's Volvo in the Bir Hassan district of West Beirut as he was on his way to play golf. Three days later, another US citizen, Joseph Cicippio, the acting controller at the American University of Beirut and another convert to Islam, was kidnapped as he left his apartment to go to the university. But astonishingly Poindexter and North continued with the policy of talking to the Iranians, deciding that a different back-channel, via the nephew of Hashemi Rafsanjani, the speaker of the Iranian parliament, would produce better results. The Activity was told to put the hostage rescue mission back on the shelf and to 'cease and desist' contacts with the Lebanese Forces. The State Department worried that the Syrians might get upset while the CIA insisted that the Lebanese Forces were not to be trusted, a concern that did not stop them trying to take over the Felix network themselves. The Christian militia agents were suspicious and refused to cooperate.[29]

The Israelis, anxious to make life difficult for Saddam Hussein's Iraq, were insistent that the talks, and the weapons supplies to Iran, should continue, and they provided an incentive to persuade North that it was worthwhile. Taking advantage of the restrictions on military aid to Nicaragua, Tel Aviv offered to supply the Contras with the weapons they needed. North told Poindexter on 15 September that

Israeli Defence Minister Yitzhak Rabin had promised 'a significant quantity of captured Soviet bloc arms for use by the Nicaraguan democratic resistance. These arms will be picked up by a foreign flag vessel this week and delivered to the Nicaraguan resistance. If [the Israeli Prime Minister Shimon] Peres raises this issue, it would be helpful if the President thanked him since the Israelis hold considerable stores of bloc ordnance compatible with what the Nicaraguan resistance uses.'

But within two weeks, with the arms-for-hostages programme falling apart and about to leak to the press, the National Security Council changed its mind yet again and the DCSINT, Deputy Chief of Staff for Intelligence, ordered the Activity to reactivate the plans for Project Round Bottle, the rescue of the hostages.[30] The Felix network had reported that three US hostages were being held in tents and caves in the Beka'a and this appeared to be confirmed by aerial reconnaissance. Two ISA operatives had just been sent into Lebanon to make preparations for the mission when the order came once again to pull out. 'Project Round Bottle was terminated without evaluation of information even though the DCSINT personally requested same,' the secret history of the unit for 1986 said. The reason for the second cancellation was that North had visited Frankfurt for talks with Rafsanjani's nephew, who 'assures us he will get two of the three US hostages held by Hezbollah in next few days'. The Iranians insisted that neither Cicippio nor Reed had been kidnapped by groups under their control, despite all the intelligence suggesting otherwise. But the whole enterprise was already unravelling. The use of the second back-channel through Rafsanjani had left the earlier negotiators furious and they leaked the story out through a small Hezbollah newspaper in Baalbek. Another American hostage, David Jacobsen, was released on Sunday 2 November 1986 in exchange for 500 TOW missiles. But on the Tuesday, Rafsanjani publicly announced that McFarlane had visited Tehran to discuss the release of the hostages. By Thursday, with both the State Department and the Pentagon rushing to distance themselves from it, the *Los Angeles Times*, citing government officials, had published an authoritative version of the arms-for-hostages affair, albeit without what was possibly the worst aspect, the use of the Israelis to illegally circumvent the congressional ban on military aid to the Contras.[31]

One senior ISA officer ridiculed the North plan to swap hostages for weapons. 'That policy was a great deal for the Iranians. "We'll give you two hostages and we'll go pick up two more." It's an endless source of money. I'd be happy to run an operation like that. You keep paying me for something, I'll make sure I've got plenty of it. Unbelievable. People in the State Department, clearly in the CIA, certainly people who understand terrorism and counter-terrorist operations were aghast at the whole thing. It was amateurish at best, absolutely amateurish. It undermined the whole thing. When you are trying to run under-cover operations and suddenly you've got some crazy operations, by any standards, being run, you've lost all credibility with those with whom you're dealing.'[32]

7 THE WAR ON COCAINE

THE NIGHT THAT Major Steve Jacoby and the rest of the guys from Falcon Aviation booked into the Bogotá Hilton in September 1989 there was a hailstorm of bomb blasts across the Colombian capital. President Virgilio Barco Vargas had clamped down on the drugs barons and a prominent *narco* had been extradited to the United States, where he faced a long prison sentence with no chance of a sympathetic hearing from a tame judge. The drugs barons, styling themselves *Los Extraditables*, declared war, warning of a 'Black September' and setting off a series of bombs in the capital and the main cartel cities of Cali and Medellín as a warning to the politicians to leave the drugs trade alone. Colombia was already one of the most dangerous places to live in the world, especially if you were male. Murder was the principal cause of death among Colombian men aged between 15 and 45, and the second among all age groups. The cocaine war threatened to make it even worse.

Officially none of that should have been of any real concern to Falcon Aviation, which was carrying out a survey of the country's aerial radio beacons. It was an insubstantial task that ought to have taken just a few weeks. But Jacoby and his men were clearly there for the long haul, and they didn't behave like some ordinary aerial survey team. They changed their hotels like most men change their underwear and when they moved outside the capital, they always travelled in bullet-proof vehicles. As with the El Salvador operations, the 'aerial survey' story was just that, a cover for the real operations being undertaken by the Activity's electronic surveillance team. As in El Salvador, Marxist guerrillas controlled much of the country. But this time the Activity was not after the rebels. It had much bigger fish to fry.

The vast majority of the cocaine arriving on America's streets was coming from Colombia, and the dollars from the drugs trade had turned the *narcos* into kings in the main drugs centres of Medellín, Cali and Antioqua. They had their own private armies equipped with military-style grenade launchers, anti-tank missiles and heavy machine guns and they were dismissive of the ability of the authorities to do anything to rein them in. They were ripping Colombia apart, with killings in Cali alone running at around 3,000 a year. When Luis Galán, the favourite in the presidential elections, promised to bring them to justice, the *narcos* simply ordered him killed. But it was a mistake. Galán's willingness to curtail the drugs trade had been backed in Washington. A few weeks later, President George Bush Snr. ordered a war on the drugs cartels. Even then, the *narcos* didn't get the message. They bombed an airliner out of the sky, killing all ten people on board, including two Americans. The response from the Bush administration was swift. They ordered Jacoby and his men to help the Colombian police take out the architects of Galán's assassination – José Rodríguez Gacha and his henchman Pablo Gavria Escobar.

Jacoby – if that was his real name – didn't fit the archetypal Hollywood image of superfit special operations forces. The major was slightly overweight and almost withdrawn. He certainly didn't stand out in a crowd but then all his training in tradecraft had conditioned him not to attract attention to himself, and what he might have lacked

153

in physical fitness he more than made up for in mental agility. Operating under the codename Centra Spike, his men used the same technique as in El Salvador, sweeping across the Colombian jungle in two specially equipped Beechcraft King Air planes, monitoring the drugs barons' cellphones. The aim was to know everything there was to know about the *narcos*. Where they worked. Where they slept. What they ate. Who they trusted. By tracking men like Rodríguez Gacha and Escobar and the people they talked to, Jacoby's men would be able to work out where they were most vulnerable. Sooner or later, that knowledge, and the Activity's extraordinary ability to locate the signal from a cellphone to within a few yards, would spell the end for the *narcos*.

Tracking down Rodríguez Gacha didn't take long. *El Mexicano*, as he was known within Colombia's criminal fraternity, was easy to find. Centra Spike followed his every move until he stopped running and holed up in a farmhouse on the Panamanian border. A team of Delta and SEAL commandos was placed on board a US warship off the coast ready to go in and capture him. But Colombia's police were in no mood to let anyone else grab the man responsible for the deaths of so many of their colleagues. Tipped off by Jacoby's team, they attacked in helicopter gunships, mowing Rodríguez Gacha and his thugs down in a hail of machine-gun fire. But Escobar was going to take much longer.[1]

President Reagan had ordered the US military, and special operations forces in particular, to act against the drugs barons in the mid-1980s. He signed a top secret National Security Directive on 8 April 1986 defining drug trafficking as a national security threat and ordering the military to take part in the operations to prevent drugs reaching the United States.[2] The President's 1988 report to Congress on national security singled out the drugs trade as a security threat and openly placed it on the same level as the threat from terrorism. It also specifically linked US intelligence operations against the drugs cartels to military operations against insurgents in Latin America. 'International terrorism and narcotics trafficking, particularly when state-supported, can threaten the security of the US and our citizens,' the President said. 'Intelligence plays a critical role in our efforts to control and reduce these threats. Intelligence collection and special operations by agencies of the US Government to protect against international terrorism and international narcotics activities will remain a high priority. The ability to conduct covert action operations is an essential element of our national security capability. Soviet, Cuban and Nicaraguan support for insurgencies in El Salvador and elsewhere in Latin America threaten nascent democracies in the region, which are already struggling with chronic poverty, economic underdevelopment, and the growing influence of narcotics cartels.' The United States was helping other countries in the interdiction and eradication of illegal drugs operations, he said. 'Measures which have proven particularly effective include aid to expand and to improve the affected country's law enforcement capabilities, to preserve the independence and integrity of its judicial system, and to provide for the sharing of intelligence and investigative capabilities.'[3]

US intelligence had been tracking links between the drugs barons and insurgents across Latin America since the early 1980s. A 1983 agency briefing on the issue reported that whereas initially the guerrillas had largely condemned drugs as evidence of the decadence of capitalism 'now, several have developed active links with the drugs trade, others extort protection money from the drugs traffickers, and some apparently use profits from the drugs to buy arms.' That made the drugs trade an important target for America's spooks, who used satellite imagery and aerial reconnaissance aircraft to pinpoint the coca fields, helping the Colombian security forces to cut back the production of cocaine. But it was not enough. For both Reagan and his vice-president George Bush Snr., the bombing of the Avianca airliner was the last straw. The Colombian drugs barons had murdered innocent Americans, putting themselves on a par with Islamic Jihad in Lebanon and the

Salvadoran FMLN. When Bush senior took over the presidency in 1989, he ordered the Pentagon to deploy special operations forces to deal with the problem. As ever, the Activity went in first to gather the intelligence and prepare the ground for the other special operators, the shooters.[4]

THE WAY THE ACTIVITY operated had been further refined under its new commander Colonel John G Lackey III. His predecessor's insistence he be reassigned, after one frustration too many caused by those senior army officers who continuously erected barriers to prevent the Activity doing its job, led Lieutenant-General Sydney T Weinstein, the Assistant Chief of Staff for Intelligence, to make clear to Inscom that the Activity fulfilled a vital role and must be allowed to carry it out.[5] Things were getting better for US special operations forces even though the generals were still opposing any attempt to give the special operators more power within the hierarchy. In November 1986, Senator Sam Nunn and his main ally William Cohen, a future Defense Secretary, persuaded Congress to pass a law creating a new US Special Operations Command (USSOCOM) and setting up a post of Assistant Secretary of Defense, Special Operations and Low-Intensity Conflict (SOLIC). The generals did their best to stymie the whole thing, and it would not be until the confirmation of Jim Locher as Assistant Secretary of Defense SOLIC in October 1989 that the system began working in anything like the way that Congress had intended.[6]

But the reaffirmation of the need for the Activity meant that under Lackey's command, the Activity was allowed to become a much more proactive operation. Lieutenant-Colonel David A McKnight, who became Lackey's operations officer, is credited in a carefully worded declassified official record with having 'changed the unit from a reactive posture to a proactive organization, and updated and improved selection and training of personnel for their highly specialized missions'. Effectively, he and Lackey reversed a lot of the changes that Floyd had put in place in his ill-fated attempts to make the very concept of the Activity acceptable to the stuffed shirts in Washington. It hadn't worked, so the ethos of King's original unit was brought back as Lackey and Dave McKnight put a bit of the maverick back into the Activity. McKnight led an Activity team which deployed to the Persian Gulf in the summer of 1987 as part of Operation Prime Chance 1, a special operations mission designed to prevent Iranian forces from attacking Kuwaiti oil tankers. The special operations force also included two SEAL teams, a US Navy Special Boat Unit, and members of the 160th Special Operations Aviation Group, the old Task Force 160, flying the AH6 Little Bird gunships. The Little Bird helicopters were renamed 'Sea Bats' after several highly effective night-time missions flying less than ten metres above the surface of the sea, during which they disabled a number of Iranian minelayers and patrol boats that were trying to attack the Kuwaiti oil tankers. McKnight took part in a number of close-in operations inside Iranian-controlled territory, looking for potential targets for pre-emptive or retaliatory attacks including launch sites for Silkworm land-to-sea missiles, coastal storage depots for mines, weapons and ammunition dumps, and other military installations. 'He made several perilous trips into denied areas to establish effective contingency-support arrangements for potential Centcom operations in the area of responsibility,' the official record states. 'His accomplishments underpinned many of the successes Centcom achieved during subsequent operations.'[7]

But the Activity was attracting too much media interest. A unit that was supposed to be so secret that no one even knew it existed had been plunged into the public limelight. As a result of the investigations of the expenses claimed by members of special forces units, Major Michael L Smith, a former adjutant of the Activity, had been indicted in connection with the theft of 200 weapons while he was in charge of procuring the weapons for the Activity during the early 1980s. Smith allegedly falsified army records to cover up the purchase of the weapons and enable him to take them home. That and the ongoing arguments over the legality and usefulness of special operations forces had made the existence of the Activity too well known. It was time to retreat back underground.[8]

Army chiefs appear to have decided to mount an elaborate deception operation to take the unit back under deep cover. On 16 March 1989, Major-General Stanley Hyman, Inscom commander, ordered the 'termination' of the ISA, adding: 'disposition of existing unit assets will be made in accordance with applicable army directives'. That the unit did not disappear but in fact continued to flourish is curious, as is the wording of an associated signal sent out by the new commander to a wide variety of senior recipients, including Caspar Weinberger, the Defense Secretary, the head of NSA and the head of JSOC. Although the signal subject heading spoke unequivocally of the 'termination' of the ISA and its associated special access programme Grantor Shadow, the body of the report was much more ambiguous: 'Effective 2400 hrs, 31 Mar 89, the term United States Army Intelligence Support Activity (USAISA) will be discontinued,' the signal said. 'USAISA or ISA should not be used in any communications/correspondence after that date.' That was precisely what Jerry King had always wanted to happen shortly after the Activity was set up. The name Intelligence Support Activity was only ever a working title. It was supposed to revert immediately to something much more bland, originally the Tactical Concept Detachment. That name had never been compromised but it appears nevertheless to have been changed slightly, possibly to make it slightly less enigmatic and therefore less likely to provoke curiosity. The new unit, if indeed it was in any way a new unit, was called the Tactical Coordination Detachment and the codename for its special access programme was Capacity Gear. The operation appears to have been timed to coincide with the arrival of a new commander. Lackey had left the previous month to take over as Director of Intelligence for JSOC, a clear sign that his period in charge

THE WAR ON COCAINE

was regarded as a success, and by implication that the Activity was now much better regarded than it had previously been. It had moved from its old base at Arlington to Fort Belvoir. If senior commanders wanted the Activity to disappear underground, they could not have picked a better time to do it. From this point on, the unit would be protected by a series of codenames which changed for every mission it undertook. During the anti-drugs operations in Colombia – which began six months after the alleged 'termination' – the Activity was known as Centra Spike.[9]

The Activity played only a small role in Operation Just Cause, the 1989 invasion of Panama, providing close-in Sigint and surveillance operators to work alongside US Navy SEALs. The Panamanian leader Manuel Noriega, who was heavily implicated in drugs trafficking, had gone from being the US-backed guardian of the Panama Canal to becoming a major bug-bear for the Bush administration. Presidential elections held in April 1989 were rigged in order to put his own puppet candidate in power. But they weren't rigged enough and when his opponent Guillermo Endara won, Noriega reacted by annulling the elections, having his thugs beat up Endara and his allies and declaring himself 'supreme leader' of Panama. The Activity had come across Noriega's involvement in the drugs trade six years earlier when it was investigating ways of penetrating the Colombian drugs cartels. 'We recruited an agent in Panama who had some potential of aiding us putting some people into the drug movement chain,' one former Activity officer said. 'It came to our attention that Noriega was a prime mover and protector of the drug traffic through Panama. We had proof of Noriega's involvement, including a warehouse which was being used to store drugs and was protected by Panamanian troops. The American ambassador and the CIA station chief were given a detailed brief. The station chief blew us off and the ambassador was totally indifferent. I was convinced that the chief of station was fully aware of Noriega's extra curriculum activities.'[10]

159

On 15 December 1989, with US action to remove him widely touted, Noriega pre-empted it by declaring a state of war with America and having a US Marine lieutenant shot. It was a stupid thing to do. The US, with large numbers of troops based in Panama, was unlikely to react kindly and in the early hours of 20 December 1989, American troops invaded Panama in overwhelming force. The role of the Activity signals intelligence operators was to support members of the navy's SEAL Team 4 tasked to prevent Noriega from escaping in his private Learjet 35A. The aircraft was fitted out with a special secret compartment to allow Noriega to ferry drugs from Colombia to Miami and was under heavy guard in a private hangar at the Punta Paitilla airfield to the east of Panama City. Noriega's control over Panama was financed by drugs money provided by the Medellín cartel, who used Panama as an entrepôt to move drugs into America, and from Noriega's own drugs deals. The Learjet's secret compartment hid the cocaine taken into America and the hundreds of millions of dollars in profits that was taken back to Punta Paitilla.

The SEALs were ordered to block the airfield and destroy the Learjet to ensure Noriega had no means of escape. Task Unit Papa was made up of three platoons from SEAL Team 4 – a total of sixty-two men – and twenty-six support operators, including the Activity Sigint team, who were there to keep tabs on any contacts between the Panamanian Defence Force troops at the airport and Noriega and his aides. In truth, the job should have been performed by a small team of four, inserted from off the shore and getting in close enough to direct an aerial attack on the hangar. That would have been the type of mission that was ideally suited to the special skills of the SEALs. But the commanders of Operation Just Cause were concerned that an aerial attack might result in collateral damage, so they decided to go in heavy, still using the SEALs instead of a more conventional unit. Task Unit Papa began its approach to Punta Paitilla, which lay to the east of Panama City, from the beach south of Howard air force base, to the west of the

ABOVE One of fifty-three Americans held hostage by Revolutionary Guards is shown off to the media, blindfolded. The scene is watched by some of the Iranian students who stormed the US embassy compound in Tehran in November 1979. (Rex Features)

BELOW The wreckage of a US helicopter which collided with a C130 aircraft at the Desert One forward operations base in Iran in April 1980, killing eight US servicemen and ending the Desert Claw hostage rescue mission. (© Bettmann/Corbis)

RIGHT Colonel Jerry King, founding commander of the Activity, visiting the Pentagon.

BELOW The headquarters of the Activity at Fort Belvoir, Virginia, the location of which led other US special operations forces to dub the ISA 'the Army of Northern Virginia'. (Terry Arthur)

NO ENTRY

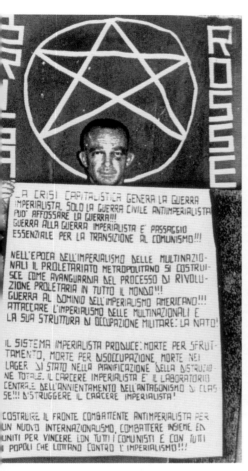

ABOVE Dozier hugged by his wife Judith after his release in January 1982. (Topfoto/AP)

ABOVE Kidnapped US General James Lee Dozier photographed by the Red Brigades holding a communiqué which denounces him as an 'assassin and hero of the American massacres in Vietnam' and adds that his 'proletarian trial' has begun. (© Bettmann/Corbis)

RIGHT The Activity's unit crest depicting an eagle carrying a claymore inscribed with the words 'Send Me', a quotation from the book of Isaiah: 'I heard the voice of the Lord, saying, "Whom shall I send, and who will go for us?" Then said I, "Here am I; send me".' The motto is Latin for 'Truth Conquers All Chains'. In the original crest, the claymore was wrapped in a chain with one of the links broken as a reminder of those killed in the Desert Claw mission. But this symbol of failure was later deemed no longer appropriate.

ABOVE Colonel Jerry King, the founder of the Activity with other members of the unit preparing to practise the HAHO (High Altitude High-Opening) parachute jump they perfected for infiltration of enemy territory.

RIGHT Colonel James 'Bo' Gritz is released by Thai police after being captured in March 1983 as he attempted to cross into Laos on a mission to 'rescue MIAs', American servicemen allegedly held prisoner by the Laotian authorities after the Vietnam War. (Sipa Press/Rex Features)

A US Marine guards the remains of the US embassy in Beirut in the wake of the truck bombing by Shi'ite terrorists in April 1983 that killed 63 people, 17 of them Americans, leading to the first of a number of Activity missions to Lebanon. (Time Life Pictures/ Getty Images)

ABOVE The aftermath of the bombing of the US Marines barracks in Beirut by Iranian-backed Shi'ite terrorists in October 1983 which killed 241 marines. The Activity's warnings that they were targets for a terrorist car-bomb had been ignored. (Eli Reed, Magnum)

RIGHT A photograph taken by an Iranian Revolutionary Guard to confirm that Iranian trained Shi'ite terrorists had bombed the US Marines barracks in Beirut in October 1983 in which 241 marines died. The photograph was obtained by an Activity agent. (Bill Cowan)

LEFT Colonel Bill Cowan, the US Marine officer (pictured in Vietnam) who chose assignment to the Activity, and two covert missions in Lebanon, over a plum posting on the White House staff. (Bill Cowan)

BELOW A wounded US marine is rescued from the ruins of his bombed Beirut barracks. (Eli Reed, Magnum)

ABOVE The aftermath of a massive bomb planted by 'rogue' agents linked to the CIA, which destroyed the West Beirut home of Hezbollah's spiritual leader, Sheikh Muhammad Hussein Fadlallah in March 1985. Fadlallah was in an armoured Land Rover and survived. (AFP/Getty Images)

BELOW Three of the US hostages kidnapped in Beirut in the mid-1980s by Islamic Jihad: Father Lawrence Jenco (left), a Catholic priest; Bill Buckley (centre), the CIA station chief in Beirut; Terry Anderson (right), Chief Middle-East Correspondent for the Associated Press news agency. These Polaroid photographs taken by the kidnappers were released to the press on 15 May 1985. Buckley, already ill, died a few weeks later. Jenco and Anderson were eventually released. (AFP/Getty Images)

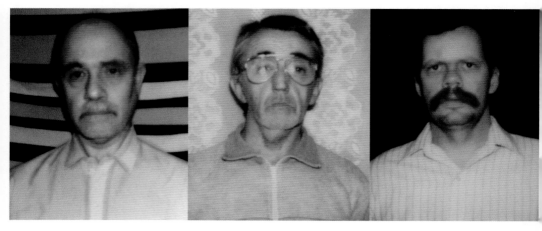

ABOVE Colonel Oliver North, who blocked Project Round Bottle, an Activity-led mission to rescue the US hostages, in a failed bid to ensure the success of his own covert talks with Iran under which hostages would be released in exchange for missiles. (© Bettmann/Corbis)

ABOVE Escobar and his bodyguard flee across the rooftops in the Los Olivos district of Medellin in November 1993 pursued by Colombian paramilitary police. (Claudia Giordanelli/Corbis Sygma)

LEFT Pablo Gavria Escobar, the Colombian drugs baron who was tracked down by the Activity's signals intelligence operators who monitored their cellphones from specially modified Beechcraft King Air fixed-wing aircraft. (Rex Features)

BELOW The body of Pablo Escobar after being shot dead on the roof of a house in the Los Olivos district of Medellin in November 1993. Did Delta take part in the assassination? (AFP/Getty Images)

TOP Aerial reconnaissance image of the Olympic Hotel in Mogadishu's Black Sea district. The target house for Task Force Raiders' snatch operation is on the opposite side of the road just off the bottom right-hand corner of the photograph. (Department of Defense)

ABOVE The damaged remains of one of the two Black Hawk helicopters that crashed during the October 1993 'Black Hawk Down' operation to snatch two leading members of the Somali National Alliance of Mohammed Farah Aideed. (Getty Images)

ABOVE The remains of the other crashed Black Hawk helicopter that crashed in the 'Black Hawk Down' operation captured in an aerial surveillance picture. (Department of Defense)

LEFT Major-General William F Garrison, Commander of Task Force Raider and himself a former member of the Activity, pictured in May 1994 giving evidence to the Senate Armed Services Committee investigation into the demise of Operation Gothic Snake. (Associated Press/Empics)

N

ABOVE Aerial reconnaissance imagery used in one of the allied special operations raids against an indicted war criminal living in Bosnia.

LEFT Stevan Todorović, who as police chief took part in the ethnic cleansing of Croats and Muslims from Bosanski Šamac, was tracked down by the Activity 'Torn Victor' signals intelligence team and snatched from a cabin 50 miles inside Serbia by the SAS. (Reuters/Paul Vreeker)

ABOVE Radovan Karadžić, the former Bosnian Serb leader who remains the main target of US and British special operations troops hunting down indicted war criminals in the former Yugoslavia. (Camera Press/David Long)

RIGHT US Special Operations troops on horseback alongside local Mujahideen fighters during the war in Afghanistan. (Department of Defense)

OPPOSITE TOP Chinook helicopter shot down on top of the Tak Urghar mountain during Operation Anaconda while bringing in a US special operations team. A SEAL commando fell from the aircraft and the crew returned to try to rescue him but were unable to prevent him being executed by Taliban/al-Qaeda fighters. The helicopter was later deliberately blown up by US troops to prevent it falling into enemy hands (Department of Defense)

OPPOSITE RIGHT A US Army Special Forces operator on an all-terrain vehicle (ATV) like those used by US special operations forces during Operation Anaconda. He shares the road with an Afghan woman in traditional burka with her children. (Getty Images)

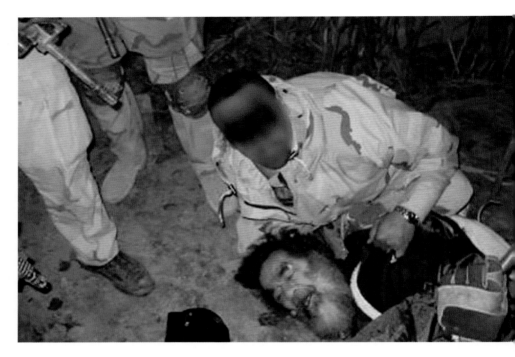

ABOVE An Iraqi interpreter shows off Saddam Hussein to the camera after he was discovered hidden in a 'spider hole' on the farm of one of his former servants at al-Dawr, ten miles south of the Iraqi dictator's home town of Tikrit, in December 2003. (Getty Images)

BELOW Thomas O'Connell, the Activity's senior intelligence officer in its formative years and now Assistant Secretary of Defense, Special Operations and Low-Intensity Conflict with overall responsibility for all special operations units, including the Activity. (Washington Times)

capital. The SEALs' fifteen Zodiac rubber combat raiding craft arrived off shore from Punta Paitilla shortly after midnight. Two SEALs swam ashore to reconnoitre and mark out landing zones. The rest of the force waited for H-hour, 0100 hours on 20 December 1989.

An intelligence report of a helicopter taking off from Colon, on Panama's northern coast and heading south towards Panama City, gave the US commanders a major problem. The Activity had tried to persuade senior army commanders that it should be allowed to put a team into Panama ahead of Operation Just Cause to provide close target reconnaissance on Noriega so he could be picked up straight away. But the offer was rebuffed. With no one knowing Noriega's precise location, there was concern that he was on the sighted helicopter and was on his way to Punta Paitilla to make good his escape on board the Learjet. The commanders of the operation had no choice but to order the SEALs to go in early. As the members of Task Unit Papa went ashore, they heard the sound of firing and explosions from the main attack on the Comandancia compound that housed the headquarters of the Panama Defence Force and realised that any hope of surprise was lost. But the southern coastal perimeter of the airfield was too far away from the private hangar where the Learjet was under close guard, to see it, let alone destroy it.

The support teams set up their positions on the southern perimeter while the three SEAL assault platoons made their way around the perimeter to the northern side of the airfield to find the hangar containing the Learjet. But as they approached, the guards opened fire. With the runway lights on behind them, the platoon members were silhouetted in the dark and the guards swiftly mowed eight of them down. There was an AC130 Spectre gunship ready in the air and prepared to bring down aerial support, but for inexplicable reasons the task unit commander had decided to leave behind the special tactics combat controller who was assigned to them, specifically to direct the Spectre's fire. The SEALs were cruelly exposed to the small arms fire of the men guarding the Learjet and without a combat controller on the ground the Spectre gunship was unable to give sustained supporting fire for fear of hitting its own men.

Chief Petty Officer Don McFaul, the 32-year-old leader of Golf platoon, which suffered the bulk of the casualties, dragged two of the wounded men to safety and was carrying a third away from the kill zone when he was himself shot. McFaul fell forward, protecting his comrade's body until help arrived. But he was mortally wounded, one of four SEALs to be killed in the raid. He was posthumously awarded the Naval Cross. The citation said that 'under heavy enemy fire and with total disregard for his personal safety, Chief Petty Officer McFaul moved into the kill zone and began carrying a seriously wounded platoon member to safety. As he was nearing the safety of his own perimeter, he was mortally wounded by enemy gunfire. His heroic actions and courage were an inspiration for other acts of heroism as the assault force prevailed in this decisive battle.' McFaul died a week before the birth of his daughter Megan. It took a good half-hour and several fierce firefights before the SEALs managed to subdue the guards and damage the Learjet sufficiently to ensure it could not be used. The mission was successful, but four SEALs died in the process and a further eight were wounded.

It subsequently turned out to have been a waste of time and, more importantly, lives. Quite apart from the flawed concept, Noriega had not even tried to escape, preferring to spend the night he was overthrown in a motel with a prostitute. 'Who would have thought, with all the warning that he had, that Noriega would decide to go to a motel and spend the evening with a whore?' one of the special operations commanders said. 'But that's what he did.' The Panamanian dictator later sought sanctuary in the Papal *Nunciatore*, the Vatican's official mission to Panama, before eventually giving himself up and being flown to America to be put on trial for drugs trafficking. Despite the problems and the FUBARs – not least the refusal to allow the Activity to track

Noriega ahead of the mission – Operation Just Cause was a successful showcase for US special operations forces.[11]

Counter-narcotics operations were now one of their main roles. The open warfare between the drugs barons and the Colombian government at the beginning of September 1989 led President Bush and British Prime Minister Margaret Thatcher to agree to send special operations teams and signals intelligence operators into Colombia to hunt down the drugs gangs. Bush promised $65 million worth of arms and equipment along with up to 100 military 'trainers', including communications, maintenance, supply and munitions specialists. A British team, including SAS officers, visited Bogotá to work out what was required. The UK military assistance included not only an SAS Sabre squadron to train the *Bloque de Busqueda*, the special Colombian paramilitary police force set up to hunt down the drugs barons, but also the latest signals intelligence equipment on board the Royal Navy frigate HMS *Alacrity*. The US contribution would include US Army Green Berets and members of the Activity's signals intelligence team, operating under the codename Centra Spike.[12]

British officials refused to confirm that the British troops being sent to Colombia were SAS and insisted that UK soldiers would not accompany Colombian forces on anti-narcotics operations. The Pentagon initially said no decision had been made on whether the American military personnel would take part in actual operations. But a secret document appearing to authorise US forces to become directly involved in operations against the drugs barons led to renewed concerns of another Vietnam, where the initial dispatch of military advisers rapidly turned into full-scale US involvement in a major war. Administration officials backtracked, insisting that American soldiers would not go on operations. 'I think there is no interest in having US troops there in operations even, I think, to accompany people on lab busts and other things,' William J Bennett, the US 'drugs czar' assured a senate sub-committee. 'I think there's very little interest in that.' While

Bennett's attempted assurance of the senators fell short of an absolute denial, Dick Cheney, the then US Defense Secretary, was unequivocal. 'US military personnel are not to accompany host country troops on operations,' he said. 'We aren't flying their helicopters for them. We are not travelling with their units as advisors into the field when they're out on operational assignments.' But in early October, the authoritative forces newspaper *Army Times* gave the game away, quoting several special operations soldiers as contradicting the administration's claims. 'It is very difficult to properly train these armies to perform long-range recon patrols for drug targets without supervising them on at least their first few missions,' an Army Special Forces master sergeant was quoted as saying. It was essential, if the US and British special operations forces were to do their job properly that they 'baby sat' their Colombian students during 'first-blood days', one special operations officer said. 'School is one thing. These jungles are another.'[13]

Initially, the Colombians simply weren't good enough and, more to the point, the drugs barons had sympathisers inside the *Bloque de Busqueda,* one former SAS soldier said. 'The initial plan had been for the SAS teams to confine themselves to training but the corrosive influence of drug money on the security forces – some helicopters would over-fly drug laboratories as an early warning on the way in to raid them – meant that most of the raids by the anti-narcotics police were failures. The SAS men then took a more direct role, leading teams of Colombians on training patrols. Each one would comb some two square miles of jungle for any trace of laboratories or trails. No prior information was given to any of the Colombian forces and when a target had been located and a raid was called in neither the troops nor the helicopter pilots were told the location until they were approaching the landing zone.'[14]

The SAS trained the police counter-narcotics force to carry out long-range surveillance operations to find the cocaine processing laboratories hidden deep in the jungle where the coca paste was turned into pure cocaine. They taught them to carry out close-in target recon-naissance, to gather the intelligence needed for a raid, how to make sure no one spotted them, and how to handle the explosives they would use to blow up the labs. 'The Colombians aimed to arrest the chemists operating the labs as well as destroying the equipment,' one former SAS soldier said. 'A new lab could be set up and running within days or even hours of a successful raid, but chemists might be harder to find in the Colombian jungle. Killing them would have put them out of the way permanently but the police were already too scared of reprisals from the cocaine gangs to countenance that.'[15] The difficulty was in knowing where to look for the labs. That's where the Activity came in.

The Centra Spike team was based in a windowless vault on the fifth floor of the US embassy in the Avenue el Dorado south of downtown Bogotá. Steve Jacoby's team were protected by reinforced walls and a six-inch-thick steel door. They had two Beechcraft King Airs, each carrying the livery of Falcon Aviation and packed with $50 million worth of intercept equipment. The aircraft were modified by Summit Aviation of Middletown, Delaware, who extended the wings to accommodate the special antennae. The knob-turners were mainly native Spanish speakers, picked out by the Activity's talent spotters on their regular trawls of the army personnel computer. The King Airs flew out of the Palencaro air base north of Bogotá. The *narcos* were addicted to cellphones, believing that the landline phones were monitored by the police. But the King Airs didn't just pick up cellphone transmissions. The shortwave radios the drugs gangs used to commu-nicate with the remote jungle labs, their personal bleeper messages and their emails were all monitored. Some of the Spanish-speaking intercept operators went on board the aircraft to monitor the radio and cellphone conversations for any piece of intelligence that required immediate action. Others stayed in the embassy, painstakingly tran-scribing the tapes the crews brought back.[16]

The Activity's well-equipped King Air intercept 'platforms' had

little problems getting 'ears on target'. A typical cellphone system is
made up of a number of base stations controlled by a mobile telephone
switching office or MTSO. When a cellphone is turned on, its trans-
ceiver automatically starts searching for the base station with the
strongest signal, like a baby animal bleating for its mother. Once it has
established contact with the base station it sets up a control link, along
which it transmits information about its identity so the network knows
where it is. This allows incoming calls to be directed to the new 'mother'
base station. The most effective way of monitoring the cellphone trans-
mission is to use a process known as 'meaconing', in which the intercept
system takes control of the cellphone. It first jams the control link,
forcing the cellphone to start scanning the available frequencies for
another base station. It then sets up a new counterfeit base station with
a much stronger signal, which attracts the target cellphone. All outgoing
and incoming calls are now redirected through the counterfeit base
station.[17]

Escobar and his colleagues believed they were immune to interception because even if their cellphone conversations were monitored,
the phone network was encrypting the transmissions in a way that
made it impossible to understand them. But the intercept systems used
by the military do not need to decrypt the transmissions. On a typical
cellphone network, it is the base station that controls the encryption. So
the intercept operator's counterfeit base section simply denies encryption, allowing the operator to listen into the calls 'in clear' without
either party knowing what is going on. The precise capabilities of the
system used by the Activity remain highly classified. But those of the
standard military cellphone interception system produced by Applied
Standard Technology, the top US company supplying such systems,
are not. The AST Model 1235 Multi-Channel Digital Receiving
System is fully computerised and has sixty independent digital
receivers, each of which can switch between the various cellphone
modes now available as required. They are also said to be 'adept' at

tracking the communications of the cellphone under attack and its base station as they switch frequency.

The systems used by the Activity in Colombia were not so sophisticated but they shared three important capabilities with their modern equivalents, quite apart from the ability to listen into the conversations between Escobar and his associates. Firstly, it is extremely easy to locate the precise position of a cellphone using modern digital direction-finding equipment. The Activity's King Airs simply flew around the target cellphone allowing the computerised DF equipment to triangulate bearings to the target phone from a number of locations and work out the precise position of the phone to within a few tens of yards.[18] They could also use Escobar's cellphone as a bug even when it was not being used to make a call. The control link with the base station is on a completely different frequency to that used to transmit the actual calls and, if the cellphone is switched on, it is active at all times. The intercept operator can use this link to turn the cellphone into a bug, even if the cellphone is not being used to make a call. So long as the phone is switched on, the intercept operator can listen in to what the owner or anyone else in the near vicinity of the cellphone is saying. The Activity's equipment also allowed them to locate the target even when he or she believed they had switched off their cellphone. Using the control link, the intercept operator could programme the telephone to ensure that if it had been switched off, it came on at precisely the time the Activity needed to be able to locate it, a useful capability given the *narcos*' willingness to move around from location to location in order to avoid being tracked down by the police.[19]

The Activity used a system known as 'traffic analysis' to study the frequency of calls to and from Escobar's cellphone. This allowed them to work out who his most important associates, hitmen and informants were, and Jacoby's intelligence analysts were eventually able to build up a detailed picture of his entire organisation. They were heavily assisted by the flood of calls that followed Gacha's death. Both the traffic analysis and the contents of those calls soon made it very clear that *El Mexicano* had in reality been just a front man. Escobar was the real leader of the cartel. The traffic analysis carried out by the Activity intelligence team was seen as the key to the campaign to bring Escobar down. His network of informants, couriers and hitmen had links into every part of Colombian society and nothing happened in the police without Escobar knowing. The Activity had to 'bring down the mountain', dismantle that network piece by piece until the protection it gave Escobar was reduced to the point where he began to get nervous. That required a systematic programme of intensive intelligence collection, building up the traffic analysis to the point where they knew every one of the people Escobar relied on and then picking them off one by one, dismantling his empire piece by piece. By the middle of January, with the *Bloque de Busqueda*, assisted by the Activity, causing him serious problems, Escobar declared a truce.[20]

But in March 1990, the plan was severely disrupted by the kind of incident that intelligence operators try desperately to avoid but politicians regularly manage to cause. By now Escobar was offering his hitmen, or *sicarios*, rewards of $8,000 for every member of the *Bloque de Busqueda* they killed. The last thing they needed was for Escobar to find out about their existence, but that was precisely what happened. One of the Activity's King Airs intercepted a telephone conversation between Escobar and the leader of his *sicarios*. They were discussing a planned assassination and it was clear the target was one of the presidential candidates, with the *sicario* to receive $625 and his family twice that amount if he died or was captured. The Activity operators realised they had no choice but to share the transcript of the conversation with the Colombian authorities if they were going to save the lives of the politicians targeted by Escobar's men. The police doubled their protection for all the candidates who had backed the extraditions. Unfortunately that did not include the politician who was actually the target, Bernardo Jaramillo of the Unión Patriótica – the political arm of one of the FARC guerrilla groups, but not particularly connected to the calls for extradition of the *narcos*. The 16-year-old *sicario* walked up to Jaramillo at Bogotá's El Dorado International Airport, making as if to welcome him before shooting him with a sub-machine gun hidden in a newspaper. The government immediately accused Escobar of being behind the attack. When he denied it, the National Security Council issued a statement alleging that 'US police' had used 'electronic listening devices' to intercept the conversation between Escobar and his head *sicario* in which the drugs lord ordered the hit, foolishly warning him that his cellphone was being monitored and hampering the Activity's operations.[21]

But still they continued to track down the *narcos*, carefully putting the pressure on Escobar, or *El Patrón* as he was known to his many admirers among the poor of Medellín and its southern suburbs. Three months later, the knob-turners directed the *Bloque de Busqueda* to the safe house of John Arías, one of Escobar's leading *sicarios*. Arías drowned while the paramilitary police were trying to force him to tell them a key piece of information. A few weeks later they captured Hernan Henao, Escobar's brother-in-law and a key associate. Then on 9 August they tracked down Gustavo Gaviria, who had been one of Escobar's closest associates since his youth when they stole cars together. He was not only the man who directly controlled the cocaine processing on Escobar's behalf, he was also the paymaster to all the *sicarios* and the agents inside the government, the police and the army. The authorities announced that he had been 'killed in a police shootout'. The *Bloque de Busqueda* were brutal killers, who once threw two suspects out of a helicopter because they were worried they just *might* have identified the Activity operators working alongside them as Americans. The words 'killed in a police shootout' on an official government bulletin meant only one thing. The target had been deliberately taken out. But it seems unlikely that someone like Gustavo Gaviria, with so much information in his head, would just have been killed outright, so some credence might be given to Escobar's angry claim that his associate had been tortured and murdered. Whatever the truth, both the US and British special operations forces were dealing with people whose willingness to indulge in torture and deliberate assassinations went far beyond what the US and British soldiers were allowed to do under laws made in Washington and London.[22]

There was now a new president, sworn in only two days before Gustavo Gaviria was killed. President César Gaviria had replaced the assassinated Luis Galán as the Liberal Party candidate and he began a highly pragmatic move towards accommodation with Escobar, eventually agreeing not to extradite him in return for his surrender. Escobar eventually ended up in *La Cathédral*, a 30,000-square-metre 'prison' compound with luxury accommodation that included wall-to-wall carpets, a 64-inch television screen, modern stereo sound systems and a Jacuzzi. There was a discothèque, a gymnasium, a football pitch and trailbikes for Escobar and his associates to ride around the compound. There were even a number of luxury chalets where Escobar and his gang could entertain prostitutes. There was no doubting it was a sell-out by the new Colombian president, but by now the men from the Activity were long gone, their attention once again switched back to the Middle East.[23]

AS HIS EYES BECAME ACCUSTOMED to the semi-dark inside the Royal Air Force Chinook helicopter, Ray Kaminski glanced around at the sixteen Brits accompanying them on the mission. A few of the Special Boat Service commandos were chatting and laughing, but most were grim-faced and quiet, some even appeared to be asleep. Special operations missions were the same the world round, Kaminski thought. Somewhere that night a Black Hawk would be taking the D-boys into action and those guys would be acting just the same. Everyone dealt with the tension in their own way, but there was only so much you could do. It was late at night on 22 January 1991. Just under six months earlier, the Iraqi President Saddam Hussein had invaded Kuwait. It was only six days since America and its allies had retaliated with awesome power, beginning the air war.

Ray Kaminski – not his real name – and his two colleagues, all technical experts from the Activity, were en route to one of the many missions allied special operations forces carried out behind enemy lines during the Gulf War. But just 30 miles from Baghdad, this was as dangerous as any. That was why they had so many British special forces with them – there were another twenty in a second Chinook flying slightly ahead and to their left. The target was the large Amariya communications centre; the mission, to obtain a length of the fibre-optic cable the Iraqis were using for the command and control links to the front-line. The cables were made of plastic-coated glass along which the messages were carried by pulses of light. The sample they needed was to be taken back to Fort Meade, Virginia, where the experts from the National Security Agency, America's electronic intelligence centre, would try to find ways of intercepting the messages. That was why they needed the Activity. The men removing the fibre-optic cable had to have both technical expertise and experience in special operations 'direct action' missions. Only one unit in the world had that combination of skills.

It was pitch black outside. They could not have mounted such an operation with even the slightest crescent of a moon. The light would have reflected off the flat desert sand, leaving them visible for miles around. There was also a sizeable distraction taking place 30 miles to the east – a major allied air raid on Baghdad. As they approached the target, they could see over to their right that it was all going off above the Iraqi capital. Anti-aircraft fire and tracer rounds lit up the horizon. The other Chinook hit the ground first and the twenty SBS men on board were immediately off and running into predetermined positions around the complex. They were to form the defensive 'baseline' of heavy machine guns and anti-tank guided missiles that would hold off any Iraqi troops who might come across the mission. The sixteen other British commandos in Kaminski's Chinook were there to blow up the main communications links when the boys from the Activity had what they wanted. Once his Chinook landed, Kaminski led the way. He had the plans of the complex, produced using imagery from US Keyhole satellites. The SBS commandos would dig down to find the right cables. Kaminski and his colleagues would cut the cable length, the SBS men would plant the explosive and then they would be off. The RAF aircrew were understandably nervous. An Iraqi military patrol might come along the road at any moment. The pilots disengaged the Chinook rotors to cut the noise but kept the engines running. They were right to be anxious. The mission was nowhere near as simple as expected. The plans produced from the satellite were not up to the job and while they managed to find a good length of cable, Kaminski wanted more. But it had already taken an hour and a half and the SBS commander decided they must pull out now or risk being discovered. The SBS explosive experts stuffed the explosive into the hole they had dug and, with most of the team already back on the helicopters, detonated it. As the Chinooks climbed away from the site and headed south towards the Saudi border, the Iraqi military were already arriving in force, but too late to stop the boys from the Activity getting away with the vital piece of cable.[24]

General Norman Schwarzkopf, the allied commander, was a staunch opponent of special operations and refused to allow them any role before the war began. The Activity managed to infiltrate a number of its own men, posing as expatriate oil workers, into Iraqi-occupied Kuwait, and sent in a number of specially trained Kuwaitis to build up a very good picture of what was going on inside the country. General Peter de la Billiere, the British commander, who was himself a member of the SAS, persuaded Schwarzkopf to allow SAS troopers to go into Iraq to collect intelligence and prevent Scud missile attacks on Tel Aviv that might lead Israel to attack Iraq, fragmenting the allies' carefully constructed coalition, which included Syrian and Saudi forces. General Wayne Downing, the JSOC commander, had less friendly relations with the allied commander and both Delta and the SEALs were kept on the sidelines. Schwarzkopf, in a previous role as army assistant chief of staff for operations, had been stymied by Downing when he tried to scratch some special operations helicopters from the budget and had not forgotten it. But when the *Washington Times* revealed that Schwarzkopf was using British special operations forces but blocking any deployment of their US counterparts, the order came down from General Colin Powell, the Chairman of the Joint Chiefs. Downing was to be allowed to send in Delta to help the SAS.[25]

The operation to collect the length of fibre-optic cable was crucial in changing Schwarzkopf's mind about the usefulness of special operations. The SBS mission commander came back with one of the Iraqi cable route markers, which he presented to the US commander as a souvenir. Schwarzkopf was 'delighted and impressed', de la Billiere said. 'This first raid made a major contribution towards establishing the reputation and capability not only of our special forces but of those of America as well.' Just as importantly, the piece of fibre-optic cable the mission collected was vital in allowing US and British technicians to work out not only how to tap it but also how to develop important new methods of intercepting communications sent along the cable. The extent to which this capability developed was revealed in a September 1991 memo from Terry Thompson, the then NSA Deputy Director of Services, who said the agency was 'much more ahead now in terms of being able to access and collect fibre-optics, cellular data, all the different modalities of communications that we are targeting, and that results in a lot of output for our analysts'. The Activity would become skilled at tapping the fibre-optic cables, going into Iraq on a number of occasions during the 1990s, to allow the allies to monitor attempts to avoid the UN weapons inspectors.[26]

SIXTEEN MONTHS AFTER the joint Activity–SBS mission inside Iraq, Pablo Escobar escaped from *La Cathédral* and the Activity returned to Bogotá to resume the hunt. The Colombian government had become deeply embarrassed by the way in which *El Patrón* continued to run his drugs operation from inside his prison compound, sending around $200 million worth of cocaine to America every month. What was the point of the top secret US and British military units hunting down Escobar if his surrender to the authorities was so meaningless? Eventually, President César Gaviria decided it was time to crack down and have Escobar transferred to a military prison. He didn't want to go and such was his control over *La Cathédral* that he was simply able to walk out through a hole in the fence. There was always someone who would look the other way for the right amount of money.

So Steve Jacoby and his men had to go back to resume the search for the renegade drugs baron, returning to the fifth-floor vault in the US embassy on Avenue El Dorado on 23 July 1992. The US ambassador, Morris D Busby, told Jacoby the SAS were no longer there to keep the *Bloque de Busqueda* on the right track. It would be good if Delta could come in to make sure they did the job right. But the Pentagon chiefs would never agree to send them. Jacoby told him it was definitely worth asking. Two years earlier, General Wayne Downing, the head of JSOC, had asked one of the Centra Spike team whether there was any role Delta could play in the hunt for Escobar. 'What are our chances of going in and not getting anybody killed?' Downing asked. 'Almost zero,' was the reply. 'None of these *narcos* is going to surrender peacefully. If you go in you either have to take them all or kill them all.' Still Downing had been interested and Bill Garrison, the Activity's former deputy commander, was now in charge of Delta, so there was every chance of a positive response. 'Don't say you want them to come in here and go after Pablo themselves,' Jacoby said, well aware of the controversy that would stir among the top brass. 'Say you want them to offer training and advice.' He knew that Delta would have to go out on the missions to make sure their training worked, just like the SAS had done. The response was swift; within days, a team of eight Delta operators arrived in Bogotá, led by Colonel William 'Jerry' Boykin, a highly religious man who prayed before each mission.

Now the whole process began all over again. The intercepts of the cellphones and radio transmissions; the aerial direction-finding figures of eight, tracking down the location of the quarry and his various associates; and the traffic analysis to evaluate who were important players in the matrix of Escobar's associates, who did he really depend on. Working in tandem with the *Bloque de Busqueda*, now trained and accompanied by Delta and SEALs, the Activity began to track down the men at the edges, working inwards, gradually closing in on Escobar himself, making him feel hunted, chipping away at his confidence. This time they weren't alone. Not only did they have Delta and SEAL commandos, it seemed at times that virtually every piece of US intelligence hardware was focusing on Colombia. US Air Force RC135 Rivet Joint signals intelligence aircraft scooping up every kind of radio signal; US Navy P3 Orions relaying back real-time video of what was happening on the ground; U2 and SR71 Blackbird spy planes; two different top secret CIA surveillance aircraft; and of course the Quasar Talent King Airs hoovering up every radio and cellnet communication the drugs barons and their men made. Everyone wanted to get in on the act. It was like the Iran hostage rescue mission all over again, only this time twice as bad. There were too many people tripping over each other, another disaster waiting to happen. Jacoby had to insist that apart from the high-altitude Blackbirds and U2s, all the other US spy planes kept below 25,000 feet. The King Airs could then at least fly at 30,000 feet and know they were safe. With the hunt for Escobar focusing on Medellín, the Activity team were given permission to set up a ground intercept site in the city's suburbs.[27]

It wasn't long before Escobar began trying to negotiate another surrender. But the Colombian government wasn't in any mood to talk.

The hunt became ever more brutal, not least because some of Escobar's former associates, men he had fallen out with badly, had joined the hunt, apparently backed by the Cali cartel which saw an easy way of eliminating its main business rival. The one-time associates of Escobar called themselves *Los Pepes*, an acronym for the People Persecuted by Escobar. They were brutal murderers and they were clearly taking part in the manhunt, killing off many of the precise targets that the Activity traffic analysis had designated for removal from the matrix. The old concerns of how involved the Activity, and now Delta, were becoming in officially sanctioned assassinations resurfaced. It wasn't just the *Bloque de Busqueda* with their willingness to ensure the targets were 'killed in a police shootout'. It was clear that, somehow, *Los Pepes* were privy to the intelligence picture that Jacoby and his men were putting together. They weren't just killing off the right guys. The Activity analysts had given the *Bloque de Busqueda* a list of people who should be left in place because their phone calls always produced the most useful intelligence. *Los Pepes* were also leaving those guys alone. There was clearly someone inside the operation feeding them intelligence and in the Pentagon the alarm bells started ringing, with some suggesting that the Activity and Delta were helping a death squad and should be pulled out.

Unfortunately for Escobar, the decision was never made. At the beginning of October 1993, the Medellín intercept site picked up his radio-telephone and located it to a farmhouse overlooking the village of Aguas Frías, to the west of the city. A few days later, on Monday 11 October, an assault team was assembled in the neighbouring valley, waiting for confirmation that *El Patrón* was still there. Shortly after four o'clock he made his regular afternoon call to his son. The radio-telephone was located to the farmhouse and the team went in. But Escobar had moved up into the woods above the house to get a better signal and saw the helicopters coming. He hid until it was dark and then fled. The raid was a failure. Nevertheless, it turned up a wealth of intelligence. One Drugs Enforcement Agency memo noted: 'Intelligence obtained at the search site and recent Title III intercepts indicate that Escobar no longer enjoys the financial freedom he once had. Escobar is extremely short of cash.' The mountain was very close to being brought down.

In late November, the Activity tracked a radio-telephone Escobar was known to use to the southern *Los Olivos* district of Medellín. He had moved into one of the large number of houses he owned. Although he usually drove round the city in a taxi when he used the radio-telephone to confuse the US direction-finding equipment, he got over-confident and, as he telephoned his family in Bogotá, was tracked down to the street in which the house was situated. When Escobar telephoned his wife an hour later, the knob-turners located the precise house and a waiting seventeen-man assault force went in. Escobar and his bodyguard were shot dead as they tried to flee out of the back of the house. The final moments of *El Patrón* remain shrouded in controversy. All the evidence is that both men went down wounded and then were shot through the head as they lay on the ground. Officially, he was killed by the members of the *Bloque de Busqueda* who certainly made up the bulk of the assault force. But there were a number of well-informed claims that they were augmented by members of Delta. Whatever the truth of the allegations, Escobar's demise was a much needed success for the Activity at the end of a year that until then had not been seen as its finest hour.[28]

8 SNATCHING WAR CRIMINALS

'SHIT. NOT A-FUCKIN'-GAIN.' Dave McKnight was a very unhappy man. He could see on the video coming through from the navy P3 Orion spy plane that the battered silver car with the red stripes down the side had stopped outside the wrong building. The local agents, recruited by the CIA, simply couldn't cut it. Twice now this guy had chickened out. General Bill Garrison, the commander of Task Force Ranger, and a former Activity man himself, had bawled McKnight out Texan-style first time round and the chief of staff and head of intelligence for the Somalia-based mission was not about to face up to that again for the sake of some CIA-recruited skinnie. They were trying to run a 'snatch' operation into the Black Sea area of Mogadishu. The Somali agents were reporting a number of 'Tier Ones' meeting in a building on Hawlwadig Road, just north of the Olympic Hotel. The agent was supposed to park his car outside the place, to 'mark' it for the snatch team from Delta. That was all he had to fucking do, and he was fucking up big time. McKnight lifted the radio handset to his mouth and pressed the tit. 'Get that guy outside the right fucking building,' he yelled. At last the guy did what he was told.

It was 1500 hours on Sunday 3 October 1993. The Activity had been sent into Mog six weeks earlier. Somalia had been ripped apart by civil war, leaving two-bit gangsters feuding over its carcass like hyenas. Admiral Jonathan Howe, the former deputy National Security Advisor who was now the UN administrator in Somalia, had been pleading for weeks with Bill Clinton to send in special operations forces to capture Mohammed Farah Aideed, the worst of the local warlords. The response was Task Force Ranger, made up of the 'shooters' from Delta, back-up from the US Rangers and 'intel' from the Activity.

The problem was, the Activity had to rely on these idiot agents recruited by the CIA. Fortunately, the Activity commander hadn't just deployed the spooks from the Activity's operations squadron. Steve Jacoby's knob-turners had been pulled out of Colombia to give a hand. There was no functioning landline telephone system in Somalia. The only way the warlords could communicate was via radio–telephone, making them easy targets for the electronic surveillance boys. The agents on the ground were reporting that two dozen members of Aideed's Somali National Alliance were meeting in the building on Hawlwadig Road, a rubbish-strewn river of dust running through the middle of the city. They included a pair of 'Tier One Personalities', Omar Salad Elmi and Mohammed Hassan Awale, two of Aideed's top aides. With the building marked for the assault, and the Delta snatch team already in the air, it was time for Jacoby's guys to cut the targets' comms. One flick of a switch and a continuous burst of noise from the Activity's jamming equipment drowned out the warlords' radio links. With luck, that should stop the targets calling for help from their *mooryan*, the gunmen who surrounded them.

The plan was for security teams of US Rangers to 'fast-rope' down from Black Hawks to seal off the building. The D-boys would then come in on Little Bird helicopter gunships to snatch Omar Salad Elmi, Awale and the rest of the targets, who would be extracted by a convoy of Humvees. One Ranger missed his rope and fell 70 feet to the ground, but mainly it went off OK. Delta got their Tier Ones and the Humvees arrived to pull them out. The mission was just about over when all hell broke loose, with gunmen allied to Aideed firing off a barrage of machine-gun fire and RPG7 rocket-propelled anti-tank grenades. The *mooryan* got lucky, taking out a Black Hawk and bringing it down 300 yards east of the target building. It was the start of a fourteen-hour rescue mission – immortalised in the book and film *Black Hawk Down* – that would leave eighteen American servicemen dead and sear into the psyche of the US military.

The Activity signals intelligence team had been called out of Colombia briefly in July 1993 to prepare for the Somalia mission. They were still tracking down someone regarded as an outlaw by the international community. But unlike Colombia, where the hunt for Pablo Escobar took place in a pretty permissive atmosphere, the search for Aideed would be carried out in an extremely hostile environment. The Somali warlord had trained as a police officer in the 1950s when his country was under Italian control, becoming the police chief in the capital Mogadishu. During the 1960s when the newly independent Somali Republic fell under Soviet influence, Aideed underwent military training in the Soviet Union and after Siad Barre seized power he became the new dictator's intelligence chief. But when the Somali president split from Moscow over his decision to invade the region's main Soviet puppet Ethiopia, Aideed was thrown into prison. He was briefly released to become ambassador, first to Turkey and then to India, but when he again fell from favour he moved to Italy to set up the dissident United Somali Congress with other members of his Hawiye tribe.[1]

Aideed led an alliance of rebel forces, the Somali National Alliance, which marched on the capital in 1991, forcibly removing Siad Barre from power. But not only did Barre's troops fight on, the SNA splintered in a power struggle between Aideed and his main rival within the Hawiye clan, Ali Mahdi. Somalia became an anarchic wasteland.

Television pictures of starving Somali children propelled the conflict up the international agenda and in December 1992, the US-led and UN-backed Operation Restore Hope went in to try to resolve the situation. Aideed agreed to disarm in early 1993 but when he saw other warlords would keep hold of their weapons he reneged on the agreement. Then in June 1993, his men ambushed a UN convoy, killing twenty-four Pakistani soldiers. Aideed was declared an outlaw by the UN, with Howe offering a $25,000 reward for information leading to his capture and pleading with his friends in DC to send in a special operations task force to sort Aideed out. With the Somali warlord now officially regarded as an international criminal, the Clinton administration decided it was time to act.

Bill Garrison, now the general in charge of JSOC, was ordered to put together a special operations force to snatch Aideed. The force was to be made up of a squadron of 130 members of Delta, led by their commander Colonel 'Jerry' Boykin; a small number of SEAL Team Six snipers; 16 helicopters from the 160th Special Operations Aviation Regiment, a small number of combat controllers from the 24th Special Tactics Squadron, to direct air support, and a back-up force provided by the 75th Ranger Regiment. They moved out to the West Coast where they began to rehearse for the operation, to 'template' the snatch missions for Aideed and his aides that would be designed to dismember the whole of the leadership of the Hawiye clan to allow the UN to take control of Mogadishu. The bulk of the intelligence was to be provided by the Activity. The CIA already had a presence on the ground in Somalia but the Activity human intelligence experts were sent in to work out what they would need to track down the Somali warlord. The fact that Garrison, a former deputy commander of the Activity, was in charge of JSOC, and that his 'J2' intelligence chief was Lieutenant-Colonel Dave McKnight – who in a previous assignment as the Activity's ops officer had set the unit back on the track charted by Jerry King – ensured that the Activity was to play a large role. Not only were the human intelligence specialists sent immediately to work out the lie of the land as part of an operational assessment team led by McKnight, the Centra Spike team was pulled out of Colombia to provide signals intelligence for the operation, and Activity imagery experts were added to the force.

Cooperation with the CIA was not going to be a problem. In the wake of the 1991 Gulf War, when there was widespread criticism of the inability of national agencies, like the CIA and the NSA, to get intelligence to military commanders in real time, the CIA had created a system of National Intelligence Support Teams, run by the CIA Office of Military Affairs, to work alongside commanders on the ground. The situation was even better for Garrison. Dave McKnight had served two tours as a special operations forces liaison with the Office of Military Affairs. His last assignment before becoming the JSOC head of intelligence was as the senior liaison officer at Langley for all special operations forces. He knew the CIA men on the ground and they were committed to helping Garrison get the best intel he could.[2]

Garrison started assembling his team immediately in consultation with General Wayne Downing, now commander-in-chief of SOCOM, and General Joseph P Hoar, who as the man in charge of US Central Command had ultimate responsibility for military operations in Somalia. 'It all was put together based upon the mission, the enemy situation as we saw it, and the terrain and the environment that we were going to have to operate in,' Garrison said. Initially, a much smaller force, codenamed Caustic Brimstone, was to deploy, but McKnight's advice from inside Mogadishu was that they needed to ramp it up. There would need to be a strong Delta force backed up by a company of Rangers who would provide force protection, holding down the fire of any resistance force while the Delta and SEAL Team Six snatch team went in. It was this requirement that led to the size of the 400-strong force assembled for Operation Gothic Snake. For a while – with the Clinton administration vacillating over whether or not to put US troops in the line of fire – there were doubts as to whether the force would go at all. But when four US soldiers were killed by a remote-controlled roadside bomb on 8 August 1993, President Clinton ordered Task Force Ranger to deploy immediately to Mogadishu. 'The company of Rangers, and the other forces that I cannot get into at this time, were determined to be the appropriate force,' Garrison said. 'We determined this because we had people that went in the country and looked at the situation and then we trained for two months before we were deployed, and this was determined to be the appropriate size force.'³ Garrison and a small advance party, including Dave McKnight, who was to be his chief of staff, left Fort Bragg for Mogadishu on 22 August. The presence in Somalia of the commander-in-chief of JSOC, and that of the other JSOC special mission units, was to be kept entirely secret. As far as anyone was to know, Task Force Ranger was to be commanded by Major-General Thomas M Montgomery, the American deputy commander of the UN force.

The Activity signals intelligence team was picking up a lot of low-level people on walkie-talkie-style radios. But Aideed had been spooked by the price put on his head by the UN and had gone underground, sleeping in as many as three different places a night and moving only by foot or donkey cart to avoid putting up any kind of signature that the intelligence teams could latch on to. The most likely source of information on his whereabouts was human intelligence. The main CIA agent was a minor warlord, the leader of a small-time clan that owed allegiance of sorts to Aideed. His handler was to be a Vietnam vet who had become a leading CIA operations officer and had run him before the Somali civil war. Codenamed Condor, the CIA officer had a key asset of his own: he was a black African American and could therefore merge into the background inside Mogadishu. The plan was for the CIA's warlord to give Aideed an ivory-handled walking stick with a homing device inserted in the handle. The hope was that Aideed would like it so much that he would carry it everywhere with him, ensuring that Garrison's force knew precisely where to find him.[4] But on 26 August, just as the main body of Task Force Ranger began arriving at Mogadishu airport in giant C5 Galaxy aircraft, the CIA's warlord shot himself in the head in a game of Russian roulette. Dave McKnight knew that they now had a major problem. He told Garrison: 'He's not dead yet but we're fucked.' Garrison's response was to quote from the opening lines of the autobiography of the American President and Unionist General Ulysses S Grant, 'Man proposes and God disposes'.[5]

Phase One of Gothic Snake had been due to last four days and was designed to give time for all the units of Task Force Ranger to become fully operational. Phase Two was a direct hunt for Aideed, which would hopefully culminate in his arrest. If that failed, then a longer term plan, Gothic Snake III, would be put in place to 'take down the mountain', just as they had done with Pablo Escobar, by dismantling his networks and taking out all the key people on whom he relied, his half a dozen top aides, or in the Activity's parlance the Tier One Personalities. If the 'Tier Ones' were removed from the picture, Aideed himself would be forced into the open to exert control over his forces.

With the CIA warlord dead and the ivory-handled walking stick now a no-go, there was a desperate lack of intel on Aideed's whereabouts. He had not been seen since 28 July. The task force needed 'current actionable intelligence' before it could go in to find him but they didn't even have the smallest piece of reliable information. No one had the faintest idea where the Somali National Alliance was. It wasn't that no one was trying. Condor was carefully organising the twenty agents the CIA and the Activity still had operating in Mogadishu into two teams. He was working in highly dangerous circumstances out of a deserted football stadium in northern Mogadishu with four members of SEAL Team Six to protect him. But the agents were highly nervous and unreliable. There was a spate of killings by Aideed's *mooryan* of people alleged to be helping the Americans. 'They murder people all the time,' one of Task Force Ranger's senior intelligence officers said. 'Most of the people they murder have nothing to do with us.' But the end result was that most of the agents refused pointblank to go out at night, which created severe difficulties both in gathering intel and reporting it. The agents were not producing enough actionable intelligence for Delta to go in, and to make matters worse the agents were deeply unreliable. Garrison had video screens up in the Joint Operations Centre (JOC) at Mogadishu airport showing real-time video from a US Navy P3 Orion circling the Somali capital and from two matt-black specially modified OH58 Kiowa observation helicopters. The agents' reports rarely seemed to match up to the video the commanders back at the JOC were watching.[6]

There was an element of relief when Dave McKnight asked the acting CIA head of station Garrett Jones about a tip-off that the Lig-Ligato compound was being used by Aideed's men as a 'command and control centre'. Jones knew the Somali National Alliance had used the compound and that Aideed had himself visited the compound on occasion. 'Yeah, that's a good target,' he said. Delta launched a snatch operation at 0300 on the morning of 30 August, roping down from helicopters and plasti-cuffing all of the occupants. They turned out to be members of the UN mission and their Somali assistants, leading to newspaper reports comparing the US troops to Keystone Cops. Garrison decided that Task Force Ranger should move to Gothic Snake III, concentrating on carefully dismantling Aideed's operation in the hope of flushing him out into the open where Delta and SEAL Team Six could go in and grab him.[7]

The Activity signals intelligence team, camped out in a tent on the side of the airport, went some way to redeeming a pretty poor intelligence picture, breaking a network of Aideed's supporters who were working for companies contracted to the UN by day while at night carrying out attacks on the peacekeeping force. At first, the knob-turners regarded the radio nets used by the UN contractors as a nuisance. They just seemed to get in the way as they scanned the air waves for Aideed's men. But then they began to notice a remarkable similarity between some of the voices and operating techniques they heard on the contractors' nets and those used by the Aideed militants carrying out the nightly mortar attacks on the airport. No one radio transmitter is exactly the same as any other. Each has its own peculiar 'fingerprint'. So the knob-turners began taking the radio fingerprints and soon realised there was a match-up between radios used on both the contractors' and the militants' networks. They then fingerprinted the voices of the operators and found similar match-ups. The result was a series of raids that netted more than a dozen militants, who were handed over to the UN force for interrogation.[8]

But intelligence successes never make as many headlines as the foul-ups and anyway, the signals intelligence team had little to offer to the hunt for the main man, Mohammed Farah Aideed, who wisely declined to use radio, preferring to pass messages and orders by courier. The close liaison between the CIA and the Activity meant that a CIA case officer, codenamed Buffalo, was stationed in the JOC while an Activity officer, codenamed Gringo II, worked permanently alongside Jones. There were some successes, most notably the capture of a primary Tier One Personality, Osman Ato, a prominent businessman who had made a fortune through his control of the lucrative trade in khat, the narcotic leaves habitually chewed by Somalis. Ato was one of Aideed's main financial backers and the man who paid for and obtained most of the warlord's weaponry. He was spotted in a car and pursued by a Black Hawk carrying a Delta team and a Little Bird with a SEAL Team Six sniper on board. The sniper leant out of the Little Bird, disabling the car by firing three shots into the car's engine block, and the Delta team fast roped down to grab Ato. But his arrest merely emphasised the complicated situation in the Somali capital. Not only was he one of Aideed's top aides, he was also one of the leading building contractors working for the UN.[9]

With the Activity's signals intelligence team unable to get a trace of any sort on Aideed, human intelligence was the key. But the unreliability of the local agents was a major problem. 'As a result of this we have experienced some weariness between [the agent-handlers and their teams] and the task force,' Garrison wrote in a memo back to Joe Hoar in Tampa. 'Generally [each team of agents] appears to believe that a second hand report from an individual who is not a member of the team should be sufficient to constitute current intelligence. I do not. Furthermore when a team member is reporting something that is totally different from what our helicopters are seeing (which we watch here back at the JOC), I naturally weigh the launch decision toward what we actually see versus what is being reported. Events such as last night, with Team 2 stating that Aideed had just left the compound in a three-vehicle convoy, when we know for a fact that no vehicles left the compound, tends to lower our confidence level even more.'[10]

As the number of raids built up, some successful, some embarrassingly unproductive, there was another problem for Garrison. The template that had been carefully rehearsed in the California training exercise was becoming well known to Aideed and his *mooryan*, many of whom had studied military tactics and guerrilla warfare in Soviet military academies. Garrison repeatedly made the point that there were only so many ways to carry out any military operation. 'You can have all the grand theories about warfare that you want,' he said. 'But ultimately there are only four options: up the middle, up the left, up the right or don't go.' The Delta snatch teams went straight up the middle. It was the way they did things. The twin elements of surprise and momentum would overwhelm the targets and, despite the odd embarrassment, the six snatch missions they had carried out thus far had been technically perfect, even if the product had not always been what they wanted. The Black Hawks would go in, the Rangers would fast rope down first to secure the perimeter of the target. Then Delta would fast rope onto or around the target building itself and snatch the quarry. The helicopters would loiter overhead to provide fire support. Once the snatch was over, one of the Black Hawks would land to pick up Delta and their target and whisk them back to the airport base. The Rangers would then be airlifted out in the remaining helicopters. It was a relatively simple and effective routine. But it had become too easy to predict. Garrison tried to maintain the element of surprise by sending the same snatch teams out twice a day, once in the morning, once in the evening, always at the same time, usually to do nothing. 'There is no question that we lost strategic surprise when we moved the force in the country, therefore, we had to maintain tactical surprise,' Garrison said. 'In each case we varied the way and manner and tactics that we used because we knew that not only did we have to maintain tactical surprise when we launched the next operation, we also had to make sure that we gave them a different look. So every operation, we used some form of different look. The other manner that we made sure that we maintained tactical surprise is that once each day we loaded the entire force and we went out and did something. Once each night that we were there, we loaded the entire force up and went out and did something. There was no way that anyone, and we assumed that they were watching us, could tell when we loaded up as to whether or not we were going out to conduct an operation.'

But these were pretty crude devices and they weren't likely to fool anyone who had made an in-depth study of the tactics used by Mao Tse Tung and Ho Chi Minh. 'If you use one tactic twice, you should not use it a third time,' said Colonel Ali Aden, one of Aideed's Soviet-trained commanders. 'And the Americans already had done basically the same thing six times.'[11]

That was the situation at 1300 hours on 3 October 1993, when Bill Garrison, Garrett Jones and Dave McKnight met in the airport JOC to discuss the latest intel situation. Just as they started talking, one of Jones's agent handlers rang through to say that a new source inside Aideed's organisation had come up with the goods on a couple of Tier

Ones. Omar Salad Elmi and Mohammed Hassan Awale were going to be meeting later that afternoon with some other Aideed supporters. The get–together would take place in a compound about fifty yards north of the Olympic Hotel, near the Bakara market, the heart of the 'Black Sea', real bandit country. McKnight told the CIA officer to get the source to park his car outside the Olympic Hotel and lift the hood as if to check the engine so the Orion's video cameras could lock onto him. He was then to drive to the target building and park outside. But the skinnie was so nervous that he rushed the stop outside the hotel, not giving enough time for the cameras to lock onto him. So he had to be ordered to do it all over again by his controller, who was talking to him over a VHF radio link. Sitting in the JOC, Garrison and McKnight watched on the video screens as the battered silver car finally pulled up outside a building. But it was the wrong building. The nervous agent had stopped short of the real target. Eventually, he was persuaded to move forward. He stopped outside the right compound and the video pictures taken from the Orion showed that Omar Salad Elmi's Volkswagen was already inside. By now it was already gone 1500 hours. The task force mounted the helicopters and, just after 1530, they lifted off, hovering briefly just feet above the ground before turning one by one and heading off towards the centre of Mogadishu and the bandit country that was the Black Sea.

Garrison, McKnight and Jones watched the assault take place on the video screens up on the wall of the JOC. At around 1540, the helicopters arrived over the target and dropped down to allow the Delta team and their Rangers support force to fast rope to the ground. Clouds of dust swirled up into the air. One Ranger missed the rope and fell 70 feet to the ground and there were some sporadic exchanges of fire with *mooryan* but nothing that constituted a major problem. The Delta boys blew down the doors, stormed into the building and plasti–cuffed twenty-four Somalis they found on the first floor, including Omar Salad Elmi and Mohammed Hassan Awale, the two Tier Ones. By

1600, the prisoners were secure and the vehicle convoy that would bring them back into the task force HQ at the airport was just about ready to load them up. The operation seemed to have been a success. Then at 1610, the first of two Black Hawk helicopters went down, taken out by *mooryan* using RPG7 rocket-propelled grenade launchers that dated back to the Second World War. From that point onwards, the mission spiralled out of control, with every attempt to rescue someone resulting in further casualties and more American servicemen to be rescued. Over the course of a little under fourteen horrific hours, Task Force Ranger lost 18 men killed in action and 84 wounded. A mission that had come so close to success was to become known as one of America's greatest military failures.[12]

But paradoxically, despite all the intelligence problems that preceded it and the dreadful loss of life, the raid achieved its mission. The intelligence had been entirely accurate. The Tier One targets were where the agent said they would be and they were captured. There had been an appalling price in loss of American life, but the intelligence system put in place by McKnight and Jones was seen as a template for future operations involving both special operations forces and the CIA. Garrison declared later: 'I was totally satisfied with the intelligence effort. Never saw anything better from the intelligence community.' Arguably, the raid was only allowed to become an operational failure by the unwillingness of US politicians to accept that deploying troops in operational theatres puts their lives at risk. Aideed's *mooryan* had taken far heavier casualties than Task Force Ranger. Bill Garrison was preparing to press home the advantage his men had gained with further raids. But the administration was not prepared to accept the possibility of any more American troops coming home in body bags and Task Force Ranger was ordered to come home without achieving its objective. There were a lot of lessons to be learned from Mogadishu and some, like the ability of the *mooryan*'s RPG7s to take out helicopters, were ignored as the US military tried to erase Somalia from its memory. But Gothic Snake only underlined the need for the special mission units like Delta to have their own intelligence team, independent of, but working with, the CIA, and provided a few more good reasons for the Activity's existence.[13]

A senior Pentagon official dealing with the problem of special operations intelligence pointed to Somalia as the moment when the concept behind the Activity was finally accepted, both within the armed forces and the CIA. The Activity had fought off an attempt by the DIA to corral it within the new Defense Humint Service it was planning to set up and was going to stand alone as a special mission unit working alongside other such units, like Delta and SEAL Team Six. 'There was a vigorous debate in recent years in the intelligence community at all levels, both military and national, about the types of intelligence that are needed for special operations – the scope, the detail, the difference between that kind of intelligence and what the 82nd Airborne, for example, needs for its missions,' said Timothy G Connolly, then the principal deputy assistant secretary of defense for special operations and low-intensity conflict. 'There was resistance in the intelligence arena to the notion that there was a need for specialized intelligence for special operations. But I have reason to believe that we've overcome that resistance, that there has been a recognition that special operations forces need specificity that no one else needs and a timeliness that perhaps other military operations can do without.'[14]

Sadly, the main lesson the administration took out of Somalia was that committing US troops anywhere risked losing lives and damaging political flak. The Clinton administration wanted to use US military power to back up its wider vision of a better world but was unable to make it over the first hurdle, preferring to fire off cruise missiles, which by and large were little more than an expensive way of rearranging rubble, rather than deploy troops with the possibility of seeing body bags returning home. Clinton pulled the US troops out of Somalia. Within weeks, the Activity had restored its reputation by tracking down Pablo Escobar. But the reluctance to risk another Mogadishu led the administration to put its plans to intervene to help UN peace-keeping forces in the former Yugoslavia on hold. 'Bosnia was already almost dead in terms of United States participation in peacekeeping,' a senior State Department official said. 'Mogadishu put the last nail in the coffin.' Fortunately, a determination in Europe to put an end to the conflict in the former Yugoslavia finally persuaded Clinton that America was the only country capable of taking a lead and forcing the main protagonists in the brutal war in Bosnia to the peace table.[15]

THE BLUE AND MAUVE uniformed Bosnian Serb special policemen standing guard by the rickety gate were happy to chat to the French army officer, gratefully accepting his Gauloise cigarettes and offering him a flask of coffee laced with *slivović*, a local plum brandy, in return. The muddy road they were guarding led to a large wooden villa that sheltered on the lush green slopes below the Yugoslav ski resort of Pale. A decade earlier, the smaller log cabins scattered among the pine trees lining the valley would have been weekend retreats for the high and mighty of the Sarajevo communist party. Now most were used by the paramilitary police guarding the main villa, home to Radovan Karadžić, the former Bosnian Serb leader. Pale was in the French-controlled sector of Bosnia, so the presence of half a dozen of their troops was unremarkable. Most French officers were sympathetic to the Serbs and this captain was typically friendly. None of the police guards spoke French so he chatted to them in broken English, happily accepting the offer of coffee and *slivović* in return for the cigarettes. His men stayed in their pale green Renault jeeps, apparently on the radio back to base. It had all the semblance of a routine French military patrol. But despite their uniforms and Renault jeeps, neither the officer nor any of his men were French. They were a mixture of shooters from Delta and knob-turners from Torn Victor, the latest codename for the Activity. Their presence in Pale was evidence of a new approach from the Clinton administration and its European allies towards the PIFWCs, pronounced 'pifwix', more formally 'persons indicted for war crimes'. It was the summer of 1997. The allies had previously steered clear of attempting to arrest war criminals. But now they had launched Amber Star, a joint operation aimed at hauling them up before the international war crimes tribunal at the Hague; and Karadžić was top of the list of the most wanted.

The new found enthusiasm for arresting war criminals, and Karadžić in particular, was welcome. But there were problems. The former psychiatrist from Montenegro had long sought to evade responsibility for the crimes carried out by his Bosnian Serb forces. He was driven from public life in 1996, and the international authorities in Bosnia were supposed to avoid any contact with him. But the French liaison officer, Major Hervé Gourmelon, was known to be close to Karadžić and there were concerns about leaks. So Delta and the Activity mounted a separate intelligence operation – codenamed Buckeye – alongside Britain's MI6 secret service and the SAS, keeping the results from the French. The Activity's knob-turners tracked Karadžić's mobile telephones and e-mails while the spooks developed agents on the ground. But the French couldn't be kept completely out of an operation that was going down in their own sector. The plans were already in place. French special forces from the *Groupement Spécial Autonome* were to be flown in by helicopter to secure the villa and disarm the police guards, while Delta, SAS and the Activity moved in on board Black Hawks to snatch Karadžić. He would be taken to a safe house before being flown on to the Hague. The men in French uniforms were part of a final recce team, one last check before the operation went ahead.

BUT IT WAS ALREADY CLEAR that something was wrong. The bogus French officer sent in by the Activity won the confidence of the guards and found out what the knob-turners had already deduced from weeks of monitoring their comms. Karadžić had vanished from the surveillance screens, slipping back across the border into his native Montenegro. There was more than a suspicion that Gourmelon had tipped him off and the raid had to be abandoned. There were furious protests from both Washington and London to President Jacques Chirac, and the Americans and British set up a separate operation, codenamed Green Light, to keep the French out of the loop. They arrested a number of PIFWCs in their own sectors. But it was clear that, without a more honest approach from the French, chasing Karadžić was a waste of energy. The Activity even began operating against them, planting a bug in the car of a female French army officer suspected of illicit links to the Serbs and monitoring her cellphone conversations. The French denied any wrongdoing of course, but when the Serbs were tipped off that their troops were about to be attacked from the air, the Activity knew who was to blame.[16]

It had all seemed so different back in December 1995, when Serbian President Slobodan Milošević, Croatian President Franjo Tudjman and Bosnian President Alija Izetbegovic signed the Dayton Accord in the studied elegance of a crystal-chandeliered ballroom in the Élysée Palace. French President Jacques Chirac had come to power in May 1995 determined to bring an end to the savage civil war that was taking place in the heart of Europe. After the signing ceremony, President Clinton and Chirac adjourned to the French president's second-floor office to discuss the next move. Chirac was angry. He had just heard that two French pilots captured by the Bosnian Serb forces had been brutally mistreated. The massacre by Bosnian Serb troops of more than 7,000 Bosnian Muslim males in the so-called safe haven of Srebrenica that July had horrified the world. Karadžić had been indicted on sixteen counts, including genocide, crimes against humanity, crimes that were perpetrated against the civilian population and against places of worship throughout the territory of the Republic of Bosnia-Herzegovina, crimes relating to the sniping campaign against civilians in Sarajevo and crimes relating to the taking of UN peacekeepers as hostages.[17]

Like Chirac, Clinton was keen to act – even though America's closest allies the British, and even his own advisers, were warning that snatching Karadžić and his military commander General Ratko Mladić could derail the Dayton Accord and put allied troops at risk of reprisals. The British Foreign Office denounced the idea as 'a high-risk adventure' that would cause more trouble than it saved and refused to send in the SAS to help the US snatch teams. 'There will be casualties, the peace deal will be dead in the water and our forces will be attacked in retaliation,' one senior British official complained. Clinton was sensitive to the last point in particular, wary of putting US troops in harm's way but nevertheless keen to ward off criticism from Republican critics that he was prepared to allow Karadžić and Mladić to get away with mass murder. The Pentagon was still paralysed by the effect of Mogadishu and the fear of body bags. General Colin Powell had just retired as Chairman of the Joint Chiefs of Staff insisting that US troops should not be sent to Bosnia. 'No American president could defend to the American people the heavy sacrifice of lives it would cost to resolve this baffling conflict,' he said. One US officer sent in with the Nato-led Implementation Force that would monitor the Dayton Accord was told by his brigade commander that 'if a mission and force protection are in conflict, then we don't do the mission'. The Pentagon insisted that US troops should not be used to hunt down war criminals. 'The mindset was that this would be a very dangerous and difficult period,' said General William Nash, the US commander during Operation Joint Endeavour. 'The war crimes thing was easily passed over. It was one of the problems we hoped would go away.'[18]

BUT IT WOULDN'T go away and, despite the doubts of their advisers, Clinton and Chirac agreed the basis of what was to become Operation Amber Star, originally simply a plan to capture Mladić and Karadžić, but later the basis for joint special operations missions to snatch indicted war criminals. By the middle of 1996, the Activity was on the ground in Bosnia, part of a combined intelligence operation that fed information into a joint planning cell. Its improved status within the special operations community and the protection of the Assistant Secretary of Defense for Special Operations and Low-Intensity Conflict meant that the Activity continued to go from strength to strength. One JSOC officer was quoted by the authoritative *Intelligence Newsletter* as saying that the Activity was still very much alive and kicking. 'The Pentagon still has the capability of the original ISA in one place and it's just being called something different, that's all,' he said. It remained focused on counter-terrorism but was also increasingly involved in economic intelligence and counter-proliferation, infiltrating agents into gangs dealing in the black markets for nuclear, biological and chemical weapons, he said. Despite the change of name, the Royal Cape special access programme continued to cover the unit's existence in the Pentagon budget and the fact that the title Tactical Coordination Detachment remained top secret meant that occasionally it was still referred to as an anonymous 'intelligence support activity', as in a 1997 statement informing Congress that it was the subject of a 'comprehensive, joint review' by a number of intelligence oversight bodies.[19]

The review posed none of the problems that the Activity had faced with earlier attempts to rein in its operations. The intel it gathered on the ground in Bosnia from its agents and electronic surveillance of telephone and radio traffic was fundamental to the joint planning cell's ability to work out a range of possible options to capture the main players, the people the International Criminal Tribunal for the Former Yugoslavia wanted arrested. The plans to capture Karadžić and Mladić weren't ready until April 1997. By now Mladić had already fled but Karadžić, although on the face of it politically sidelined, was still living in Pale, and still a key player in the Bosnian Serb 'capital'. The Amber Star plan ran to more than sixty pages of operational data, maps and diagrams, bound in an orange cover. The *Groupement Spécial Autonome*, the French equivalent of Delta, would mount a heliborne attack on Karadžić's villa to take out the guards while Delta went in to snatch him and take him to the International Criminal Tribunal for the Former Yugoslavia in the Hague. The election of Tony Blair as British prime minister a few weeks later reversed the UK position, making the SAS available for the snatches and providing a dynamism the process had lacked until that point. It led to an agreement between America, France, the UK, Germany and Holland that they were all prepared to use their respective special operations forces to hunt down war criminals. The special operations snatch squads were to fly into Bosnia for each mission, coming under the control of the Combined Joint Special Operations Task Force commanded initially by Brigadier Cedric Delves, a British officer. Delves had commanded the 1982 SAS raid that destroyed eleven Argentinian Pucaras on Pebble Island during the Falklands conflict. His name had become synonymous with Bosnia just over a year earlier when as Director Special Forces, the British equivalent of the JSOC commander-in-chief, he and his SAS escorts had been stopped by Serb troops during a visit to Sarajevo and stripped of all of their weapons and equipment and most of their clothes. Delves was not amused by the anecdote circulating at his regiment's Hereford base that he had been left 'wriggling and giggling' by the side of the road, wearing only his boxer shorts, which according to SAS legend were emblazoned with the Union Flag.[20]

Both Delves and the Americans were even less amused when the carefully formulated Amber Star plans were stymied almost immediately by the French liaison officer Major Hervé Gourmelon. He allegedly passed them on to Karadžić as part of secret discussions that looked suspiciously like sanctioned negotiations aimed at getting the former Bosnian Serb president to surrender to the French. When the Americans complained, Gourmelon was immediately withdrawn. The French denied that his betrayal had compromised plans to arrest

Karadžić saying he 'maintained various contacts consonant with his orders. As soon as the course of these contacts could have appeared questionable, this officer was immediately given a new assignment in France.' But one US official said: 'We know, definitely, that he passed information about NATO operations related to efforts to eventually get Karadžić.'[21]

Over the following months, the special operations mission to capture war criminals stalled over the reluctance of the Pentagon to put US troops into dangerous situations and America's refusal to share any more intelligence with the French. But the Activity operations and signals intelligence squadrons continued to gather intelligence on the ground, running a number of agents and monitoring telephone and radio communications under the codename Torn Victor. They were part of a large-scale US intelligence operation, codenamed Buckeye, which was led by the Activity, but also included teams from Britain's secretive 14 Int, an undercover military intelligence unit, the CIA, the NSA and Delta. The Buckeye operation provided a useful vehicle for covert US involvement in a number of snatch operations by the British SAS and the Dutch 108th Special Operations Corps to deliver war criminals to the Hague. The low-profile American connection was seen as a way of being there without taking the risk that high-profile snatches might lead to US casualties or the reprisals against US troops the Pentagon feared.[22]

The first joint snatch operation with the SAS came on Thursday 10 July 1997. It had been approved during a private meeting between Bill Clinton and Tony Blair at the Nato summit in Madrid four days earlier. By now, the international tribunal had agreed to start issuing the allies with sealed indictments, secret arrest warrants that would ensure any snatch operation achieved the necessary element of surprise. With the plan to arrest Karadžić on hold, the joint British-US snatch, codenamed Operation Tango, would target one of his main henchmen. Simo Drljaca, a former Serb paramilitary leader, carried out ethnic cleansing

of the northern town of Prijedor in 1992, reducing its Muslim population from nearly 50,000 to practically zero. Drljaca's men murdered
thousands of Muslims and ethnic Croats in concentration camps at
Omarska, an iron ore mine 10 miles east of Prijedor; the notorious
murder camp at Trnopolje; and the Keraterm ceramics factory in
Prijedor. The international tribunal's sealed indictment charged that
'Bosnian Serb military and police personnel in charge of these facilities,
their staff and other persons...killed, sexually assaulted, tortured and
otherwise physically and psychologically abused the detainees.
Detainees were continuously subjected to or forced to witness inhumane
acts, including murder, rape and sexual assaults, torture, beatings and
robbery, as well as other forms of mental and physical abuse.' As the
leading figures in the local paramilitary organisation, Drljaca and his
brother-in-law Milan 'Mico' Kovačević, an anaesthetist who super-
vised the day-to-day running of the camps, were guilty of 'complic-
ity in genocide'.[23]

The flamboyant Drljaca was now logistics assistant to Dragan Kijac,
the Bosnian Serb Interior Minister. That seemingly innocuous position
hid the fact that he was a key figure in the intelligence and protection
system set up to protect Karadžić and the other indicted war criminals
by providing them with false documents and safe houses. Despite being
removed from his post as police chief of Prijedor by Nato forces, all
the Activity intelligence revealed that he continued to control police
operations while at the same time being a leading member of the local
mafia, running protection rackets, expropriating private businesses
and controlling organised crime. The Torn Victor intelligence reports
showed that he spent much of his time by a nearby lake at Gradine,
fishing and drinking with his associates, and seemed to have no idea
that he was a target for the allied intelligence operations. At the time of
the snatch operation, 0930 on the morning of 10 July, he would be at the
lake fishing. Kovačević would be in his office in the town's hospital
where he had taken over as director. Two SAS snatch squads, who had

spent the past week training on the Brecon Beacons in Wales, were flown in the day before the operation. One of the squads, wearing the uniform of the British contingent to what had now become the Operation Joint Guard S-FOR Stabilisation Force, was flown by US Black Hawk helicopter straight to the lake. Drljaca heard the helicopter, saw the troops and, realising what was coming, opened fire. He hit one of the SAS soldiers in the leg, but was gunned down in a hail of automatic rifle fire. His son Sisa and brother-in-law Spiro Milanović swiftly threw up their hands and were arrested. At the same time, the second SAS team, this time in civilian clothes, tricked their way into Kovačević's office. He took one look at their weapons and surrendered. Kovačević, Sisa Drljaca and Spiro Milanović were bundled into a helicopter and taken to the US base at Tuzla where a C130 Hercules aircraft was waiting to fly them to the Hague.[24]

The next raid came on 18 December 1997 when Dutch army commandos from the 108th Special Operations Corps, backed up by members of the SAS, snatched two Bosnian Croats accused of taking part in the massacre of more than 100 Bosnian Muslims at Ahmici, a Muslim village near Vitez, in October 1992 and April 1993. Vlatko Kupreškic was wounded in the chest, arm and leg after grabbing an automatic rifle and opening fire on the Dutch commandos who smashed their way into his apartment in Ahmici in the early hours of the morning. Kupreškic's HVO Croat militia unit allegedly took part in a series of ethnic cleansing operations against Muslims in Ahmici and eight other villages along the Lašva River. He was found guilty of crimes against humanity but freed on appeal. The other suspect, Anto Furundzija, was the leader of a Bosnian Croat paramilitary group called 'The Jokers', whose members murdered, raped and tortured captured Muslims. He was arrested after coming home from a night out drinking with friends. The arrest was almost aborted when he drove straight past his home in Vitez, leading the Dutch commandos to believe that the mission might have been compromised. But when he turned around, pulled up onto his drive and staggered out of his car it became clear that he was simply drunk and had missed his turning. He surrendered without incident. Yet again the Americans stayed in the background, providing the logistical back-up, with the intel coming from the Activity.[25]

SEAL Team Six was to have carried out its own raid in December 1997, this time to snatch a Bosnian Serb indicted by the Hague tribunal. More than sixty members of the special mission unit were smuggled into the Tuzla air base in metal containers unloaded from a C17 Globe-master aircraft and taken to safe houses prepared by the Activity. But General Eric Shinseki, the US commander of S-FOR vetoed the operation because he believed it was too dangerous. The SEALs were ordered back to their base at Dam Neck, Virginia. International observers, unaware that the Americans were providing a substantial back-up organisation in the form of Buckeye, indeed unaware of the existence of the operation at all, were scathing of the apparent lack of US involvement in the arrests of suspected war criminals. Richard Goldstone, a South African judge who had been the first chief war crimes prosecutor for the Hague tribunal, ridiculed the unwillingness of US commanders to put their troops in harm's way, saying: 'It's like saying firemen should not be sent to put out fires. Why have a fire brigade then?'[26]

Goldstone's allegations might have been a fair condemnation of the attitude of senior Pentagon and US Army commanders but as an overall criticism of US policy on the ground in Bosnia they were misplaced. General Shinseki was undoubtedly reluctant to put his men in harm's way, but he had been overruled by General Wesley Clark, the Supreme Allied Commander Europe. DevGru was sent back into Bosnia in January 1998. They first arrested Goran Jelisić, a Bosnian Serb who had commanded the notorious Luka detention camp in Brcko, where hundreds of Muslims and Croats were tortured, raped or killed. Jelisić revelled in the self-coined sobriquet, 'the Serb Adolf'.

US intelligence sources had reported through late 1992 and into 1993 that several thousand Muslims had been murdered and then cremated at the camp. Jelisić's daily routine made the intelligence operation easy. He was snatched by the SEALs as he walked from his apartment to the nearby bookshop he owned in the north-eastern city of Bijeljina. The US commandos were hidden in two unmarked vans parked outside Jelisić's apartment block. Over the next few weeks, DevGru struck twice more, arresting three Bosnian Serbs who had taken part in the ethnic cleansing of the northern town of Bosanski Samac. Simo Zarić, Milan Simić and Miroslav Tadić all surrendered meekly to the SEALs sent to arrest them. The SAS and Dutch commando raids had made a point to those indicted for war crimes. Resisting arrest was likely to get you killed.[27]

The continuing French reluctance to arrest any of the indicted Bosnian Serbs living in their sector, which included Karadžić's Pale villa, would have been a much fairer target for Goldstone's criticism. His replacement Louise Arbour had described the French sector as a 'safe haven' for war criminals. When the pressure built up by the US and British raids persuaded Dragoljub Kunarac, a Bosnian Serb indicted on charges of 'gang rape, torture, and enslavement' of Muslim women, to surrender to the French in the town of Pilipovic in eastern Bosnia in late February 1998, they refused to arrest him. It was not until more than a week later, after senior members of the Bosnian Serb community had assured French military commanders that it would be alright to take Kunarac to the Hague, that they finally agreed to turn him over to the Hague tribunal.[28]

The SAS continued to lead the way, in public at least, snatching two Bosnian Serbs, Miroslav Kvoćka and Mladen Radić, in Prijedor on 8 April. Both were wanted for crimes against humanity committed at the Omarska camp where US intelligence sources had spoken of nightly murders of groups of Muslims by Bosnian Serb paramilitaries. The French finally arrested an indicted war criminal on 15 June, in a move that was clearly designed to avert criticism of their inaction at a conference that was convening that morning in Rome to write a treaty establishing a permanent war crimes court. Miorad Krnojelac, the former commander of the Foča prison, where scores of Muslims were tortured and at least twenty-nine murdered, surrendered in Foča to French and German troops.[29]

The Activity played a leading role in Operation Ensue, the most dramatic of the snatches mounted by the SAS. The capture of Stevan Todorović took place 50 miles inside Serbia on 27 September 1998. Todorović had murdered, tortured and sexually assaulted Croats and Muslims during the ethnic cleansing of Bosanski Samac. He was tracked down by mobile telephone intercepts carried out by the Activity knob-turners to a log cabin in the remote Zlatibor region of western Serbia. The SAS snatch team stormed the cabin, gagged and blind-folded him and bundled him into the back of a black sports utility vehicle, which then drove back to the Drina river that forms the border between Bosnia and Serbia. Todorović was smuggled across the river into Bosnia by rubber dinghy and taken by helicopter to Tuzla where an American officer confronted him with the words: 'So you thought you were safe over there did you?' One British officer described it as 'a classic mission', adding that the authorities were happy for the Serbs to know that the SAS had carried out the raid. 'It's a deliberate frightener for [Serb leader Slobodan] Milošević. That's policy now. The guys are getting very good and they've got a list of options in Yugoslavia. Many of them now speak Serbian and they know the ground pretty well.'[30]

But it was DevGru who seized the biggest prize when they arrested Radislav Krstić, the Bosnian Serb general who commanded the notorious Drina Corps, which had captured the so-called UN Safe Haven at Srebrenica in July 1995 and proceeded to massacre more than 7,000 Muslim men and boys. The US commandos tracked his chauffeur-driven car as it drove from Bijeljina towards Brcko in north-eastern Bosnia, stopping it and arresting him and a number of his associates, two of whom were themselves indicted war criminals. They gave up quietly rather than risk taking on the heavily armed SEAL commandos. Krstić's trial heard tapes of a number of different radio conversations between the Drina Corps commander and his junior officers in which he ordered them to murder the Muslim men they captured. The conversations were allegedly intercepted by the Bosnian Muslim Army, the *Armija Bosna i Hercegovina*, but there were suspicions that some of the intercepts provided to the tribunal for Krstić's trial were from US sources on the ground, most likely the Torn Victor signals intelligence team. The State Department had initially insisted that no US intercepts would be made public but the White House took a more nuanced stance. 'Theoretically, there may be some information we cannot provide for national security reasons,' White House spokesman Mike McCurry said. But he went on to add that the administration was confident that there were 'ways of repackaging the information' to avoid revealing intelligence sources and methods. The Hague tribunal found Krstić guilty of 'genocide; persecution through murders, cruel and inhumane treatment, terrorising the civilian population, forcible transfer and destruction of personal property; and murder as a violation of the laws or customs of war'. He was sentenced to forty-six years in prison.[31]

There has been a steady stream of arrests of indicted war criminals since that time, many carried out by allied special operations forces, and a number of them on the basis of intelligence provided by the Activity. In a tacit reflection of its silent role in many of the snatch operations, General James L Jones, Commander US European Command, said in March 2004 that despite the criticism that most of the arrests have been carried out by the SAS, the work of US special operations forces in the capture of PIFWCs remained 'one of the great under-recognized success stories of our mission in the Balkans.'[32]

9 'AMERICA'S AVENGING ANGELS'

It was pitch black as the team from Task Force Sword watched the small convoy of two oil tankers and one truck cross the Toba mountains, heading for the main road from Quetta to Kandahar. The rough border track leading from Iran was a favourite route for smugglers taking raw opium out of Afghanistan and bringing back any commodity they could sell. It was Friday 16 November 2001, just over two months after the 9/11 attacks, and the first day of Ramadan. The truckers parked up beside the road just outside the small Afghan village of Tungi, ten miles inside the border with Pakistan. Observing the strict rules of Ramadan, they waited until it was dark before eating their first meal of the day, and then hunkered down for the night. They would later claim that the $16,000-worth of gasoline and kerosene they were carrying was being delivered to 'ordinary people'. But the intelligence collected by the Activity from human sources on the ground was very clear. Once it reached the main road, the truckers would head north to sell their load where it was likely to make the most money, in Kandahar, the headquarters of the Taliban, the hardline Islamic rulers of Afghanistan who, as a result of their support for Osama bin Laden, were now fighting a desperate war against America and its allies.

US and British special operations forces had been on the ground inside Afghanistan for more than a month, liaising with the Northern Alliance and other factions like the Shi'ite Hazara, Mongoloid descendants of members of Genghis Khan's forces whose Hazarajat mountain fortress had never been subjugated by the Taliban. But in the south, the US and British troops had fewer allies and were seeking more brutal ways of undermining their opponents. This operation was set up by the Activity, now using the codename Grey Fox, but normally referred to on the ground as Task Force Orange. The Activity's agent-handlers, the spooks, had recruited sources among those Pushtun tribesmen who once supported the Taliban but were clever, and pragmatic, enough to realise that the old regime's days were numbered. Now the shooters were taking over, creeping up on the convoy without a sound. The first the startled truckers knew of what was going on was when they were hauled out of their cabs at gunpoint, flung to the ground and had their wrists and feet bound together with white plasti-cuff restraints. They struggled in vain as they were dragged off and dumped behind the rocks above their trucks. Totally disorientated and terrified that they were about to be killed by bandits, the smugglers barely had time to work out that their captors, who were talking into microphones attached to their black hockey-style helmets and wearing night-vision goggles that glinted green, must be American troops before they heard the staccato whack-whack-whack of the rotor blades of approaching helicopters. Suddenly there was a series of flashes and the whoosh of missiles passing overhead followed by massive explosions as the two tankers burst into flames, sending out a wave of intense heat, and the oil drums on the back of the flat-bed were catapulted hundreds of feet into the air. The US special operations forces cut the plasti-cuff restraints from the wrists of their captives and paid one of the villagers twenty dollars to take the disgruntled truckers to the nearest town, telling them in basic Farsi to make sure they spread the word about what the American forces could do. While attention focused on CIA and Army Special Forces operations in the north, the Activity was busy making a name for itself in the south.[1]

THE OPERATION TO DISRUPT the smugglers was just part of the emphatic response by the US and its allies to the 9/11 attacks. The destruction of New York's Twin Towers and the Pentagon's West Wall by Islamic terrorists who managed to infiltrate American society led to suggestions that insufficient attention had been paid to Osama bin Laden and his al-Qa'eda network. The failings within the FBI, the Federal Aviation Authority, and to a lesser extent the CIA, that led to the success of the attacks were undeniable. But there had been no lack of interest inside the Clinton administration in trying to track bin Laden down, with the President issuing directives that the CIA and military special operations forces could use lethal force if need be to eliminate the man widely seen within the intelligence services, even then, as America's Public Enemy Number One. This determination to try to track him down was blocked by the Joint Chiefs of Staff who, on presidential orders, developed no fewer than thirteen different options to attack or capture bin Laden, but then failed to recommend any of them. Perhaps the most audacious was an Activity proposal in the mid 1990s to 'eliminate' Osama bin Laden in the Sudanese capital Khartoum, one former US intelligence officer said. The Activity already had the al-Qa'eda leader under observation. Assisted by the CIA, they constructed a 'blind', a camouflaged observation post, on top of a house opposite a building the al-Qa'eda leader was known to visit frequently. It was disguised as a rooftop garden and allowed the Activity personnel to watch the al-Qa'eda leader come and go. But a suggestion that the surveillance operation should be extended to include 'eliminating' bin Laden was vetoed.[2]

The attempts to snatch bin Laden and bring him back to America for trial began in 1997 and were intensified in May 1998 after he was secretly indicted by a New York federal grand jury. The CIA went into Afghanistan to try to track him down, employing around thirty locally recruited Afghan 'tribal assets', former members of the mujahideen who were codenamed the GE/Seniors, to help them snatch him. The CIA was in daily secure communications with the Afghan agents, paying them a total of around $10,000 a month. A plan was devised under which they would mount a full-scale assault on al-Qa'eda's Tarnak Farms training camp just south of Kandahar, on the outskirts of the city's airport, to snatch bin Laden. The camp was made up of about eighty mud-brick buildings surrounded by a ten-foot wall. US intelligence was able to sketch out a detailed plan of the compound, recording who lived or worked in which buildings, right down to the houses used by bin Laden's wives, even to the one with whom he was most likely to sleep.

The idea of a raid on the Tarnak Farms compound had originated in the fall of 1997 with plans going so far that two full-scale rehearsals took place in America. One group comprising the Afghans and members of the CIA's paramilitary Special Activities Division would enter the compound, subdue the guards, snatch bin Laden and drive him to a desert rendezvous. A second group would then pick him up and take him to a remote airfield where a CIA aircraft would be waiting to fly him to America. It was shown to Lieutenant-General Michael Canavan, the commander-in-chief of JSOC, who regarded it as an attempt to secure results 'on the cheap' that could be better managed by his own men. But it was nevertheless, he said, pretty much along the lines that JSOC would have come up with had they been asked to carry out the operation. Fresh rehearsals took place between 20 and 24 May 1998, with some of the Afghans flown to America to take part, but in the end the plans were deemed to be too risky. The attackers were likely to be killed; there would be collateral losses among the women and children in bin Laden's entourage that would almost certainly result in bad publicity; and the al-Qa'eda leader would be unlikely to come easily, making it a near certainty that he would be killed. The mission would be labelled a deliberate assassination and therefore illegal under the executive orders laid down by Presidents Ford and Reagan. On 29 May 1998, senior CIA officers called off the operation.[3]

Little more than two months later, on 7 August 1998, al-Qa'eda carried out bomb attacks on the US embassies in Kenya and Tanzania, killing 224 people, only twelve of whom were US citizens. The attacks led President Clinton to order cruise missile attacks on facilities linked to al-Qa'eda in Afghanistan and, most controversially, Sudan. Those long-distance attacks were denounced as a sign of US impotence, as indeed they were. The seventy-five cruise missiles, each of them costing $1 million, merely rearranged the rubble at primitive al-Qa'eda training camps inside Afghanistan, while the attack on a pharmaceuticals factory in Khartoum, which was allegedly producing precursors for chemical weapons, caused an international outcry. But the long-range remote control attacks were attractive to US politicians who had become terrified of the effect on the electorate of television pictures of body bags returning home. Behind the scenes, Clinton tried to be more effective, signing a series of Presidential Findings authorising the use of lethal force during any operations to capture bin Laden and his main lieutenants, a move that effectively allowed their assassination. Under a National Security Council plan codenamed Delenda, diplomatic and financial persuasion would be combined with covert action and special operations missions aimed at preventing countries from giving al-Qa'eda sanctuary. Saudi Arabia played a key role in trying to persuade the Taliban to give up bin Laden, or at the very least force him to leave Afghanistan. One of the executive orders actually foresaw a situation where the Taliban would not extradite the al-Qa'eda leader but were prepared to force him to fly to another country. In those circumstances, US forces would have authority to shoot down bin Laden's aircraft. But there remained significant opposition, within both the CIA and the Joint Chiefs of Staff, to covert or clandestine missions, whether by special operations forces or the CIA's Special Activities Division. President Clinton ordered a number of special operations missions designed either to snatch or take out senior members of al-Qa'eda. Richard Clarke, the National Security Council official responsible for counter-terrorist operations under Clinton, said that plans for such missions were put together by the Activity and other special operations planning teams. There was no lack of commitment from within the US special operations community to the idea of mounting missions to snatch or kill bin Laden and between fifteen and thirty special operations personnel were killed or injured in rehearsals. But the Joint Chiefs failed to recommend a single one of the plans their special operations experts produced.[4]

Alan Holmes, the then Assistant Secretary of Defense for Special Operations and Low-Intensity Conflict, proposed several missions but 'ran into a lot of resistance from the uniformed military on the notion of actually staging special operations against bin Laden,' Clarke said. 'On several occasions, the Defense Department was asked to develop snatch operations, and they did usually what they were asked to do. But the overwhelming message to the White House from the uniformed military was we don't want to do this. We spent an awful lot of time and money developing the Special Operations Command, the special operations forces, but whenever in the 1990s it was suggested that we might want to use them, the uniformed military leadership in the Pentagon thought that was a very bad idea. And when you would go to the Special Operations Command and the units involved, they always thought it was the White House that was stopping them from being used. They always wanted to do the operations.'[5]

The Activity was asked in 1998 to put together a plan to arrest a leading al-Qa'eda theologian, Mahfouz Walad al-Walid, otherwise known as Abu Hafs the Mauritanian, who was believed to be the architect of a number of the organisation's terrorist attacks. Signals intelligence revealed that he would be in the Sudanese capital Khartoum for a number of months and in this case at least there was no shortage of actionable intelligence. 'We knew what hotel he was in,' Clarke told the commission looking into the 9/11 attacks. 'We knew what room he was in, in the hotel, and we couldn't get him because the CIA did not have a snatch capability.' When the military were asked to mount a special operations mission, they replied: 'Well, that would never work. We couldn't do it. It would be too hard.' Some months afterwards, Clarke met a special operations officer who lambasted him for blocking the mission. 'You guys at the White House stopped us from doing that snatch operation,' the officer said. 'We had it all planned. We were going to do it with five people.' The plans had not made it to the National Security Council or anywhere in the White House 'because the uniformed military leadership didn't want it to happen,' Clarke said. 'But they told their troops that the White House was stopping it, and we never had anybody who would go through that door of that hotel that day, despite repeated requests.'[6]

Another special operations plan involved a forty-man team being flown 900 miles to snatch bin Laden from inside Afghanistan but General Henry 'Hugh' Shelton, Chairman of the Joint Chiefs of Staff, recommended against it. His main reason was that the wives and children of bin Laden and other al-Qa'eda leaders were likely to be killed. Less than a year before the 9/11 attacks, the Special Operations Command drew up a plan that would attack bin Laden by taking out 'five key nodes' but again Hugh Shelton refused to back it. His main argument was that there was never enough 'actionable intelligence' to carry out a raid. The response from one senior special operations officer questioned on this by the 9/11 Commission was: 'If you give me the action, I'll give you the intelligence.' To the special operations community this was a statement of the obvious. The Activity was set up precisely to collect the intelligence needed to carry out such operations but it was never used in a snatch operation against bin Laden because senior US commanders were not prepared to risk 'another

Mogadishu'. Hugh Shelton claimed he was not asked to put boots on the ground to obtain the 'actionable intelligence' needed for a mission against bin Laden and 'the military does what it is told'. It was a catch-22 situation. The Joint Chiefs were tasked to set up operations that needed 'actionable intelligence' but were not prepared to put the Activity or any other special operations forces on the ground to collect it unless somehow it already existed.[7]

The unwillingness to take effective action against bin Laden was not confined to the military. Senior CIA officers declined to use lethal force believing, wrongly, Clarke said, that it would not have been legal. The GE/Seniors claimed to have ambushed convoys bin Laden was in, on two occasions becoming involved in firefights, but Gary Schroen, the CIA station chief in Islamabad, apparently unaware of Clinton's intention in making the lethal force rulings, warned them against killing the al-Qa'eda leader. During October 2000, the CIA flew a number of Predator flights over Afghanistan, finding bin Laden on two separate occasions. But because they were only experimental flights, the Agency refused to use them to target the al-Qa'eda leader. There was a good deal of intelligence on bin Laden's whereabouts and what he was doing, the vast majority coming from signals intelligence provided by the British, who were monitoring bin Laden's cellphone. But the CIA was no happier about the prospects for covert action to capture the al-Qa'eda leader than the Joint Chiefs of Staff. The CIA Director of Operations was particularly hostile to the idea believing that any such missions 'could go bad, could end up in corruption or drug-running'.[8]

The CIA had, on paper at least, a far more limited ability to mount snatch operations in a hostile environment. That problem could have been overcome by melding a CIA team with a special operations forces task force. But the Joint Chiefs blocked any suggestion of a combined CIA-special operations mission against al-Qa'eda installations inside Afghanistan. 'The military repeatedly came back with recommendations that their capability not be utilized for military operations in

Afghanistan,' Clarke said. 'The military was asked to develop plans and they did reluctantly and they came back and they said here is a plan but we really recommend against it. What we continue to have is a military that is very capable but doesn't want to use its capability and a CIA that doesn't have much capability and therefore justifiably doesn't want to use it.'[9]

The CIA did at least keep trying to find ways of damaging al-Qa'eda, and just a week before the 9/11 attacks, on 4 September 2001, obtained authorisation to use between $125 million and $200 million a year arming Afghanistan's Northern Alliance. The alliance was an ill-mixed assortment of Tajiks, Uzbeks and Hazara who were fighting the Taliban and its al-Qa'eda backers under the command of the charismatic Ahmed Shah Masood, leader of the Jamiat-i-Islami faction. Masood was a former mujahideen commander with strong links to the West, and in particular Britain's MI6. But five days after the CIA got the OK to give Masood its backing, disaster struck. The Northern Alliance leader agreed to meet two Arab journalists, a television reporter and his cameraman, at his base in the Panjshir Valley in northern Afghanistan. The two men had been waiting for more than a week to interview him and claimed to be Moroccans whose families had moved to Belgium. They carried a letter of introduction from a London-based Islamic organisation. Masood insisted that they tell him before the interview what they would be asking him. Every question concerned his attitude to bin Laden. An aide warned him that the 'journalists' were almost certainly from al-Qa'eda, but he insisted on going ahead with the interview, telling the two men: 'You can start filming now.' The cameraman immediately detonated explosives packed into his camera battery, killing a number of people, including himself and Masood. The West's best friend in Afghanistan was dead.[10]

Two days later, four US airliners were hijacked and three of them used as manned missiles to attack the Twin Towers and the Pentagon. A total of 2,749 people were killed. President Bush wanted swift and effective retribution. There were to be no 'photo opportunity attacks', he said. It had to be something that would really hurt the terrorists in their bases in Afghanistan, something that would cripple al-Qa'eda, preferably getting rid of bin Laden forever. But the Pentagon, where shelves bulged with plans for virtually every possible contingency, had no plan at all for an attack on Afghanistan. US military planners looked at three possibilities: 1) the Clinton option of firing cruise missiles at a mixture of targets, including al-Qa'eda training camps; 2) A combination of cruise missiles and massed air attacks using smart bombs, much like the 1998 Desert Fox attacks on Iraq; 3) A mixture of those options with the addition of large numbers of 'boots on the ground', including some special operations forces but mainly US Marines and airborne units.

The CIA, heavily influenced by the British Secret Intelligence Service MI6, was much more forward-looking. It favoured using the Northern Alliance as a proxy force, with a small number of CIA operatives and special operations forces on the ground directing them. The British, who had used such proxy forces in a succession of colonial wars during their long post-war retreat from empire, were staunch backers of this plan. Despite their reputation for gratuitous brutality, Afghan mujahideen were pragmatic fighters, willing to switch allegiances rather than come out on the losing side. There were many local warlords who now supported the Taliban, but who might be persuaded to switch sides. Both MI6 and Brigadier Graeme Lamb, Britain's Director Special Forces, the equivalent of the JSOC commander, saw the British operations in Oman during the 1970s as the perfect model for Afghanistan. There the SAS, supported by Omani Air Force Jaguar ground attack aircraft flown by seconded RAF pilots, used the tough local tribesmen to put down a widespread insurgency by rebels sent across the border from the communist People's Democratic Republic of South Yemen. As a result, Oman was now one of the West's staunchest allies in the region and was ready to allow US and British forces to use its territory as a staging post for any attack on Afghanistan. The State Department and senior US military commanders, with their continuing distrust of special operations, were unenthusiastic about the CIA plans. Only a few months earlier, State Department officials had dismissed the Northern Alliance as 'part of the problem, not part of the solution'. But a barnstorming briefing two days after 9/11 from the Director of the CIA's Counter-Terrorism Center, Cofer Black, persuaded President Bush it would work. He authorised George Tenet, the CIA Director, to spend up to $1 billion buying allegiances among the Afghan factions. Tenet couldn't say for sure how much it would take to destroy the Taliban but it would be 'very expensive'. Bush authorised it without question, saying simply: 'Whatever it takes.'[11]

On Saturday 15 September, Tenet outlined his plans for an invasion by proxy to a full meeting of Bush's war cabinet held around a large table in the wood-panelled Laurel Lodge at Camp David. The meeting had begun with a prayer. After some brief updates on the situation, Tenet laid out a highly imaginative plan. Entitled simply 'Going to War', it envisaged members of the Agency's Special Activities Division and small teams of special operations forces building up the anti-Taliban forces on the ground and directing allied air attacks on the enemy front line. The Taliban leader Mullah Mohammed Omar wouldn't have a chance of holding territory against a full onslaught of US air power. Although support for the Americans would be most easily obtained in the north, both the CIA and MI6 had been wooing allies like the GE/Seniors in the Pushtun south who would help to build up a network of Taliban opponents and support for a broad-based replacement government friendly to the West and hostile to al-Qa'eda. Hugh Shelton now had plans in place for a full-scale air attack on Taliban positions, but his idea of how the ground war would be fought involved far more conventional US troops and looked decidedly unimaginative and lack-lustre alongside Tenet's visionary concept.[12]

At around midday on Monday 17 September, Bush was briefed in the Pentagon by the JSOC commander-in-chief Major-General Del Dailey on the special operations forces that would take part in the attacks on the Taliban. Afterwards, the President addressed a number of reservists called up for the war in Afghanistan. Asked if he wanted bin Laden killed, Bush replied: 'There's an old poster out West as I recall that said: "Wanted Dead or Alive".' That afternoon, back in the White House, he signed a Memorandum of Notification, effectively removing any barrier to the assassination of bin Laden. The al-Qa'eda leader was now quite literally 'wanted dead or alive'. The President also officially authorised Tenet's plans to fight the war by proxy, using the Northern Alliance as the main ground force, assisted by CIA para-militaries and allied special operations forces.[13]

A little over a week later, Gary Schroen arrived in Afghanistan as head of the ten-man CIA team codenamed Jawbreaker. True to the President's words, Cofer Black had briefed Shroen and his deputy with the words: 'Your job is to capture bin Laden, kill him and bring his head back in a box full of dry ice.' Quite how they were supposed to get hold of a box of dry ice in a country that was still rooted in the Middle Ages was not clear to Shroen but he got the message. He and his Jawbreaker team flew from Tajikistan into the Panjshir Valley in a CIA Russian-built Hip Mi17 helicopter with $3 million in $100 bills stashed in a large metal suitcase. This was the money that was to be handed out to Afghan tribal leaders to bring them, or keep them, on side.[14] The British Secret Intelligence Service MI6 was also sending in a team of eight officers to make contact with its agents inside Afghanistan. While both MI6 and the CIA had strong links to Masood, the British traditionally had a better presence in Afghanistan than the Americans. During the Soviet occupation of the 1980s, the CIA had unwisely tied its hands by striking a deal with Pakistan's Inter-Service Intelligence Service (ISI) under which the Americans would not conduct unilateral operations against the Russians inside Afghanistan. As a result, it relied heavily on MI6, using it as a proxy to carry out operations that were deemed too secret to involve the Pakistanis. It was MI6 that first forged the close links with the Northern Alliance that Gary Shroen and his men, officially known as the Northern Afghanistan Liaison Team, were about to exploit. Masood had been cultivated by the British since the summer of 1981 when a five-man MI6 team had made the difficult journey over the Hindu Kush into the Panjshir by foot to offer the Jamiat-i-Islami leader and his mujahideen fighters the financial backing and modern communications equipment they needed to fight the Soviet occupation forces.

MI6 also had better links than the Americans with a number of other Afghan tribal factions, particularly in the south, where the ill-advised deal with the Pakistanis had its greatest effect. There was a good deal of mutual respect between Shroen and the MI6 Afghan experts. They had worked with each other on numerous occasions before. Much of the MI6 clout with the mujahideen during the Soviet occupation stemmed from the money and weapons that their CIA col-leagues gave them to pass on to people like Masood. But the British were not just the CIA's front-men. They had a wealth of experience in Afghanistan, and not only during the Soviet occupation. It went back to the 19th century when a series of disastrous defeats for red-coated British invasion troops had given way to a somewhat subtler approach that was more effective in dealing with the many tribal factions that inhabited the country. During the latter part of the 19th century, in what became known as the Great Game, British intelli-gence officers sent into Afghanistan learned how to use the various tribal rivalries to wrong-foot the Russians and further the influence of Queen Victoria's government at the expense of the Tsar's. The trick was to work out what made the people you needed on your side tick. Money was certainly an important element, but the British officers who played the Great Game always had to keep in mind one adage: 'You cannot buy the loyalty of an Afghan, you can only rent it.'[15]

The British respect for Shroen was based on a long history of co-operation going back to before the Soviet occupation. He was 59 and his retirement had been held up for this particular operation for very good reasons. He was quite simply the CIA officer with the most experience in the region, having run agents inside the Iranian and Pakistani governments during stints in Tehran and Islamabad. He had been the CIA station chief in Kabul until the Soviet invasion, when he moved to Islamabad to work with both the ISI and MI6 on operations inside Afghanistan, making frequent trips up to the northern city of Peshawar, which was home to most of the Afghan resistance movements. During the 1990s, he ran a series of covert operations inside Iran from a secret overseas station. His experience in the region was unequalled on either side of the Atlantic. Shroen met first with General Mohammad Qasim Fahim Khan, the former mujahideen commander who had taken over the leadership of Jamiat-i-Islami, and by extension the Northern Alliance. Masood enjoyed widespread respect among the various tribal factions that made up the Northern Alliance. He was its natural leader. But even under Masood, the alliance had been brittle. Shroen knew that Fahim's position had to be bolstered if the alliance was to provide the united force it would have to be if it were to defeat the Taliban.[16]

Gary Shroen and the other members of the Jawbreaker team travelled across Northern Afghanistan, talking not just to Fahim but to other Northern Alliance leaders. They included Mohammed Atta, the outwardly sophisticated, urbane Jamiat-i-Islami leader in the north-western city of Mazar-i-Sharif; the Hazara leader Karim Khalili; General Ismail Khan, the Iranian-backed warlord who controlled the western city of Herat; and the brutal Uzbek warlord General Abdul Rashid Dostum, whose willingness to change sides – he had fought both for and against the Russians during the occupation – epitomised the problems, and the possibilities, the CIA and MI6 officers faced as they tried to knit together an anti-Taliban coalition. Dostum's brutality was legendary. When one of his fighters was caught stealing, the warlord had him tied to one of the tracks of a tank, which was then driven around, turning the unfortunate man into mincemeat.

The CIA officers explained the plans and told the Afghan commanders that they should expect small 'A-teams' of US Army Special Forces who would help coordinate the attacks on the Taliban and would include US Air Force combat controllers to direct the aerial bombardment. On Monday 1 October, five days after arriving in the Panjshir, Gary Shroen sent a secret assessment back to CIA headquarters at Langley, Virginia, saying he believed that a concerted aerial bombardment of the Taliban front lines would precipitate a major collapse, with most of their support swiftly disappearing. 'A Taliban collapse could be rapid with the enemy shrinking to a small number of hard-core Mullah Omar supporters in the early days or weeks of a military campaign,' Shroen said.[17]

The American special operations forces and the CIA special activities operatives working in northern Afghanistan were to be based at 'K2', the Karshi-Khanabad air base in southern Uzbekistan. This was to be the headquarters of Joint Special Operations Task Force – North, otherwise known as Task Force Dagger, which was largely built around Central Command's 5th Special Forces Group (Airborne) and led by the group's commanding officer, Colonel John Mulholland, who had himself once commanded the Activity's operations squadron. During the initial phases of the war, Mulholland reported direct to General Tommy Franks, the Centcom commander. Uzbekistan was one of a number of countries across the region that agreed to provide bases or over-flight rights for US military aircraft. The deals were done through a mixture of arm-twisting and promises of long-term economic and political support, with Uzbek President Karimov one of the last to come on board, holding out until a visit by Rumsfeld on Saturday 6 October, just hours before the aerial bombardment of Afghanistan was to begin.[18]

By now members of the Activity were already inside southern Afghanistan – sometimes wearing unmarked combat uniform, sometimes *shalwar kamiz*, the traditional baggy shirt and trousers favoured by the tribesmen. They steadily worked up networks of friendly Afghan sources on the ground. They were collecting human intelligence, preparing the way for operations by Delta. A lack of intelligence was one of the biggest problems the Americans faced. They could get ground attack aircraft in place easily enough. It was knowing what to hit. There was also a continuing reluctance to send in special operations forces without 'actionable intelligence'. The Activity was doing what it could but it was becoming apparent that it was too small to do everything that was required for a war that was going to be special operations heavy. The issue of whether there was sufficient 'intelligence support' for US special operations forces – and whether it was capable of providing the 'high-quality intelligence on a real time or near real time basis' that operations to capture or kill specific individuals and groups needed – was at the top of a list of issues produced for Congress to address on the SOF issue.[19]

The air attacks began on Sunday 7 October, with more than fifty allied aircraft and a similar number of Tomahawk cruise missiles bombarding Taliban or al-Qa'eda targets across Afghanistan. But the lack of intelligence limited their effectiveness, with one senior British intelligence officer complaining that the two British $1 million cruise missiles fired 'did little more than rearrange the rubble' at deserted and derelict al-Qa'eda training camps.[20] It was vital that special operations forces were infiltrated into northern Afghanistan to work with the Northern Alliance and to collect intelligence, but bad weather was causing delays. Finally, on Friday 19 October, the first Operational Detachment Alpha, or A-team, landed by two MH53 Pave Low helicopters on the Shomali plain to be met by Shroen, who took them to link up with Fahim. Eight others would follow them into northern Afghanistan, their primary mission to act as liaison with the Northern Alliance and to use the SOFLAM laser designators to guide US aircraft onto their targets. At their pre-mission briefing, the US troops were left in no doubt as to why they were going into Afghanistan. 'This is not a war as you have ever known it before,' a senior special operations commander said. 'This is vengeance for the women and children they murdered on 9/11. Our responsibility is to implement that vengeance. Fight as though your own families were killed in New York. You are America's avenging angels. Your goal is justice and you are authorized to use all means necessary towards that end.'[21]

The US special operations forces working with Dostum were swiftly made to realise that this was a war unlike any other they had known. They were a little bemused to have to go into battle with him on horseback but the first supplies they asked for when they radioed back to their command centre was a batch of leather saddles. The Special Forces captain who commanded Tiger 02, the A-team that was working with Dostum, had been a high school rodeo rider. But none of the US troops ever got entirely used to the wooden saddles used by Dostum's men. In a report back to commanders concerned that the A-teams appeared to be having little effect, the commander of Tiger 02 wrote: 'I am advising a man on how best to employ light infantry and horse cavalry in the attack against Taliban Russian T55 tanks, Russian armoured personnel carriers, BTRs, mortars, artillery, ZSU anti-aircraft guns and machine guns. I can't recall the US fighting like this since the Gatling gun destroyed Pancho Villa's charges in the Mexican Civil War in the early 19th century. We are doing amazingly well with what we have. We have killed over 125 Taliban and captured over 100 while losing 8 KIA. Frankly, I am surprised we have not been slaughtered. We will get better at working things out as we go. It is a challenge just to have food and water for a few days. These folks have nothing. I have ridden 15 miles a day since arriving, yet everywhere I go the civilians and "muj" soldiers are always telling me they are glad the USA has come here with planes to kill the Taliban. They speak of their hopes for a better Afghanistan once the Taliban are gone. We killed the bastards by the bushel-full today and we'll get more tomorrow.'[22]

Only a matter of hours after the first A-team arrived in the north, early on Saturday 20 October, US special operations forces mounted two apparently spectacular raids in southern Afghanistan. More than 100 US Rangers parachuted onto a lightly defended air base 60 miles south-west of Kandahar. A grainy green video of the operation was handed over to the networks for no other reason than to demonstrate to the US public that their soldiers were actually doing something inside Afghanistan. At the same time, Task Force Gecko, a reinforced squadron of Delta troops, attacked a compound just outside Kandahar that was known to be used by Mullah Omar. Announcing the raids at the Pentagon the next day, US Air Force General Richard B Myers, the newly appointed Chairman of the Joint Chiefs of Staff, said the troops met 'light' resistance. 'The mission overall was successful,' Myers said. 'We accomplished our objectives.' But in the words of one Delta operative, the Gecko raid on Mullah Omar's compound was 'a total goat-fuck'. The truth was somewhere in between, one US official said. He admitted that Gecko did not go entirely to plan and that the 'cosmetic' raids were actually designed to provide a show of something happening on the ground, both for the psychological impact on the Taliban and to appease a US public increasingly frustrated with the slow pace of the war. 'It was a television show,' one Delta operative complained.

At his Pentagon press conference, Dick Myers was keen to point out that the video footage showed US special operations forces 'were able to deploy, manoeuvre, and operate inside Afghanistan without significant interference from Taliban forces'. But his claim that resistance at the Delta target was light was a long way from the truth. 'The raid was a success from the intelligence point of view,' the official said. 'We got lots of intelligence. But our men were surprised by the amount of resistance they ran into. The speed with which the Taliban launched a counter-attack came as a bit of a shock. They fought like maniacs. We didn't expect that. Intelligence got it wrong.' A dozen or so US soldiers were wounded, several of them seriously, in the ensuing firefight. To make matters worse, two US Rangers were killed when their helicopter was 'browned out' in a dust storm and crashed inside Pakistan ahead of the raid. Another helicopter landed so quickly while attempting to get troops out of the firefight at the Delta target that it lost part of its undercarriage, which was later shown to the television cameras by the Taliban, who claimed to have shot it down.

The commanders of Delta were furious at the way in which their men were used as a large-scale force. The unit had been set up and designed to operate in small four or six-man teams, based on the SAS model and designed to get in quick, do the job, and get out quick, preferably with as little fuss as possible. They demanded that the SAS – who had been kept on the sidelines by Tommy Franks, the allied commander – should be brought in to help and expressed dismay at the continued lack of understanding of special operations among senior US commanders. They 'think we can perform fucking magic', one Delta operative said. 'We can't. Don't put us in an environment we weren't prepared for. Next time, we're going to lose a company.' The hope was that British Special Forces commanders might be able to make Franks and his planners see sense. It was a vain hope. Throughout the operations inside Afghanistan, both Delta and the SAS repeatedly found themselves used in a role for which they were never intended, carrying out large-scale assaults on enemy positions.[23]

About a week after the Delta raid on the Mullah Omar compound, two squadrons of SAS were infiltrated into the Hazirud valley in the western foothills of the Hindu Kush to carry out reconnaissance of Taliban targets in northern Afghanistan. Despite the primary importance of collecting intelligence that would assist the bombing campaign, the elite British troops regarded it very much as a second-rate job. They were grateful when they were reassigned to Combined Joint Special Operations Task Force – Sword, the elite special mission unit task force, which was put together and commanded by Del Dailey to carry out the more difficult operations in the south. Task Force Sword was more than 2,000 men, made up of Delta, DevGru (the old SEAL Team Six), and the Activity, augmented by A and G squadrons of Britain's 22 SAS Regiment. It operated from bases in Pakistan and on the Omani island of Masirah – where Dailey had his headquarters – and from the US aircraft carrier *Kitty Hawk*, which was in the Persian Gulf with Black Hawk and Pave Low special operations helicopters replacing some of the fixed-wing aircraft normally lined up on its flight deck. The main role of Task Force Sword was to pursue high value targets and to cut off the Taliban and al-Qa'eda troops as they attempted to flee the US air bombardment by crossing into Pakistan's Tribal Areas. The Activity signals intelligence operators had an important role to play, intercepting the communications of the fleeing al-Qa'eda and Taliban members. In early November, the allies had a major success when a CIA Predator unmanned aerial vehicle armed with Hellfire anti-tank missiles spotted a Taliban convoy parked outside a three-storey hotel near Gardez, 80 miles south of Kabul, and destroyed it. British signals intelligence experts subsequently inter-cepted satellite telephone messages showing that Mohammed Atif, the 57-year-old deputy to bin Laden, was among those killed in the attack.[24]

But the real measure of the success of the innovative use of CIA and MI6 teams alongside special operations forces and a local proxy force of Afghan fighters was in the astonishing four days it took for the Taliban to be forced out of northern Afghanistan. The victory was set up in advance by the CIA and MI6 liaison teams on the ground. Gary Shroen's caseful of dollars was a major factor. But the key to winning support was rarely if ever money alone; sometimes it was the opportunity to avenge a long-held grudge against someone who had only been a temporary ally, sometimes a promise of US and British support in the post-war carve-up of Afghanistan. Often the motive that might lead a key commander to switch sides was simply pragma-tism, a wish to be on the winning side. Whatever the motives of their new allies, the US and British teams had spent the past month carefully putting together a game-plan, creating a situation where a few deft moves at the right moment would bring down the Taliban like a house of cards.

The first sign of their success came on Friday 9 November when the key northern town of Mazar-i-Sharif fell to a combined force of Dostum's National Movement, Jamiat-i-Islami troops and Shi'ite Hazaras. The CIA and MI6 teams waited until precisely the right moment before using their agents to press all the right buttons, getting the people they needed on side to defect at the most advantageous moment for the allied advance. The next day, Saturday 10 November, the combined Northern Alliance force moved west, taking Sar-i-Pol and Shiberghan, Dostum's personal fiefdom. By the Sunday, 11 November, with the carefully laid plans of the CIA and MI6 teams encouraging a series of defections by key commanders, the Taliban retreat had turned into a full-blown stampede. In the west, the Northern Alliance captured the town of Qala-i-Now, while in the north-east Fahim's men swept through Taloqan, Pol-i-Khomri and Bamiyan. The following day, the main western city of Herat fell and on Tuesday 13 November, with the Taliban now in headlong flight, Fahim's men occupied the capital Kabul, allowing the top secret allied special operations forces and intelligence teams to set up their base inside Afghanistan at the old Soviet air base at Bagram, north of the capital. But their main targets, bin Laden and his ally and protector Mullah Omar, would get away.

The al-Qa'eda leader had been located by British signals intelligence experts in a series of caves at Tora Bora in the White Mountains, 25 miles south-west of Jalalabad, almost as soon as the US bombing attack began. Activity agent-handlers and signals intelligence specialists were sent into Tora Bora and at the end of November gained confirmation from human intelligence sources recruited on the ground that bin Laden was in the caves. Teams from Task Force Sword moved into the Tora Bora region, intent on preventing bin Laden from escaping. They were joined by elements from Joint Special Operations Task Force – South, codenamed Task Force K–Bar, which was led by US Navy SEALs but also included special forces from Denmark, Germany, Australia, Norway, Canada and New Zealand, and by elements of Task Force Dagger. K–Bar's main role was to raid sites inside southern Afghanistan where al-Qa'eda or Taliban personnel were believed to be hiding. The assault on the Tora Bora caves was its first mission and it was badly botched. Allied commanders relied too much on local Afghan forces and large numbers of special operations whose forte was really small-scale operations. Allied commanders on the ground wanted a sizeable number of conventional forces deployed to block any attempt by the Taliban and al-Qa'eda fighters to flee across the border into Pakistan. But the US generals feared this might produce many more casualties and the 'risk aversion' mentality won the day. 'Their attitude was, "We must kill the enemy, but we must remain absolutely safe",' one Afghan commander said. 'This is crazy. If they had been willing to take casualties to capture Osama then, perhaps they'd have to take fewer casualties now.' The lack of major numbers of ground troops along the border allowed leading players in the al-Qa'eda and Taliban organisations to escape over the border into the sanctuary of Pakistan's lawless Tribal Areas. They included bin Laden himself, who was confirmed as being in Tora Bora in early December by an intercepted message in which he could be heard speaking personally to one of his lieutenants. The al-Qa'eda leader slipped through the disjointed allied lines and across the border into Pakistan in the second week of December. He could have been stopped. A combined force of SAS and SBS commandos tracked him down and was just twenty minutes behind him but they were then pulled off to allow US troops to go in for the kill. It took several hours for the US special operations team to get there, by which time bin Laden had escaped. Task Force Sword not only pursued the fleeing terrorists across the border, it also provided intelligence assistance to the Pakistani special operations troops who were trying to track down al-Qa'eda members inside the Tribal Areas, with the Activity using its signals intelligence skills to locate houses and compounds where the terrorists were hiding.[25]

Tommy Franks decided to improve the intelligence picture by setting up a fusion cell under Brigadier-General Gary 'Shooter' Harrell, a burly Delta officer who had taken part in the hunts for the Colombian drugs baron Pablo Escobar and the maverick Somali warlord Mohammed Farah Aideed. Harrell set up his cell – the Joint Inter-Agency Task Force – Counter Terrorism – at Bagram air base under the codename Task Force Bowie. It was made up of around 100 intelligence specialists, more than half of them civilian. They included members of the CIA, NSA, DIA and FBI as well as US, British and Australian special operations personnel, among them members of the Activity. Attached to Harrell's organisation was Advance Force Operations (AFO), a collection of around forty-five special operators led by another veteran Delta officer, Lieutenant-Colonel Pete Blaber. The AFO included half-a-dozen recce teams, each custom-made for the mission it was to perform, using a combination of Delta or DevGru shooters, Activity intelligence experts and Air Force Special Tactics combat controllers, whose role was to call in close air support to destroy any targets the teams decided to take out. The AFO's job was to go in first to prep the battlefield for the special operations teams from Task Force 11, as Task Force Sword had now become.[26]

MASTER SERGEANT KRIS K was the commander of Juliet, one of the AFO recce teams sent into the Shah-i-Kot to recce Operation Anaconda. It was Thursday 28 February 2002. Kris was watching five men heading along the same route his Juliet special operations team had used to climb the mountainside in the early hours of that morning. They were following the tracks that Juliet's tiny ATV all-terrain vehicles had left in the snow. The five men looked like Afghans. They wore turbans and the ubiquitous pyjama-like *shalwar kamiz*. They had been headed down the mountain towards Serkhankhel, one of four villages in the valley below. But when they saw the tracks they turned and followed them. The main Anaconda force was not due to enter the Shah-i-Kot for several days, but it was beginning to look like the shooting might start a little early.

For weeks, CIA sources had been reporting large numbers of 'AQT' – the shorthand for al-Qa'eda terrorists – assembling in the valley, just under 70 miles south of the capital Kabul. It looked suspiciously like a last stand before they followed Osama bin Laden across the border into Pakistan or melted into the landscape and returned to their farms. A joint CIA and Special Forces team, backed up by friendly militias, had ventured into the valley a couple of weeks earlier, only to withdraw amid suspicions they were being set up for an ambush. The signals intelligence specialists were reporting an increase in Arabic cellphone traffic from the villages clustered around the river that ran through the middle of the valley. So US commanders began planning Operation Anaconda, in which allied special operations forces, backed up by two infantry battalions, one from the 101st Airborne Division and another from the 10th Mountain Division, and by local Afghan forces, would end any large-scale Taliban or AQT resistance for good.[27]

Pete Blaber needed some Delta recce specialists to head up the teams he was sending into the valley to gather intelligence on the AQT positions, ahead of the main force. So Kris and the four other members of the recce team of Delta's B Squadron had been pulled off an exercise in Europe and ordered to Bagram before being deployed forward to an AFO safe house in the town of Gardez, just a few miles north of the Shah-i-Kot. The Juliet team had made their way up the mountain the previous night, headed for Takur Ghar, the 10,469ft mountain that dominated the eastern side of the valley. But after stopping up here for the night, Kris had decided this spot gave them a better, and safer, view down the valley.

Now he was on watch with Jay, a Special Tactics combat controller.

Jason, the Activity signals intelligence specialist, was scanning the air waves for AQT radio and cellphone traffic. Jay could bring in close air support but it was already too late for that, the aircraft would never get there in time. Three of the fighters on the track below were carrying Kalashnikov AK47 assault rifles. The other two had RPG rocket-propelled grenade launchers, the rockets strung over their shoulders like the quivers of mediaeval archers. Kris needed some extra firepower and he needed it fast. He talked softly into his short-range personal radio to wake up Bill and Dave, the two other members of Juliet, both highly experienced Delta operators, who were asleep in the tent down the slope and dangerously close to the vehicles.

The five Afghans had come from a cave complex half a mile to the east, to the left of Juliet's position high on the snow-covered mountain ridge at the north-eastern end of the Shah-i-Kot. The name meant 'the place of kings'. The snowy mountains and ridges that rose sharply on either side of the valley were littered with caves and foxholes that had been used by the 'muj' during the Soviet occupation in the 1980s. This particular cave complex was known to be used now by the AQT, with bin Laden himself said to have rested there before fleeing across the border into Pakistan. The presence of the cave complex only added to Kris's concern. It wouldn't be long before the five Afghans came across the ATVs, a cross between a motorbike and a four-wheel-drive golf buggy, where Juliet had hidden them, behind a rock formation. If they got there, the shit would really hit the fan. They would quickly realise that a small team of Americans was somewhere nearby. Five on five was an even match but the firefight would echo across the mountains, waking up everyone for miles around, and with large numbers of AQT thought to be inside the cave complex, Juliet would be on the run with very little hope of evading capture, followed by the inevitably brutal Afghan torture and death.

All five members of Juliet now had the laser-sights on their M4 carbines trained on the Afghans below. 'Hold your fire,' Kris whispered.

Suddenly, the Afghans stopped. They were clearly puzzled by the tracks. They looked more like they had been made by toys than by real vehicles. The five men seemed uncertain as to whether it was worth following the tracks further. They talked to each other for a few moments, debating whether to continue. Briefly, they elected to keep going but even as the Juliet team adjusted their rifles ready to fire, they agreed it was a wasted effort and turned back. Still one last Afghan remained undecided. He kept going, moving ever closer to the hidden ATVs until, to quote Juliet's after-action report, 'at what would have been his last moment', he too gave up, turned back and followed the others down the mountainside towards Serkhankhel. Then in a minor miracle, a sudden blizzard whipped up, sending the five Afghans rushing to the shelter of the village below and covering the tracks from further investigation.

The two other Delta recce specialists, the athletic Kevin 'Speedy' Short and his stocky buddy Bob were part of India, another of the intelligence-gathering teams sent into the Shah-i-Kot. India was above the south-east fork out of the valley, perfectly placed to cover anything Juliet couldn't see. Both Kevin and Bob were master sergeants, aged 36 and 38 respectively, a measure of the experience and maturity of judgement deemed necessary to carry out the recce role. There was only one other member in the India team, Dan, the second Activity knob-turner. Nowadays there were no knobs on the high-tech scanners the Task Force Orange operators used. It was all about pressing buttons. But within the Activity at least, the old nickname still stuck. Dan and Jason picked out the relevant cellphone and radio comms, worked out what was going on and relayed the frequencies and network details to the RC135 Rivet Joint signals intelligence aircraft overhead and back to Bagram so the NSA-controlled satellites could be tasked to track the signals and provide back-up. Despite unexpectedly fierce resistance from large numbers of Taliban and AQT forces, and some extraordinary decision-making that saw control of the Task Force 11 element switch from Delta to DevGru commanders halfway through the operation, Anaconda was a success. It was close air support brought in by the recce teams, and in particular Jay, Juliet's combat controller, that won the day. Between them, the recce teams were estimated to have killed far more Afghan fighters than the main force. Juliet, whose kills included many of those inside the cave complex, courtesy of a powerful thermobaric bomb, was the only team to stay in place through-out the battle, finally riding their ATVs onto the back of a Chinook and flying back to the Gardez safe house ten days after they had orig-inally begun their climb up the mountain.[28]

FORCED OUT OF ITS BASES in Afghanistan, al-Qa'eda began looking at Somalia as a possible location for its training bases. The US and its allies responded by stepping up intelligence operations in the region. Special operations forces were moved to a French base in Djibouti. US, British and French imagery intelligence surveillance aircraft began criss-crossing Somalia looking for any al-Qa'eda presence and the US opened negotiations to set up a signals intelligence base on the Yemeni island of Socotra. The Activity was sent into Somalia clandestinely, flying in by helicopter from a US warship based off the coast. Assisted by local clan members and disguised in local clothing, they liaised with friendly tribes and tracked down members of al-Qa'eda who were trying to prepare the ground for bin Laden and his main cohorts to find a safe sanctuary in southern Somalia. The intelligence the Activity found was undoubtedly 'actionable'. But memories of Mogadishu remained strong and there was a continued reluctance at senior levels within the US military to get involved in firefights inside Somalia. Fortunately, the Activity had developed strong links with the Jordanian special forces, training them and assisting them in arresting terrorists who threatened the government of King Abdullah II, the Sandhurst-educated ruler in Amman. The Jordanians were happy to take over the Somalia mission from the Americans, killing the al-Qa'eda terrorists and reducing the threat that bin Laden might set up bases there.[29]

The problems obtaining authority for the type of risky but indispensable operations the Activity was designed to carry out clearly still remained. But that situation was about to change. Rumsfeld was sick of being told that US forces could not go after the terrorists who needed to be hunted down because there was a lack of 'actionable intelligence'. He was furious that the joint chiefs appeared to believe that special operations forces needed the CIA to prepare the battlefield for them, particularly given that the Activity existed to carry out precisely that role and that many of the personnel used by the CIA's Special Activities Division had to be seconded from special operations units in the first place.[30] At the end of 2001, aides to the US Defense Secretary commissioned a secret report into why special operations forces were not used to take out al-Qa'eda before the 9/11 attacks. Written by Professor Richard Shultz, an expert on special operations and Professor of Security Studies at Tufts University, Medford, Massachusetts, it accused senior military commanders of invoking a series of 'show-stoppers' to prevent the Activity and other special mission units from being deployed.[31]

Senior officers were not interested in combating terrorism, regarding it as a crime rather than a 'clear and present danger', Shultz said. This problem was exacerbated by the fact that special operations forces were seen by the top brass as 'cowboys' whose operations would only get senior officers into trouble and damage their careers. 'Risk aversion' was at the centre of US military policy, Shultz said. The Joint Chiefs insisted on failsafe requirements for special operations missions – principally that no one would be killed – but no one could ever make such guarantees about military missions, which were by their very nature dangerous. General Pete Schoomaker, former commander-in-chief of SOCOM, summed it up when he told Shultz: 'Rumsfeld might think we're at war with terrorism but I'll bet he thinks he is at war within the Pentagon. The real war's happening right there in his building. It's a war of the culture. He can't go to war because he can't get his team up for it.'[32]

Senior levels of the armed forces had become 'Somalia-ized', Shultz said. 'The firefight in Mogadishu had a profound impact on the unwillingness of the US to use SOF on offensive counter-terrorist missions for the rest of the decade,' his report said. 'It reinforced an already jaded view. For the mainstream military, the lesson of Somalia was that here was yet another example of those reckless SOF units attempting operations that end up in disaster. Somalia had a profound effect on the Clinton administration. Among the lessons it learned was SOF units can get you into trouble.' Discussing the vexed issue of 'actionable intelligence', Shultz made a direct reference to the Activity and the fact that it had never been allowed to do its job properly. 'The lack of actionable intelligence was invoked often to stop the employment of SOF counter-terrorist units,' he said. 'Special operators considered it one of the chief challenges for executing counter-terrorist operations. Counter-terrorist units did not have the necessary operational intelligence/infrastructure support in denied and hostile areas. They lacked Operational Preparation of the Battlefield (OPB). A unit was created in the 1980s to establish OPB in areas with the potential for SOF CT missions. But it was never permitted to implement the full range of OPB activities. Therefore, terrorist sanctuaries in the denied areas were off limits.'[33]

Things were about to change. On 1 July 2002, Rumsfeld sent a two-line memo to Douglas Feith, his Under-Secretary for Defense Policy, designed to find a way round the problem. 'How do we organize the Department of Defense for manhunts?' he asked. 'We are obviously not well organized at the present time.' Three weeks later, clearly already firm in his own mind of what he needed to do, Rumsfeld sent a secret order to General Myers telling him to get General Charlie Holland, the commander-in-chief of Special Operations Command, to develop a plan to deal with terrorists. He left no doubt that, if necessary, the terrorists should be killed. 'The objective is to capture terrorists for interrogation or, if necessary, to kill them, not simply to arrest them in a law enforcement exercise.'[34]

The Activity's time had come. As Rumsfeld cast around for a unit that could actually carry out the manhunts he was demanding, a secret Pentagon report singled out the Activity as having 'the potential, if nurtured, to fight the kind of war the Secretary envisages fighting'. But he would need to sort out the problem that had hampered Activity operations since the unit was set up more than twenty years earlier, the excessive number of hoops they had to jump through to obtain authorization for even the smallest of missions. The US Defense Secretary was determined to make sure that special operations forces could obtain the authority for both deployment and the use of lethal force 'in minutes and hours, not days and weeks'. He also ordered a ramping-up of the ability to carry out the 'operational preparation of the battlespace', the precise role of the Activity. In an echo of the initiative taken by Jerry King when he set up the ISA, Rumsfeld told Special Operations Command to scan the personal files of every member of the armed forces for anyone with 'languages, ethnic connections and other attributes needed for clandestine or covert activities'. The size of the Activity was to be dramatically increased. In order to ensure that SOCOM commanders were not prevented from obtaining the people they needed, they were to keep Rumsfeld informed of the results. Finally, he moved the Activity, its identity on the army's books now covered by the top secret special access programme Titrant Ranger, out of the control of army intelligence chiefs and under the direct control of Special Operations Command. It now had the ability not only to go in first to gather the intelligence without needing to jump through a never-ending series of hoops to obtain authorisation, but where necessary it could kill anyone who got in its way.[35]

THREE MONTHS LATER, it very publicly demonstrated that capability. The Horn of Africa and the surrounding region was an important one for America to control if it was to clamp down on bin Laden's ability to operate. One of the key countries in the region that had been brought in on the US side in the war on terror was Yemen. It was bin Laden's ancestral home and al-Qa'eda had previously operated there with virtual impunity, most notably in the October 2000 bombing of the USS *Cole*, in which seventeen US sailors died. During talks at the White House in December 2001, President Bush offered Yemeni President Ali Abdullah Salih training teams that would help his security forces track down the al-Qa'eda terrorists. By the beginning of November 2002, US influence in the region was improving. The Pentagon announced it was setting up a task force with 800 special operations forces and 400 US Marines, based in the former French colony of Djibouti. General Myers said there were a number of countries in the region that 'you could call ungoverned, or at least not under some government's tight control, where terrorists can gather and either do operational planning or training and so forth. So, we're very interested in the area for that reason and have positioned forces there to take appropriate action.'

The policy of greater US involvement in the region was already proving itself in Yemen where the position was beginning to show radical improvement. While the al-Qa'eda presence remained strong, the US and Yemeni forces were beginning to get a handle on their activities, watching and waiting for their moment. 'There is no question but that there are al-Qa'eda in Yemen,' Rumsfeld said. 'We have some folks in that country that have been working with the government and helping them think through ways of doing things. It's been a good cooperation, and we've shared some information and we think that over time it ought to be beneficial.'

The training teams sent to Yemen included members of the Activity, in particular its signals intelligence experts, the knob-turners.

When the training came to an end, they stayed on to track down senior al-Qa'eda targets. In April, they foiled a bomb attack on the US embassy in Sana'a and prevented the assassination of one of the Yemeni intelligence officials who was working alongside them. Six months later, the training and assistance paid off with the assassination of a leading member of al-Qa'eda, the first to take place outside of Afghanistan and a breakthrough in the new US policy of using lethal force to take out the terrorists.

THERE WAS LITTLE DOUBT that the Toyota Land Cruiser that could be seen bumping along the rocky desert road on the screens at CIA headquarters in Langley, Virginia, contained the high-value target the US was after. The Activity had matched the location of Qa'ed Sunyan al-Harethi's cellphone to the dusty Toyota 4x4 vehicle. Al-Harethi was the most senior al-Qa'eda terrorist in Yemen, bin Laden's personal representative in the mountainous desert country and one of the top dozen members of al-Qa'eda. He was suspected of masterminding the attack on the USS *Cole*. His cellphone was at the centre of a matrix of terrorist contacts logged by the Activity's traffic analysts. They had been waiting for the moment when they could remotely programme it to switch itself on, providing the right target in the right place for an attack and allowing the Activity to take out the main subject of the manhunt in Yemen. CIA Predators, based across the Gulf of Aden in the former French colony of Djibouti, flew regular flights over the country, looking for al-Qa'eda targets. The 27-foot-long unmanned aerial vehicle could fly at heights of up to 25,000 feet and had a camera pod that could rotate through 360 degrees, providing real-time video, infra-red and radar imagery of anything moving below it. The operator watching the screens in Langley could pinpoint the target with a laser designator before launching one of the two deadly Hellfire anti-tank missiles the Predator carried.

The Activity picked up al-Harethi's cellphone 100 miles east of the capital Sana'a, on Sunday 3 November 2002. He appeared to be heading for the town of Marib, which the US Ambassador, Edmund J Hull, was due to visit the following day. The five other al-Qa'eda terrorists travelling alongside al-Harethi in the Toyota Land Cruiser included Kamal Derwish, a US citizen apparently connected to one of the terrorist cells that carried out the 9/11 attacks. It was unclear whether or not there was any connection between their apparent intention to drive to Marib and Hull's impending visit but it scarcely mattered anyway. Al-Harethi was the target of the nine-month manhunt, and Bush's authorisation of assassination meant that the US CIA and special operations commanders could kill him the moment they got eyeball on him.

With the Activity tracking his cellphone, it was a relatively easy task to move the Predator into position above him, following the Land Cruiser as it made its way along the rocky dirt road towards Marib. The order to press the button was given in Langley but it could just as easily have been made by one of the military commanders on the ground. Even if al-Harethi and his men had been aware of the Predator loitering above them, they would have had no place to hide. The first missile launched hit its target, setting off a secondary explosion, possibly of a bomb intended for Hull. By the time anyone got there, the Land Cruiser and its six occupants were little more than a few pieces of mangled metal and a dark brown scorch mark on the desert road. Yemeni security forces said they found traces of explosives and the remnants of communications devices in the wreckage. Bush was unapologetic over the change in US policy with regard to the assassination of enemies of America. 'The only way to treat them is as what they are – international killers,' he said. 'And the only way to find them is to be patient, and steadfast, and hunt them down.' But by now, the US President was already concentrating on hunting down another enemy of America and the Bush family in particular – Iraqi President Saddam Hussein.[36]

10 A REAL KILLER ELITE

IT WAS SHORTLY BEFORE TEN o'clock on the morning of Tuesday 22 July 2003 and the temperatures in central Iraq were already well above 100 degrees. Troops from the 101st Airborne Division moved quietly into place to secure the area around the large three-storey villa in the al-Falah district of north-east Mosul. The Activity had been running a number of Iraqi agents inside the Sunni triangle north-west of Baghdad as part of the hunt for 'Black List One' – Saddam Hussein. Now one of the former Iraqi generals they were using as go-betweens and trackers had come up trumps. A con-man who had served three years in jail for impersonating a relative of Saddam had tipped the general off that the Iraqi dictator's two sons Uday and Qusay were hiding in his villa. With a $15 million award on each of their heads, it had been only a matter of time before someone decided to sell them out.

A small SAS team had been sent in to carry out close target reconnaissance of the villa the previous evening. They were part of a thirty-man UK detachment based in Mosul alongside the Delta and Activity operators. The British special forces had proven adept at merging into the local population. The SAS det commander was confident that his team could storm the building and kill the four occupants swiftly that night. It was the sort of operation that the SAS trained for routinely at their close-quarter battle training facility at Pontrilas, ten miles south of Hereford. They had a proven track record of success in such operations. But the US commanders were sceptical that the SAS team would be sufficient. More to the point, it was important that if there was a major success against Saddam and the insurgency it was American soldiers who produced that success. The word came up from Baghdad that this operation was to be carried out by Delta.

Once the US troops were in place, an Iraqi interpreter used a bullhorn to urge the brothers to surrender – to come out with their hands up. The response from inside the house was a burst of automatic gunfire, which missed the Americans and wounded an Iraqi standing outside a mosque across the road. As the airborne troops provided covering fire, 'shooters' from the Activity and Delta went in. They were part of Task Force 20, the special operations task force set up to capture the leading members of Saddam's regime who were designated as 'High-Value Targets'. The Delta and Activity men stormed through the iron front gates of the walled compound around the villa. Some broke down the front door and began clearing the ground floor. Others entered through the basement garage where a new black Mercedes was parked and climbed the stairs at the back of the building, checking possible entry and exit points. Three of the shooters were halfway up the stairs to the first floor when they came under fire from behind barricades. The two brothers themselves were holed up in a bedroom at the front of the house. The shooters used stun grenades to try to shock them into dropping their defences but without success and were forced back after a heavy exchange of small arms fire. Still they had at least discovered where the targets were.

COLONEL JOE ANDERSON, a former US Ranger who was commanding the operation, called in the Night Stalkers' MH6 Little Bird attack helicopters to use their armour-piercing missiles, to try to flush the defenders out, and put Apache helicopter gunships and A10 Thunderbolts on standby. The first Little Bird mistook several Delta operators who were on the roof for the Iraqis, nearly causing a blue-on-blue, but fortunately the difficult approach meant all but one of his missiles missed the building completely. A second Little Bird had no more luck so Joe Anderson ordered the troops from 101st Airborne in front of the house to open fire with Humvee-mounted TOW anti-tank rockets. One missile cut a telegraph pole outside the villa in half before hitting home in the front left bedroom, blowing the window frames out onto a BMW parked in the street below.

Meanwhile, Lieutenant-General David Petraeus, the command-ing general of 101st Airborne, who was circling overhead in his Black Hawk helicopter, spotted activity in a pink-painted villa 80 yards down the street from the target house. Uday's bodyguards had been cut off by the American cordon and were preparing to fire on the US troops from behind. Petraeus swiftly ordered his men into place and the body-guards' opening burst of fire from an AK47 Kalashnikov assault rifle was cut short by a volley of tracer from an American .50in calibre heavy machine gun.

A total of eighteen TOW missiles were fired into the villa where Uday and Qusay were hiding. The force of the attack on the target house was so strong that four special operations forces trying to find an entry point at the rear were wounded by shrapnel from TOW anti-tank rockets that went straight through the house and out the other side. The acrid stench of smoke and carbon enveloped the villa as its façade crumbled in the face of the battering from missiles designed to penetrate the heaviest armour. Fragments of decorative tiles added small splashes of colour to the rubble dropping down in front of the building. Thousands of .50in calibre and 5.56mm tracer and armour-piercing rounds were pumped into the villa. The US troops even fired a surface-to-air missile through a window. But still the four men inside continued to respond with AKs on automatic. Eventually, after four hours of intensive exchanges of fire, the shooting from inside the house tailed off and the special operations shooters were ordered back in, only to be engaged by automatic rifle fire from an AK47 held by Qusay's son, who was hiding under the bed in a bedroom at the rear of the house. The 14-year-old was killed by the first burst of return fire from the Delta operators. The US troops found the battered body of Uday – whose connection to the Activity had begun two decades earlier during the attempt to obtain a T72 tank – in the front bedroom where he and his brother Qusay had chosen to make their last stand. Their internal organs were quite literally battered to the point of disintegration by the shock waves from the barrage of missiles. All four of the bodies were collected up, wrapped in green ponchos and placed in the back of the waiting Humvees. They were taken back to Baghdad where their faces were shaved and they were then photographed before being moved to a secret location where they were buried.[1]

As the Activity's human intelligence operators were celebrating their success, the knob-turners in the electronic surveillance team picked up what promised to be an even more valuable lead. They intercepted a satellite telephone call from 'Black List One' himself. Spooked by the shooting but unaware of what was going on, Saddam wanted his aides to move him to a new safe house. The satphone's location was immediately pinpointed but by the time the rapid response teams got there the former Iraqi dictator had gone. The Activity now set out to 'take down the mountain', finding and arresting Saddam's main allies one by one as they had with Pablo Escobar, until the former Iraqi dictator had no one left to support him. Shortly after Task Force 20 killed Uday and Qusay, it was combined with Task Force 5, as its counterpart in Afghanistan was now called, to form a new hit squad, Task Force 121, a combination of Delta, DevGru, Activity, CIA, SAS and SBS commandos whose sole purpose was to capture or kill America's main enemies in the region. In Afghanistan, that meant Osama bin

Laden and his ally Mullah Mohammed Omar, the Taliban leader. In Iraq, a British special forces officer said Task Force 121 had one role alone, 'pure and simple to find Number One'.

THE IDEA OF ATTACKING Iraq to remove Saddam Hussein from power was always on the cards once the Bush administration came to power. The Iraqi dictator had tried to assassinate the President's father and there were a number of senior members of the administration, like the Vice-President Dick Cheney, who had been there the first time, in the 1991 Gulf War, and regretted letting him off the hook then. Donald Rumsfeld was speaking for a number of others when, during a National Security Council meeting the day after the 9/11 attacks, he raised the possibility of using them as an excuse for invading Iraq. But the idea was pushed to one side in favour of concentrating on Osama bin Laden, the man directly behind the attacks. Nevertheless, the Pentagon, where Paul Wolfowitz, the chief advocate of deposing Saddam, was Rumsfeld's deputy, continued pressing for an attack on Iraq, and in December 2001, with the war in Afghanistan almost over, General Tommy Franks, the commander-in-chief of Central Command, was called to the President's ranch retreat at Crawford in Texas to brief him on plans for an invasion. Franks, under pressure from Donald Rumsfeld to keep it ultra-light, told the President he had already decided that the plans were too heavy. They envisaged a large ground force of up to half a million troops. Franks said he had told his planning staff to go away and come back with an 'Afghanistan-style' invasion plan, representing the other end of the spectrum and largely using special operations forces. These two plans would form the outer 'bookends' of his planning options, he said. Somewhere between them would be the optimum plan that would suit Iraq. Tommy Franks himself preferred the idea of a medium force with around five front-line divisions and a total of up to 250,000 men. His problem was that Rumsfeld was determined to keep it ultra-light, to fit in with his plans to downsize the US military, making it a much lighter, slimmer force. The arguments between the two men over the size of the invasion force were to bedevil planning for the Iraq War.[2]

In his first State of the Union address on 29 January 2002, President Bush specifically named Iraq as part of an 'Axis of Evil' that threatened America and its allies. 'By seeking weapons of mass destruction, these regimes pose a grave and growing danger,' the President said. Two and a half weeks later, he signed a secret National Security Council directive establishing the reasons for invading Iraq. Bush had reportedly told one aide: 'Fuck Saddam. We're taking him out.' It no longer seemed to be a question of if; all the discussion was of how soon, with increasing talk of an invasion that autumn when conditions on the ground in Iraq would be ideal. It was causing jitters across Europe, where only Tony Blair could be counted on to back a US-led invasion.[3] But even the British Prime Minister's advisers were warning that an outright invasion would be illegal, and there was significant unrest within his own party. Two cabinet ministers, Robin Cook and Clare Short, were known to be ready to resign if Britain went to war with Iraq. A Secret UK Eyes Only Cabinet Office Options Paper warned that there were essentially two options: a strengthening of the containment policy that was already in place, or regime change. But tougher sanctions and inspections would not be enough to get rid of Saddam. More importantly, it would not be enough for Washington. 'The US has lost confidence in containment,' the paper warned. There was increasing pressure within the administration to invade Iraq and it had less to do with the War on Terror than a desire to finish the job that the President's father had begun in the Gulf War. 'The success of Operation Enduring Freedom, distrust of UN sanctions and inspection regimes, and unfinished business from 1991 are all factors,' the paper said. But there would be major problems finding a legal justification to use military force, it warned starkly. 'Subject to law officers' advice, none currently exists.'[4]

Mr Blair spent the weekend of 9 and 10 March 2002 reading the doom-laden Cabinet Office options paper at his Chequers retreat ahead of talks with US Vice-President Dick Cheney the next day. Speaking at a Downing Street press conference after the talks, Mr Blair insisted that no decisions had been taken on how to deal with the threat from Iraq, 'but that there is a threat from Saddam Hussein and the weapons of mass destruction that he has acquired is not in doubt at all.' The Prime Minister then cut the press conference short. He knew that he and Mr Cheney were only the warm-up act. A few minutes later, Mr Bush would step up to a podium in the White House Rose Garden to address 1,300 guests assembled to mark six months since the 11 September attacks. The President did not talk specifically about Iraq but he did warn that the War on Terror was about to get more difficult. 'Inaction is not an option,' he said. 'Men with no respect for life must never be allowed to control the ultimate instruments of death.' No one had any doubt who he had in mind.[5]

The next day, Tuesday 12 March, the Joint Chiefs of Staff began a two-day exercise designed to test the US military's part in the War on Terror. Exercise Prominent Hammer I was the first US military exercise to play out an invasion of Iraq. As the exercise came to an end, Condoleeza Rice was having dinner in Washington with Sir David Manning, Mr Blair's foreign policy adviser, who had gone to Washington to prepare the ground for a summit between President Bush and Mr Blair to be held at Crawford at the beginning of April. In a report of their discussions, Sir David warned the Prime Minister there were worrying signs that President Bush and his advisers did not realise the pitfalls ahead: 'Bush has yet to find the answers to the big questions: how to persuade international opinion that military action against Iraq is necessary and justified; what value to put on the exiled Iraqi opposition; how to coordinate a US/allied military campaign with internal opposition (assuming there is any); what happens on the morning after? I think there is a real risk that the Administration underestimates the difficulties. They may agree that failure isn't an option, but this does not mean that they will avoid it.'[6]

Peter Ricketts, the Foreign Office Policy Director, was scathing of attempts in Washington to link Saddam Hussein to al-Qa'eda and by extension to the 9/11 attacks. 'US scrambling to establish a link between Iraq and al-Qa'eda is so far frankly unconvincing,' he said. 'To get public and Parliamentary support for military options we have to be convincing that the threat is so serious/imminent that it is worth sending our troops to die for. Even the best survey of Iraq's WMD programmes will not show much advance in recent years. Military operations need clear and compelling military objectives. For Iraq, "regime change" does not stack up. It sounds like a grudge match between Bush and Saddam.'[7]

The British were particularly concerned over the apparent lack of planning for a post-war Iraq. Jack Straw, the British Foreign Secretary, warned Mr Blair in a letter marked 'Secret and Personal' that no one seemed to have a clear idea of what would happen afterwards. 'There seems to be a larger hole in this than anything,' Mr Straw said. Most of the US assessments argued for regime change as a means of eliminating Iraq's weapons of mass destruction. 'But no one has satisfactorily answered how there can be any certainty that the replacement regime will be any better. Iraq has no history of democracy so no one has this habit or experience.' The Secret UK Eyes Only Cabinet Office Options Paper was even blunter. 'The only certain means to remove Saddam and his elite is to invade and impose a new government,' it said. 'But this would involve nation-building over many years.' Without a long-term allied occupation, 'there would be a strong risk of the Iraqi system reverting to type. Military coup could succeed coup until an autocratic Sunni dictator emerged who protected Sunni interests. With time he could acquire WMD.' The allies would be back where they started.[8]

A sombre Mr Blair flew into Mr Bush's Prairie Chapel Ranch on board a presidential helicopter late on Friday 5 April. He was wearing a black suit and tie in mourning for the Queen Mother who had died the previous week. President Bush, wearing blue jeans and work boots, drove him to the ranch house in a pick-up truck. The contrast could not have been starker, in more ways than one. The Prime Minister was cautious when asked about Iraq in a pre-summit interview with a US network. His aides had been insisting all week that this was not a 'council of war'. Mr Blair told NBC that he and the President were 'not proposing military action at this point in time'. But Mr Bush, in his corresponding pre-summit interview with the British Independent Television News, said: 'I made up my mind that Saddam needs to go.' There was, in fact, little doubt that the Crawford summit was a council of war. 'I explained to the Prime Minister that the policy of my government is the removal of Saddam, and that all options are on the table,' Mr Bush said later. 'The world would be better off without him and so will the future.' Tony Blair, determined to keep the transatlantic alliance alive but desperate to get the UN backing that would make an invasion legal, persuaded Mr Bush to hold off going to war that autumn, to wait a few months, in the hope of getting UN backing. But Secret UK Eyes Only documents later revealed that it was here at Crawford that Mr Blair agreed to 'support military action to bring about regime change'. It was a hugely dangerous step for the British Prime Minister, since as the papers warned: 'regime change per se is not a proper basis for military action under international law'. The civil servants drafting the papers added that it was now 'necessary to create the conditions in which we could legally support military action.'[9]

On Saturday 11 May, Rumsfeld and Franks went to Camp David to brief the President on the war plan. There were still arguments going on over the precise size of the ground forces but the allies would attack from the south, through Kuwait and from the north through Turkey, with large numbers of US, British and Australian special operations forces infiltrating Iraq well ahead of the attack to prepare the battlefield and collect intelligence. The only part of the plan where there was any real similarity with Afghanistan was in northern Iraq, where allied special operations forces were already in place to link up with the Kurdish Peshmerga. But even here, Tommy Franks intended to send in US and British troops to provide the main fighting force.[10]

The most novel element of the war plan was the air war. The Southern and Northern Watch patrols by US and British military aircraft over the no-fly zones set up to prevent Iraq attacking the Shia in the south and the Kurds in the north remained in place. This gave the allies the opportunity to mount a covert air war. Ostensibly, the rules of engagement dictated that attacks by allied patrols had to be 'a necessary and proportionate response to actual or imminent attack from Iraqi ground systems'. The Northern Watch patrols were mounted from the eastern Turkish base at Incirlik and the Turks had to be told the precise details of every operation mounted from their territory. But in the south, the allies had a free rein. Franks wanted to start 'spikes of activity' designed to provoke a reaction from the Iraqis that would constitute the justification for war that they needed to create, allowing allied aircraft to start taking out the Iraqi air defences one by one. The plan, codenamed Southern Focus, was given the go-ahead and, immediately after that Camp David briefing, the 'spikes of activity' began.[11]

At the end of August, with the increased allied attacks having failed to provoke the excuse for retaliation that the allies wanted, they began the air war anyway, degrading the Iraqi air defences one by one in a deliberately targeted series of raids. During March 2002, no bombs at all were dropped in the southern no-fly zone and the following month only 0.3 tons of ordnance was used. But in May the figure rose to 7.3 tons, then 10.4 in June, dipping to 9.5 in July before rising again to 14.1 in August and then 54.6 tons in September as a full-scale air war began. Bush would not receive the necessary Congressional sanction for military action but it was already underway. The first major air raid in September, involving more than 100 allied aircraft, was against the air defences at the H3 airfield in western Iraq. Located at the furthest extreme of the southern no-fly zone, far away from the areas that needed to be patrolled to prevent attacks on the Shia, they were attacked solely in order to allow allied special operations forces to fly undetected into Iraq from West Wing, the codename for their base at the Shaheed Muwaffaq airfield at Azraq in eastern Jordan.[12]

The US already had large numbers of aircraft and armoured vehicles in the region in case Iraq attacked one of its neighbours but both the Joint Chiefs and their British equivalents now began moving military units and ships out to the Gulf, often under cover of joint exercises with their allies in the region. The RAF staged a joint live-fire exercise, Desert Thunderclap, with its Jordanian counterpart, using it as cover to move aircraft to the Azraq base to support SAS operations. But while Tony Blair, facing considerable domestic opposition to invading Iraq, did not give the go-ahead to start deploying troops until early December, the American build-up in the Gulf was steady and unrestrained throughout the second half of 2002.[13]

By October 2002, allied special operations forces were already infiltrating Iraq, their passage made easier by the continuing destruction of the Iraqi air defences. They included members of the Activity, who were tapping fibre-optic cables, monitoring the communications of senior Iraqi officials and developing agents on the ground inside Baghdad itself. But the debate over how much power units like Delta, DevGru and the Activity should have to carry out their own missions without jumping through hoops to get authority was still going on. Donald Rumsfeld had no doubt. He wanted special operations forces to be able to track down terrorists anywhere in the world and snatch them or kill them as swiftly as possible without suffering the delays of gaining authority to do so that had hampered special operations from Tehran to Mogadishu. But General Charlie Holland, the head of Socom, was holding back, reluctant to tread on the toes of the five regional commanders who split up the world and controlled all US military operations in each of their sectors. Socom's only role was to support those theatre commands. It could not initiate its own operations. Rumsfeld rightly saw this as a barrier to the War on Terror. He wanted it changed.[14]

The Shultz report, with its emphasis on the failure to use the special operations capabilities developed in the wake of Operation Eagle Claw, and in particular the Activity itself, had been followed in August 2002 by a special study conducted by the Defense Science Board, a Pentagon advisory body. Rumsfeld, angry at the way in which the CIA had muscled in on the Pentagon's territory during the war in Afghanistan, had made it clear that he wanted to see the US special operations intelligence capability dramatically expanded, with more units like the Activity that could carry out covert operations around the world, preparing the battlefield for potential future conflicts long before they began. Although the initial focus was on tracking members of al-Qa'eda, Rumsfeld had made it clear that he wanted US special operations forces to pre-empt any future threats. The blueprint drawn up by the Defense Science Board appeared to mirror the original 1981 plans for the Intelligence Support Activity. It suggested an elite counterterrorism organisation reporting directly to the National Security Council, which it called P2OG, standing for Proactive Pre-emptive Operations Group.[15]

P2OG operatives would operate all over the world, going into countries where there was no threat to recruit agents and collect intelligence that would allow the US to react swiftly if that country did become a threat. The group members would include operators skilled in collecting both human and technical intelligence as well as shooters able to provoke the right responses. They would be able to 'pre-emptively evoke responses from adversary/terrorist groups' in order to obtain the intelligence they needed. Their databases would be so extensive that three-dimensional computerised maps of the landscape and of each important building could be prepared. The intelligence analysts would not only speak the language of their opponents, they

would be able to bury themselves in their culture so they could understand and predict what the enemy might do at any turn. Much of this,
right down to the three-dimensional computerised mapping, mirrored
the capabilities that the Activity had created but had been prevented
from using by bureaucratic superiors. But the Defense Science Board's
ambitions for P2OG were not limited by such considerations and only
concerned with how best to prosecute the Global War on Terrorism. It
envisaged a web of worldwide sensors to track the movement of
weapons of mass destruction with a 'SWAT-like' counter-proliferation team standing by to prevent terrorists or rogue states gaining
control of them. There would be a special 'Red Team' to get into the
minds of the terrorists and biological or chemical tags that could be
secretly attached to individuals so they could be tracked anywhere
around the world. The focus was on the need to 'exploit the special
operations forces' inherent intelligence collection capabilities' and
giving them a presence worldwide on a day-to-day basis 'to exploit
human and geographic access in potential crisis locations' so they could
'hold states/sub-state actors accountable'. It was, in short, a dramatic
expansion and vindication of the plans put in place by Jerry King and
his colleagues in the ISA more than twenty years earlier.[16]

The report was presented to Rumsfeld in October 2002. The US
Defense Secretary was now convinced that if the War on Terror was to
be prosecuted efficiently, Special Operations Command had to be given
the power to act on its own initiative, to take out terrorists within hours,
not wait for permission from Pentagon lawyers or Congress with all
the risk that the target would move on or the mission plan leak out. A
few weeks after receiving the Defense Science Board report, he commissioned another, asking the government-funded Institute for Defense
Analyses [IDA] to look at the role of special operations and devise a
way of reorganising them, 'to start with a "blank sheet" and re-design
US SOCOM to fight the war on terrorism'. Although the review was
ostensibly carried out by a panel, it was in fact effectively the work of

former special operations commanders, and in particular Generals
Pete Schoomaker and Carl Stiner, both ex-commanders-in-chief of
SOCOM. The study unequivocally backed Rumsfeld's gut instincts,
calling for special operations forces to be given much more control
over their own activities and much bigger budgets.[17]

The US Defense Secretary responded immediately, giving Special
Operations Command new powers to initiate the terrorist 'manhunts'
he wanted. The war on terrorism had been hampered by the inability
of the special operations forces to act on their own initiative, he said.
Special Operations Command could not plan its own missions. It was,
in the jargon of the US military, a 'supporting command'. Its forces
deployed in Afghanistan and Iraq did so in support of Central
Command and acting on its orders. But the US Defense Secretary had
decided to make Special Operations Command a 'supported command',
allowing it to plan and execute its own hunt-and-destroy missions.
'The challenge we face in the global war on terror is to root out those
terrorists and terrorist networks that threaten our people; to find them,
disrupt them, capture, drive them from their safe havens and prevent
them from murdering more of our citizens,' Mr Rumsfeld said. 'In
Afghanistan and elsewhere, we've seen the indispensable role that
special operations forces have and are currently playing. We're taking
a number of steps to strengthen the US Special Operations Command
so it can make even greater contributions to the global war on terror.
The global nature of the war, the nature of the enemy and the need
for fast, efficient operations in hunting down and rooting out terrorist
networks around the world have all contributed to the need for an
expanded role for the special operations forces. We are transforming
that command to meet that need.' At the same time, he moved the
Activity under the direct control of JSOC to concentrate on giving
Delta and DevGru the actionable intelligence they needed to do their
job.[18]

As US special operations forces prepared the ground inside Iraq, they had never been more powerful. Unlike the 1991 war, where General Schwarzkopf refused to give them their rein, they had backing and support at the highest levels within the Pentagon. It was no longer potentially damaging to their careers for senior commanders to support special operations missions; it was politically dangerous not to support them. The result was unprecedented. Some 10,000 special operations forces were involved in the war in Iraq, more than during any conflict since the Second World War, including Vietnam. Led by Brigadier-General Gary 'Shooter' Harrell, who was now commander of Centcom's special operations component, they called down air strikes; hunted senior Baath Party officials; searched for weapons of mass destruction; seized airfields; secured vital bridges; took control of oilfields to prevent Saddam torching them; sought out Scud missile launchers; and made surreptitious contact with Iraqi opposition figures.[19]

On the early evening of Wednesday 19 March 2003, about eight hours before the war began, allied special operations forces flew into southern and western Iraq to destroy Iraqi command posts, in particular those expected to be used to launch chemical and biological weapons. They also destroyed key junctions in the fibre-optic communications links in order to disrupt the Iraqis' command and control system and force their communications up onto the airwaves where they could be monitored by the allies. The western front was supplied entirely by the Combined Joint Special Operations Task Force – West, codenamed Task Force Dagger, based at Azraq in Jordan and made up of US Rangers, US Army Special Forces, and British and Australian SAS. Little Bird helicopter gunships from 160th Special Operations Aviation Regiment mounted simultaneous attacks against Iraqi border posts to open up corridors that British and Australian SAS could use to fly in to take the H2 and H3 airfields to deny them to the Iraqi military and to provide the task force with forward operating bases inside Iraq. US Rangers staged a daring airborne assault on H1 airbase. They also seized the Haditha Dam, north of Karbala, to prevent the Iraqis from flooding the approaches to Baghdad.

But the main role of Task Force Dagger was to hunt for Scud missile launchers. During a series of pre-war infiltrations, the US, UK and Australian special operations forces had reconnoitred around 100 'Scud pans', areas of hard ground, amid the mainly soft sand of the western desert, from which Scud missiles could safely be fired. They secured fifty of these sites on the first night, and the remaining fifty the next. Their other roles included seeking out potential targets for allied air attack and blocking off lines of escape through Syria or Jordan for senior figures in the regime. This last role was to lead to some of the fiercest fighting of the war, when US Army Special Forces and British SAS troops clashed with Iraqi troops protecting what was believed to be an escape route for Saddam and his entourage near Qaim on the Syrian border. In the south, US Navy SEALs and the British Special Boat Service (SBS), which specialised in protecting the North Sea oilfields from terrorist attack, secured oil wells to prevent the Iraqis from setting them on fire. They also carried out reconnaissance for the amphibious assault on the Faw peninsula by British Royal Marine Commandos and secured vital bridges on the route north. The SBS and 3 Commando Brigade's pathfinding Brigade Patrol Troop then began operating under cover inside Basra, bringing down aerial attacks on key targets and helping MI6 debrief its agents in the city, an operation that led to the eventual British takeover of the city with only very few casualties.[20]

When Turkey refused to allow the 4th Infantry Division and the British 1st Armoured Division to use its territory to invade northern Iraq, blocking a key part of the allied plan, the gap was filled by large numbers of special operations forces, mainly US Army Special Forces, who used the Kurdish Peshmerga guerrillas to hold down the whole of the northern front. The Combined Joint Special Operations Task Force – North, codenamed Task Force Viking, organised the

Peshmerga forces to seize the key cities of Kirkuk and Mosul and directed air support for their attacks in an operation that mirrored the use of the Northern Alliance in Afghanistan. Despite facing, on paper at least, a total of thirteen Iraqi Army divisions, they swiftly forced enemy troops out of the major cities while still managing to prevent them falling back on Baghdad. The capture of Mosul followed one of the most celebrated firefights of the war, the Battle of the Debecka Pass, when thirty-six US Army Special Forces and eighty Peshmerga took on at least one Iraqi mechanised infantry brigade. The Special Forces found themselves defending a plateau armed only with heavy machine guns and Javelin shoulder-launched anti-tank missiles. They fought off two armoured counter-attacks before calling in air support to repel a third. Tragically, a US Navy aircraft responding to the call bombed a disabled Iraqi T55 tank that was being examined by a group of Peshmerga and US Special Forces. The attack killed a dozen Peshmerga in one of the worst friendly fire incidents of the war. Three Special Forces soldiers were awarded the Silver Star for their part in the battle, including Staff Sergeant Jeffrey M Adamec. 'We all made a mental promise,' he said. 'Nobody had to yell out commands. Everybody just knew. We were not going to move back from that point. We were not going to give up that ground. We called that spot the Alamo.'[21]

The special mission units of JSOC, including the Activity, were part of Task Force 20, which was based initially in Kuwait and directly subordinate to Tommy Franks. The task force's main role was searching for possible weapons of mass destruction sites and capturing senior members of the regime, working through a list of more than 100 'High-Value Targets' who were to be captured or killed. But it also played a role in the securing of the southern oil installations to prevent the Iraqis blowing them up. As the front moved north, Task Force 20 set up a forward operating base at Tallil. The Activity enjoyed an extremely good war, particularly the knob-turners of the electronic surveillance team, who infiltrated the Iraqi capital itself, merging into the Iraqi population to carry out 'close-in' monitoring of the communications of senior Iraqi officials. Their tapping of the Iraqi fibre-optic cables, now an Activity speciality, also provided vital information. The Activity's ability to provide precise locations for the radio and satellite telephones of Saddam's henchmen led to a series of successful strikes by US aircraft and Tomahawk cruise missiles. Its human intelligence operators worked with CIA officers recruiting agents and trying to persuade senior Iraqis to defect and, with Delta and Special Tactics combat controllers, bringing down allied air attacks on key targets in the Iraqi capital. Given the difficulties of operating in such a brutal regime, the allies had a surprising number of agents in pre-war Iraq, including long-term penetration agents. Human intelligence played a key role throughout the 2003 war on Iraq, beginning with the opening air strike in the early hours of 20 March in which thirty cruise missiles and smart bombs dropped by two F117A Nighthawk stealth strike aircraft slammed into the Dora Farm complex belonging to Saddam's youngest daughter Hala. The intelligence came from a 'very good' CIA source, described later by President Bush as 'a guy on the ground' who 'was convinced that not only Saddam Hussein would be in the complex, but Uday and Qusay, his two sons, would be there as well.' Tragically, the attack failed to kill anyone of any importance apart from the CIA's own agent, who was in the Dora Farm complex when the cruise missiles hit it. The Activity collated all of the available intelligence, giving allied special operations forces direct real-time access to the intelligence product of national agencies like the CIA and the NSA. Brigadier-General Donald Wurster, Director of the Socom Centre for Intelligence and Information Operations told the Senate Armed Services Committee that 'special operations forces signals intelligence capability has routinely proven itself in ongoing combat operations throughout Afghanistan and Iraq,' while special operations human intelligence resources had 'proven to be one of the greatest contributors to the successes enjoyed by special operations forces to date'. The 'high quality intelligence' available to US special operations forces had helped Task Force Viking 'to establish early footholds and successful operations in northern Iraq', enabled Task Force Dagger to dominate western Iraq, denying it to Saddam's forces, and 'assisted in the seizure of key airfields, the capture of Iraqi senior leadership and the prevention of potential ecological disaster through the intentional destruction of oil wells and infrastructure'.[22]

Once the war was officially declared over, Rumsfeld pushed forward with his plans to ensure special operations forces stayed at the centre of US military tactics, making three key appointments. Given the way in which special operations missions had been repeatedly blocked by senior military commanders, the first was perhaps the most important. The US Defense Secretary asked Pete Schoomaker to come out of retirement to become the army chief of staff in a clear sign that he was unhappy at the failure of conventional military commanders to understand the value of special operations forces. The 57-year-old Schoomaker had impeccable special operations credentials, twice commanding a Delta squadron before taking command of Delta itself, then commanding general of JSOC followed by Army Special Operations Command and finally serving as commander-in-chief Special Operations Command. He had also taken part in the failed mission to rescue the Tehran hostages that led to the creation of the Activity. 'If it wasn't for Desert One, we wouldn't have the [special operations] force we have today,' he said. The successes in Afghanistan and Iraq were 'the result of 20 to 25 years investment in special operations. The investment is wisely paying off.'[23]

A few weeks later, Rumsfeld followed the advice given by Professor Richard Shultz eighteen months earlier and appointed an Assistant Secretary of Defense for Special Operations and Low-Intensity Conflict who had what Shulz described as 'the knowledge and confidence to provide policy advice even when it does not coincide with the views of the Joint Chiefs of Staff'. The new appointment was good news for the Activity. Tom O'Connell had been Jerry King's senior intelligence officer in the old ISA. Like King he had served in Vietnam, where O'Connell had taken part in the controversial Phoenix programme, which sent out teams to collect intelligence and 'neutralize' Viet Cong suspects. O'Connell had been the JSOC Director of Intelligence and a special operations liaison officer with the CIA before going into industry as a senior manager in Raytheon's Intelligence and Information Systems division.[24] The third key appointment came when Charlie Holland retired in September 2003 to be replaced by his deputy General Bryan 'Doug' Brown. Appointing Brown as SOCOM commander-in-chief, Rumsfeld said he had a wealth of special operations experience. 'He served in a Special Forces "A Team", was one of the first Army Aviators in special ops, a combat assault pilot in Vietnam, and a plank-holder in Task Force 160. He served as Commanding General of the Joint Special Operations Command, Commanding General of the US Army Special Operations Command, deputy here to Charlie Holland, and I believe, has probably participated in one way or another in almost every special operations forces combat campaign since Vietnam.' The appointment of these key officials set the scene for a major expansion of intelligence support for special operations.[25]

IN IRAQ, TASK FORCE 121 was carefully following up every reported sighting of Saddam Hussein, but months went by with no sign of success. By the end of the summer, the US troops had received so many unsubstantiated sightings of the former Iraqi dictator that they had taken to referring to him as 'Elvis'. But in the background, the Activity and their CIA colleagues were working away on contact analysis, tracking the links between Saddam and his various henchmen. Operating out of their tiny headquarters inside the 'Green Zone', the heavily defended allied stronghold in Baghdad, they used a combination of intercepts of satellite and radio telephones and human intelligence from agents on the ground, and from Iraqis anxious to collect the $25 million reward, to narrow their search down to the area around Saddam's family stronghold of Tikrit, north-west of the Iraqi capital. The bulk of the material was human intelligence, since the small groups protecting Saddam were aware that any use of a satellite phone would immediately be picked up and the site located. The bulk of communications were via face-to-face meetings, with the use of satellite telephones restricted to emergencies.

THERE WERE NO FEWER than eleven raids aimed at trying to catch Saddam during September and October 2003 alone. Task Force 121's commanders knew they had to take a fresh approach if they were going to get the former Iraqi dictator. At the end of October, they mounted a major raid on the village of Awja, about five miles south of Tikrit, where Saddam had been brought up, arresting and questioning more than 500 Iraqis, many of whom had direct links to Saddam's family. Those interrogations added a host of additional detail to the intelligence picture and formed the start point for a renewed, sustained hunt for Black List One. Delta, DevGru or SAS shooters now began to snatch relatives or henchmen of the Iraqi dictator to order, taking his inner circle apart piece by piece, ratcheting-up the pressure. The intelligence experts interrogated every new prisoner, adding any new information he provided to the accumulated intelligence picture. They then worked out which of Saddam's remaining cronies was best able to provide the next missing piece of the jigsaw and sent the shooters out on a 'shopping expedition' to snatch the man they needed to fill in that gap.

By early December, Task Force 121 knew they were right on Saddam's tail. The shooters had brought in half a dozen close relatives of the former Iraqi dictator over the past few days and, while none of them had told their interrogators where he was, the cumulative effect of the detail had provided a very clear picture of Saddam's life on the run. They now knew that a reported sighting of him being driven around Baghdad in a battered orange and white Toyota Corolla taxi was almost certainly correct, and that for most of the time he had been using a taxi matching that description to move between any of several dozen safe houses, each with a secret hiding place in case American troops came knocking. Sometimes he might stay in one place for a few days, sometimes only for a few hours, often moving out only just ahead of the special operations forces tracking him down. 'They've been so close at times that they have picked up his slippers and they've been warm,' one British member of Task Force 121 said. Sooner or later, someone would get greedy for the $25 million bounty and give him up or just get careless and let that key piece of the jigsaw slip.

At ten minutes to eleven on the morning of Saturday 13 December 2003, they got the tip-off they were waiting for. A new detainee, one of Saddam's bodyguards, said he was hiding up in a farm in the village of al-Dawr, ten miles south of Tikrit. The farm was owned by one of the Iraqi dictator's former servants, a man called Qais al-Nameq. The Activity intelligence specialists downloaded satellite imagery of the area indicated by the tip-off. There appeared to be two sets of buildings which task force commanders codenamed Wolverine 1 and Wolverine 2, putting together a plan to close down the whole area. At 2000 hours, all electricity supplies to the two farms were cut off, plunging them into darkness, and 600 troops from the Raider Brigade of the 4th Infantry Division's 1st Brigade Combat Team moved in to seal them off. Once a tight outer perimeter was established, quarantining the two farms and any possible escape routes, around forty shooters and intelligence operators from Delta and the Activity moved in.

This time there were going to be no members of the SAS involved. The British had blotted their copy book with poor security. A Foreign Office official attended a meeting at which it was disclosed on a 'Secret Close Hold' basis that the task force was right on Saddam's tail. That information should not have left the room in which the meeting was held. But the Foreign Office official telephoned London, setting off a series of telephone calls that compromised the operation and left the US special operations troops understandably wary of British officials. An SAS team was on standby to provide back-up but the decree had come down from on high. The capture of Saddam Hussein had to be 100 per cent 'made in the US of A'. As the US special operations troops combed the two farms, a CIA Predator loitered overhead, relaying back live infra-red video images to task force commanders watching back in Baghdad. But there was no trace of 'Black List One'. Perhaps this was yet another false trail. The Activity interrogators went back to their man. Saddam was definitely there, he said. If they couldn't find him, they should look for an underground bunker, 'that's where he'll be'.

The US special operations forces began a thorough search of the whole of the area. It led them to a small mud-brick building, little more than a hut, sandwiched between Wolverine 1 and Wolverine 2. Parked outside was a battered orange and white Toyota Corolla taxi. One man, armed with an AK47 Kalashnikov rifle, tried to make a run for it and was detained. Another man was arrested inside the mud-brick house. It had just two rooms, a makeshift kitchen and a bedroom with a single bed covered in new clothes, some of them still in their packaging. Underneath the bed there was a box containing $750,000 in $100 bills. But there was no sign of Black List One.

Then one of the US soldiers noticed a crack in the ground, alongside a dirty rug. He pulled the rug aside and dug down to expose a dirty piece of Styrofoam that appeared to be covering a hole in the ground. A Delta shooter readied a hand grenade, in case anyone in the hole started shooting up at them. Another carefully lifted the Styrofoam lid. Underneath it was a 6ft deep hole, its walls braced with pieces of wood. At the bottom the hole opened out into a wider cavity, barely high enough to crawl in but just long enough to let a man lie down, and there, flat out with a pistol stuck in his belt, was the unmistakable figure of the self-styled Lion of Babylon, aka Elvis. He was 'caught like a rat in a trap,' one US commander said. Wearing an unkempt white beard, Saddam looked shattered, almost as if he was too tired to carry on and was just glad that his nine months on the run were over. The former Iraqi dictator raised both hands in surrender and said: 'I am Saddam Hussein, I am the president of Iraq and I'm willing to negotiate.' One of the Delta operators looked down at him, trying to work out how this tired, shaken old man had imposed a reign of terror on the Iraqi people, and said, dismissively: 'President Bush sends his regards.'[26]

FOLLOWING ITS SUCCESS in the hunt for Saddam, the bulk of Task Force 121 moved to Afghanistan to apply the same techniques to the search for bin Laden and Mullah Omar. The Pakistani government put thousands of troops into the operation, focusing on the Tribal Area and arresting large numbers of people suspected of supporting or sheltering al-Qa'eda members. This allowed the Activity to build up a computerised intelligence directory and carry out intensive 'contact analysis' of the links between al-Qa'eda terrorists and their supporters in the Tribal Area. Even if it produced few 'High-Value Targets', such an operation would make the area too dangerous for al-Qa'eda to use. But maintaining adequate cooperation with Pakistani organisations that previously fostered the Taliban government was always going to be difficult and there were soon complaints that the mission was being hampered by the unwillingness of President Pervez Musharraf to upset tribal leaders whose support he needed if he were to stay in power.[27]

There were now more than 6,000 special operations forces on active service across the world and the Activity was too small to provide the actionable intelligence for all those missions. It concentrated on supplying intelligence for Delta and DevGru as part of Task Force 121, developing the new intelligence techniques that had led to the capture of Saddam Hussein. Meanwhile, Tom O'Connell, Doug Brown, and O'Connell's military deputy Jerry Boykin, who had commanded Delta in Mogadishu in 1993 and was now a lieutenant-general, set about expanding the intelligence capabilities available to US special operations forces. Donald Rumsfeld was keen to build up the military's intelligence capabilities and in particular the 'preparation of the battlefield' role performed by the Activity. The shortage of intelligence support units had been exposed when the dire warnings of the problems of a post-war Iraq proved correct. Members of the DIA's Defence Humint Service had been drafted in to help provide human intelligence on the ground as allied troops struggled to control the insurgency in Iraq. It was an ad hoc arrangement that didn't work. The Defence Humint Service had developed during the latter stages of the Cold War and, while it had good Middle East specialists, they were largely deskmen without the battlefield awareness needed to support front-line special operations missions, and there simply weren't enough of them. So often the human intelligence operators sent to Iraq had no grounding in the Arabic language or culture. The obvious flaws of such an ad hoc system were cruelly exposed by the Iraqi insurgency.

The DIA set up a new organisation, the Strategic Support Branch to send out small teams of interrogators, analysts and agent-runners who understood the counter-terrorism/counter-insurgency threat and would also be able to brief task force commanders on all the intelligence available on their area of operations, be it from national agencies that had traditionally not allowed their intelligence to be passed to front-line commanders, or had been unable to do it in real time – like the NSA and the CIA – or basic tactical intelligence collected on the front line by GIs, the sort of intel that had too often in the past been ignored at command level. Many of the new intelligence operators would be civilians. Most would not have to acquire the high levels of physical fitness demanded for members of the Activity. They would be out of the line of fire, directing the intelligence effort to ensure that every piece of available intelligence was used to back up the front-line attempts to track down terrorists.

'We're trying to operationalize intelligence,' Jerry Boykin said. 'We are going to spend a lot more time in the future finding the enemy, determining who he's connected to, how he's trained, how he's financed, how he's supported, than we are manoeuvring in the battle-space. What we're trying to do is achieve the kind of synergy where our analysts are driving our collections. We caught Saddam Hussein because we had analysts putting a puzzle together where they were literally turning to operators across the room and saying: "Here's what I need you to get." The operator would then get imagery or capture an individual and interrogate him and then feed that information directly back to the analyst, who would put that into the puzzle and say: "OK, the next thing I need is the following".'[28]

At the same time as the DIA was expanding its human intelligence specialists to back up the special operations forces involved in the Global War on Terror, Doug Brown added 700 intelligence specialists to the teams planning and preparing special operations missions, both at Special Operations Command in Tampa, and in the five theatre commands covering the different parts of the world, in order to provide the actionable intelligence the special operations forces needed to do their job.[29]

None of this appeared particularly controversial, but one part of the expansion of the military intelligence machine was, and it sparked something resembling a turf war between the Pentagon and the CIA. Alongside the expansion of basic human intelligence collection measures to support the War on Terror, Rumsfeld was expanding the number of undercover special operations intelligence operatives sent into countries that might become targets in the future to carry out battlefield preparation, looking for potential targets and scouting routes for infiltration and exfiltration of the special operations forces that could carry out any attacks. Such operations were of course nothing new. Most of these missions were being carried out by the Activity, which had been mounting similar operations for a quarter of a century.

The difference was that they had never been carried out on quite the same scale and had only rarely received the kind of support at the highest levels that they were now getting from the US Defense Secretary, who also persuaded Congress to authorise the payment of up to $25 million a year 'to foreign forces, irregular forces, groups or individuals' to side with America against terrorists, another activity that had traditionally been the remit of the CIA. The number of operators and analysts in the Activity had to be dramatically increased to cope with all the new intelligence.[30]

It soon emerged that the countries being targeted by the heavily expanded Activity included not only those deemed to pose a threat to American interests, like Iran, North Korea and China, or where al-Qa'eda might operate unimpeded, like Somalia and Yemen, but also countries that were on America's side in the War on Terror like Indonesia, the Philippines and Georgia. The veteran American investigative journalist Seymour Hersh revealed at the beginning of 2005 that US special operations forces had been inside Iran for some months – in what appeared to be a reprise of the Activity's 1987 Prime Chance missions. They had been collecting intelligence on several dozen targets, including Iran's nuclear facilities. The aim of the mission was to provide targets that might be attacked by cruise missiles or a swift 'in-and-out' special operations mission. The special operations forces – almost certainly members of the Activity – had recruited local agents to gather intelligence on the nuclear facilities and had planted 'sniffer' sensors to sample the atmosphere and report any evidence of radioactive emissions. A separate operation to fly Global Hawk unmanned aerial vehicles over Iran sparked a UFO frenzy after 'red flashes, streaks of green and blue, and low, racing lights' were spotted in the skies above Iran.[31]

Tom O'Connell dismissed any suggestion that the expansion of undercover operations abroad meant that the military was muscling in on the CIA's territory. 'I have heard it said that there is a conspiracy within the Department of Defense to go and rip off the agency's capabilities,' he said. 'I can assure you that nothing could be further from the truth. One, there is enough work for everybody. Two, I don't think the relationship between the CIA and special operations forces has ever been closer, and, three, both have their own distinct role. The CIA can certainly provide many considerable advantages to special operations forces, but their primary mission is still to recruit spies, and the special operations forces are much larger than the CIA.'[32]

But the Pentagon admission that it had 'dramatically expanded' the number of clandestine reconnaissance missions inside countries with which America was not at war also raised a series of potential legal difficulties, quite apart from the fact that soldiers carrying out such missions would not be entitled to be treated as legal combatants under the terms of the Geneva Convention. Traditionally, the CIA was the only US organisation allowed to carry out 'covert' missions – a term widely understood in US government and legislative circles to mean operations that were deniable – and all such operations had to have been authorised by the President in advance. The military was entitled to carry out 'clandestine' missions, operations that although conducted secretively would be admitted if they came to light. But while the Pentagon insisted that the missions being carried out in a range of countries were 'clandestine', it also held open the possibility that if such operations were uncovered they would be denied. The US military was also obliged by law to inform both Congress and the State Department in advance of any 'significant' intelligence activities in foreign countries, which had always been taken to include operations where those taking part might be killed or where US foreign policy objectives might be damaged if the mission became public.[33]

Rumsfeld, who wanted to remove the bureaucratic barriers that had prevented the Activity doing its job in the past, had already side-stepped the rules, persuading President Bush to sign a number of Presidential Findings, including one authorising the military 'to find and finish' terrorist targets. The Defense Secretary received important support for his expansion of special operations intelligence capability from the National Commission on Terrorist Attacks upon the United States in July 2004. The commission, which had examined the reaction to the al-Qa'eda threat ahead of the 9/11 attacks, recommended that the military take responsibility for all paramilitary operations 'whether clandestine or covert'. The CIA should divest itself of its paramilitary Special Activities Division, despite the latter's success working alongside special operations forces in Afghanistan and Iraq, and all such operations should become the responsibility of the Pentagon.[34]

President Bush also made it clear in November 2004, in a consolidated War Powers Report to Congress, that special operations forces would carry out missions around the world as part of the Global War on Terror and that it was not possible to predict what form those missions might take. 'I will direct additional measures as necessary in the exercise of the US right to self-defense and to protect U.S. citizens and interests,' the President said. 'Such measures may include short-notice deployments of special operations and other forces for sensitive operations in various locations throughout the world. It is not possible to know at this time either the precise duration of combat operations or the precise scope and duration of the deployment of U.S. Armed Forces necessary to counter the terrorist threat to the United States.' That presidential report to Congress arguably legitimised any special operations counter-terrorist mission ordered by Rumsfeld. At any event, Tom O'Connell rejected any suggestion that the undercover spying missions might be illegal. 'Many of the restrictions imposed on the Defense Department were imposed by tradition, by legislation, and by interpretations of various leaders and legal advisors,' he said. 'The interpretations take on the force of law and may preclude activities that are legal.' The Pentagon had always had the authority to carry out such missions but these had been 'winnowed away over the years'. He praised Rumsfeld's attitude to special operations forces, saying that the Defense Secretary had forced officials to discard the old 'hide-bound way of thinking' and 'risk-averse mentalities' previously prevalent within the Pentagon, and he warned that any country which failed to live up to its international responsibilities and allowed terrorists to use its territory was likely to be a target of US special operations forces. 'Those responsibilities include the requirement to stop terrorism within its borders,' O'Connell said. 'And if you can't do that as a sovereign nation, you can expect the United States to have to respond.'[35]

Another graphic example of the US willingness to attack terrorists wherever they might try to hide occurred in May 2005, shortly after the arrest by Pakistani security forces of a senior member of al-Qa'eda, Abu Faraj al-Libbi. He was tracked down by US signals intelligence operators on the ground in Pakistan, almost certainly members of the Activity, who pinpointed the location of his cellphone. Analysis of al-Libbi's previous calls led the US team to one of his colleagues, a Libyan member of al-Qa'eda known as Haitham al-Yemeni. On 7 May, six days after al-Libbi was arrested, al-Yemeni's cellphone was tracked to a car in the small village of Toorikhel, close to the town of Mirali in North Waziristan, the heart of the Tribal Areas. The Pakistani newspaper *Dawn*[36] reported that a bomb inside a car containing two men had exploded, killing both al-Yemeni and another man, Samiullah Khan. But in fact, as in the incident in Yemen more than two years earlier, the car and its occupants had been destroyed by a Hellfire missile, fired by a CIA Predator unmanned aerial vehicle. Amnesty International accused the US of an illegal 'extrajudicial killing' and pointed out that the UN Special Rapporteur on extrajudicial, summary or arbitrary executions had been highly critical of the US approach. But the US dismissed the criticism. Al-Qa'eda terrorists were 'enemy combatants' and as such 'lawful subjects of armed attacks'.

THE USE OF special operations forces to prosecute the Global War on Terror is arguably the only way forward, but it will remain controversial, particularly given the willingness of at least one of its key architects to compare it to the Phoenix programme in Vietnam, which led to the deaths of more than 20,000 people. 'I think we're running that kind of programme,' Boykin said. 'We're going after these people. Killing or capturing these people is a legitimate mission for the department. I think we're doing what the Phoenix programme was designed to do, without all of the secrecy.'[37] Having finally been accepted as an indispensable part of the special operations community, the Activity is likely to be at the heart of that programme for some years to come. Whether running agents into terrorist groups, tracking down their satellite or mobile telephones and computers, or simply providing the 'eyeball' on the ground that commanders need ahead of any military operation, the Activity is a top secret, elite force at the forefront of the War on Terror, dedicated to finding America's enemies, wherever they are and, if all else fails, taking them out. It is finally a true Killer Elite.

NOTES

Chapter 1

1 King from correspondence with Colonel Jerry M King, September to December 2004; background to rescue attempt and Vaught quote from Lucien S Vandenbroucke, *Perilous Options: Special Operations as an Instrument of US Foreign Policy*, OUP, New York, 1993; Susan L Marquis, *Unconventional Warfare: Rebuilding US Special Operations Forces*, Brookings Institute Press, Washington DC, 1997

2 Colonel John T Carney and Benjamin F Schemmer, *No Room for Error: The Covert Operations of America's Special Tactics Units from Iran to Afghanistan*, Ballantine Books, New York, 2002

3 Correspondence with Jerry M King, September–December 2004; for a good outline of the Studies and Observations Group and its activities see: *SOG: An Overview*, by Lieutenant-Colonel Robert L Turkoly-Joczik, Ph.D. (USA, Retired), at http://www.specialoperations.com/MACVSOG/Overview.htm

4 Correspondence with Jerry M King, September–December 2004

5 *ibid*

6 Lucien S Vandenbroucke, *Perilous Options: Special Operations as an Instrument of US Foreign Policy*

7 Colonel Charlie A Beckwith (Ret) and Donald Knox, *Delta Force: The Inside Story of America's Super-secret Counterterrorist Unit*, Fontana/Collins, Glasgow, 1985

8 Stansfield Turner, Intelligence for a New World Order, *Foreign Affairs*, Fall 1991

9 Steven Emerson, *Secret Warriors: Inside the Covert Military Operations of the Reagan Era*, Putnams, New York, 1988

10 Colonel John T Carney and Benjamin F Schemmer, *No Room for Error: The Covert Operations of America's Special Tactics Units from Iran to Afghanistan*

11 Correspondence with Jerry M King, September–December 2004

12 *ibid*

13 *ibid*

14 David C Martin and John Walcott, *Best Laid Plans: The Inside Story of America's War Against Terrorism*, Touchstone, New York, 1988; quote from former special forces intelligence officer from: William V Cowan, Clandestine and Covert Operations in Lt-Col H T Hayden USMC, *Shadow War: Special Operations and Low Intensity Conflict*, Pacific Aero Press, Vista CA, 1992

15 Correspondence with Jerry M King, September–December 2004

16 Colonel John T Carney in Colonel John T Carney and Benjamin F Schemmer, *No Room for Error: The Covert Operations of America's Special Tactics Units from Iran to Afghanistan*

17 Special Operations Review Group, *Rescue Mission Report*, Washington DC, August 23, 1980

18 Correspondence with Jerry M King, September–December 2004

19 Noel Koch, Objecting to Reality in Loren B Thompson, *Low-Intensity Conflict: The Pattern of Warfare in the Modern World*, Lexington Books, Lexington, 1989

20 Colonel John M Collins, 1946–1972: First Rejection and Resurrection in Benjamin F Schemmer & Col John T Carney Jr, *US Special Operations Forces*, Special Operations Warrior Foundation, Tampa, 2003; Tom Clancy with General Carl Stiner, *Shadow Warriors: Inside the Special Forces*, Pan, London, 2002; *SOG: An Overview*, by Lieutenant-Colonel Robert L Turkoly-Joczik, Ph.D. (USA, Retired), at http://www.specialoperations.com/MACVSOG/Overview.htm

21 William C Westmoreland, *A Soldier Reports*, New York, Doubleday, 1976; Charles N. Simpson, *Inside the Green Berets*, Navato, California: Presidio Press, 1983

22 *The Strategic Lessons Learned in Vietnam*, Vol 6, McLean, Virginia: BDM Corporation, 1979

23 Tim Weiner, *Blank Check: The Pentagon's Black Budget*, Warner, New York, 1990

24 Correspondence with Jerry M King, September–December 2004

25 *ibid*; Steven Emerson, *Secret Warriors: Inside the Covert Military Operations of the Reagan Era*; Tim Weiner, *Blank Check: The Pentagon's Black Budget*

26 Special Operations Review Group, *Rescue Mission Report*, Washington DC, August 23, 1980

27 Steven Emerson, *Secret Warriors: Inside the Covert Military Operations of the Reagan Era*; John M Collins, *Special Operations Forces: An Assessment*, National Defense University Press, Washington DC, 1994

28 Colonel John T Carney and Benjamin F Schemmer, *No Room for Error: The Covert Operations of America's Special Tactics Units from Iran to Afghanistan*; Geoffrey T Barker, *A Concise History of US Army Special Operations Forces*, Anglo-American, Fayatteville, 1988; Steven Emerson, *Secret Warriors: Inside the Covert Military Operations of the Reagan Era*; A Warrior Elite For the Dirty Jobs; America's growing Special Forces seek a role, *Time Magazine*, 13 January 1986. Task Force 160 is now the 160th Special Operations Aviation Regiment, known as 'The Night Stalkers', while Detachment One, Military Airlift Command Operations Staff is now 24th Special Tactics Squadron. Both remain special mission units under the operational control of the JSOC.

29 Memorandum for Director, Defense Intelligence Agency, Subject: Intelligence Capability, dated 10 December 1980, obtained under the FOIA by Jeffrey Richelson

30 Steven Emerson, *Secret Warriors: Inside the Covert Military Operations of the Reagan Era*

31 Jeffrey T Richelson, 'Truth Conquers All Chains': The US Army Intelligence Support Activity, 1981–1989, in *International Journal of Intelligence and Counter-intelligence*, Volume 12, Number 2; White House to Put Limits on Secret Army Spy Unit, *Los Angeles Times*, 15 May, 1983; Secret Army Intelligence Unit lived on after 1980 Iran Mission, *Washington Post*, 23 August, 1983

32 Information supplied to the author in confidence; Susan L Marquis, *Unconventional Warfare: Rebuilding US Special Operations Forces*, Brookings Institute Press, Washington DC, 1997

33 USAISA Brief History of Unit, *circa* 1985, obtained under FOIA by Jeffrey T Richelson

Chapter 2

1 Information supplied to the author in confidence; Dozier's 42 Days in a Tent, *Newsweek*, 15 February 1982; 'Please dear God... make it the right time', *United Press International*, 5 February 1982; Dozier: The Captive General Safe at Home, *Newsweek*, 23 January 1984; Steven Emerson, *Secret Warriors: Inside the Covert Military Operations of the Reagan Era*, Putnams, New York, 1988; David C Martin and John Walcott, *Best Laid Plans: The Inside Story of America's War Against Terrorism*, Touchstone, New York, 1988; Police raid suspect hideouts for kidnapped general, Associated Press, 19 December 1981

2 Steven Emerson, *Secret Warriors: Inside the Covert Military Operations of the Reagan Era*; David C Martin and John Walcott, *Best Laid Plans: The Inside Story of America's*

War Against Terrorism; Fat Man, Tailor, Soldier, Spy; How the US and Italy got the Mafia to help find General Dozier, *Time Magazine*, 28 February 1983

3 *ibid*

4 Steven Emerson, *Secret Warriors: Inside the Covert Military Operations of the Reagan Era*

5 Information supplied to the author in confidence; Jeffrey T Richelson, 'Truth Conquers All Chains': The US Army Intelligence Support Activity, 1981-1989, in *International Journal of Intelligence and Counterintelligence*, Volume 12, Number 2

6 Information supplied to the author in confidence

7 *ibid*

8 Information supplied to the author in confidence; Operation Betrayal: Delta/SEAL Rescue Force Poised to Snatch American Hostages in Lebanon, *Soldier of Fortune*, October 1989

9 Information supplied to the author in confidence

10 *ibid*

11 Information supplied to the author in confidence; USAISA Brief History of Unit, *circa* 1985, obtained under Freedom of Information Act by Jeffrey T Richelson

12 Information supplied to the author in confidence

13 *ibid*

14 Jeffrey T Richelson, 'Truth Conquers All Chains': The US Army Intelligence Support Activity, 1981-1989, in *International Journal of Intelligence and Counterintelligence*, Volume 12, Number 2; USAISA Brief History of Unit, *circa* 1985, obtained under Freedom of Information Act by Jeffrey T Richelson

15 Information supplied to the author in confidence

16 How Dozier Was Rescued, *Newsweek*, 8 February 1982

17 Information supplied to the author in confidence

18 Steven Emerson, *Secret Warriors: Inside the Covert Military Operations of the Reagan Era*

19 Major blow to Europe's terrorism, *Christian Science Monitor*, 29 January 1982; Italy warned Nato of terror threat, *United Press International*, 11 January 1982; Capture two more Red Brigades suspects, *United Press International*, 12 January 1982; More clues linked to Dozier kidnap, *United Press International*, 14 January 1982

20 Fat Man, Tailor, Soldier, Spy; How the US and Italy got the Mafia to help find General Dozier, *Time Magazine*, 28 February 1983

21 Information provided to the author in confidence; Dozier tells his story, and the Red Brigades crackdown goes on, *Time Magazine*, 15 February 1982

22 Information provided to the author in confidence; How Dozier Was Rescued, *Newsweek*, 8 February 1982; In a dramatic raid, Italian commandos free a kidnapped US general, *Time Magazine*, 8 February 1982; Dozier tells his story, and the Red Brigades crackdown goes on, *Time Magazine*, 15 February 1982

23 David C Martin and John Walcott, *Best Laid Plans: The Inside Story of America's War Against Terrorism*

24 Washington News, *United Press International*, 10 February 1982

25 Information supplied to the author in confidence; Steven Emerson, *Secret Warriors: Inside the Covert Military Operations of the Reagan Era*

26 Information supplied to the author in confidence; Jeffrey T Richelson, 'Truth Conquers All Chains': The US Army Intelligence Support Activity, 1981–1989, in *International Journal of Intelligence and Counterintelligence*, Volume 12, Number 2

27 Information supplied to the author in confidence; Steven Emerson, *Secret Warriors: Inside the Covert Military Operations of the Reagan Era*; David C Martin and John Walcott, *Best Laid Plans: The Inside Story of America's War Against Terrorism*; Thomas K Adams, *US Special Operations Forces in Action: The Challenge of Unconventional Warfare*, Frank Cass, London, 1998

28 Secret Justice: Army Trials Could Cripple Covert Operations, *Washington Post*, 18 May 1986; Who's in Charge Here?, *The New York Times*, 20 December 1987

29 Information supplied to the author in confidence; Army's Covert Role Scrutinized; Financial Probe Raises Fear That Special Units 'Got Carried Away', *The Washington Post*, 29 November 1985

30 Information supplied to the author in confidence; Steven Emerson, *Secret Warriors: Inside the Covert Military Operations of the Reagan Era*; Tim Weiner, *Blank Check: The Pentagon's Black Budget*, Warner, New York, 1990

31 Information supplied to the author in confidence; Steven Emerson, *Secret Warriors: Inside the Covert Military Operations of the Reagan Era*; The Secret Army: Ambitious Goals, Exotic Names – But Disappointing Results, *Time Magazine*, 31 August 1987; David C Martin and John Walcott, *Best Laid Plans: The Inside Story of America's War Against Terrorism*; Tim Weiner, *Blank Check: The Pentagon's Black Budget*

Chapter 3

1 Information supplied to the author in confidence; Steven Emerson, *Secret Warriors: Inside the Covert Military Operations of the Reagan Era*, Putnams, New York, 1988

2 Kill Two Americans and Government Official, *The Associated Press*, 4 January 1981; Salvadoran Junta enacts Martial Law, *The New York Times*, 12 January 1981; US

Sending Salvador Weapons and Supplies Valued at $5million, *The New York Times*, 18 January 1981; El Salvador's Future – and How U.S. Can Influence It, *US News & World Report*, 26 January 1981

3 US white paper on El Salvador, *Christian Science Monitor*, 26 February 1981

4 Fred Woerner, The Strategic Imperatives for the US in Latin America, *Military Review*, February 1989; Special Report; The Secret Wars Of The CIA, *Newsweek*, 5 October 1987; Playing for High Stakes; Reagan dispatches more 'trainers' to El Salvador, *Time Magazine*, 16 March 1981; Eric L Haney, *Inside Delta Force*, Dell, New York, 2002

5 Lieutenant-Colonel David H A Shepherd, The British Experience in Counter-insurgency, in Lt-Col H T Hayden (ed), *Shadow War: Special Operations and Low Intensity Conflict*, Pacific Aero Press, Vista, CA., 1992

6 US Army Training and Doctrine Command, Joint Low-Intensity Conflict Project, Analytical Review of Low-Intensity Conflict, Ft. Monroe, Virginia, 1986

7 Dr James S Corum, The Air War in El Salvador, *Aerospace Power Journal*, Summer 1998

8 Ross Kelly, Special operations In El Salvador, *Defense and Foreign Affairs*, August/September 1986; James Adams, *Secret Armies: The Full Story of the SAS, Delta Force, and Spetsnaz*, Pan, London, 1988

9 Holly Sklar, *Washington's War on Nicaragua*, South End Press, Cambridge, 1988; James Adams, *Secret Armies: The Full Story of the SAS, Delta Force, and Spetsnaz*; Steven Emerson, *Secret Warriors: Inside the Covert Military Operations of the Reagan Era*

10 Information supplied to the author in confidence; Steven Emerson, *Secret Warriors: Inside the Covert Military Operations of the Reagan Era*

11 Information supplied to the author in confidence; Ross Kelly, Special Operations in Honduras, *Defense and Foreign Affairs*, October 1986

12 Information supplied to the author in confidence; Steven Emerson, *Secret Warriors: Inside the Covert Military Operations of the Reagan Era*; Secret Warriors, *US News & World Report*, March 21, 1988

13 Steven Emerson, *Secret Warriors: Inside the Covert Military Operations of the Reagan Era*

14 US Congress, Senate Select Committee on POW/MIA Affairs, *POWs/MIA*, Washington DC, US Government Printing Office, 1993

15 James 'Bo' Gritz, *A Nation Betrayed*, Lazarus, Boulder City, 1988

16 The Americans Left Behind, *Time Magazine*, 17 October 1994

17 James 'Bo' Gritz, *A Nation Betrayed*; New Evidence Rekindles POW Issue,

Chicago Sun-Times, 3 June 1992; The Americans Left Behind, *Time Magazine*, 17 October 1994

18 James 'Bo' Gritz, *A Nation Betrayed*; Eric L Haney, *Inside Delta Force*

19 James 'Bo' Gritz, *A Nation Betrayed*

20 Information provided to the author in confidence

21 James 'Bo' Gritz, *A Nation Betrayed*

22 Information provided to the author in confidence; James 'Bo' Gritz, *A Nation Betrayed*

23 *ibid*

24 James 'Bo' Gritz, *A Nation Betrayed*

25 Information provided to the author in confidence

26 Information provided to the author in confidence; James 'Bo' Gritz, *A Nation Betrayed*

27 Information provided to the author in confidence

28 James 'Bo' Gritz, *A Nation Betrayed*

29 Information provided to the author in confidence

30 Information provided to the author in confidence; Steven Emerson, *Secret Warriors: Inside the Covert Military Operations of the Reagan Era*; Jeffrey T Richelson, 'Truth Conquers All Chains': The US Army Intelligence Support Activity, 1981–1989, in *International Journal of Intelligence and Counterintelligence*, Volume 12, Number 2

31 Steven Emerson, *Secret Warriors: Inside the Covert Military Operations of the Reagan Era*; Jeffrey T Richelson, 'Truth Conquers All Chains': The US Army Intelligence Support Activity, 1981–1989, in *International Journal of Intelligence and Counterintelligence*, Volume 12, Number 2

32 *ibid*

33 Memorandum to the Deputy Under-Secretary for Policy from Frank C Carlucci, Deputy Defense Secretary, dated 26 May 1982. Obtained under FOIA by Jeffrey T Richelson

34 White House To Put Limits On Army's Secret Spy Unit, *Los Angeles Times*, 15 May 1983; White House To Put Limits On Secret Army Spy Unit, Paper Says, *The Associated Press*, 15 May 1983; Steven Emerson, *Secret Warriors: Inside the Covert Military Operations of the Reagan Era*; Jeffrey T Richelson, 'Truth Conquers All Chains': The US Army Intelligence Support Activity, 1981–1989, in *International Journal of Intelligence and Counterintelligence*, Volume 12, Number 2

35 Information provided to the author in confidence

36 Correspondence with Jerry King, November 2004

37 Charter of the US Army Intelligence Support Activity, obtained under FOIA by Jeffrey T Richelson; Executive Order 12333–United States intelligence activities, dated 4 December 1981, available at http://www.cia.gov/cia/information/eo12333.html

Chapter Four

1 US Consular Officer Tells of Explosion, *Associated Press*, 20 April 1983; Death van delivers bomb to the U.S. Embassy, *United Press International*, 22 April 1983

2 Death van delivers bomb to the U.S. Embassy, *United Press International*, 22 April 1983; Streets Filled With Lunchtime Strollers, *Associated Press*, 18 April 1983; Evidence Lacking In Bombing at Beirut Embassy, *The Washington Post*, 20 May 1983; US Embassy in Lebanon Devastated by Bomb Blast; Dozens Killed, Pro-Iran Group Named, *Facts on File World News Digest*, 22 April 1983; Eric Haney, *Inside Delta Force*, Dell, New York, 2002

3 The Explosion at the US Embassy in Beirut, Radio Free Lebanon 1345 gmt and 1645 gmt, 18 April 1983, *BBC Summary of World Broadcasts, Part IV*, 20 April 1983; A Beirut Whodunnit with the Last Page Missing, *The Economist*, 23 April 1983

4 Information provided to the author in confidence; Standing Firm in Lebanon, *Heritage Foundation Reports*, 24 October 1983; What America hasn't learned from its greatest peacekeeping disaster, *Washington Monthly*, October 1989

5 Steven Emerson, *Secret Warriors: Inside the Covert Military Operations of the Reagan Era*, Putnams, New York, 1988

6 Correspondence with Bill Cowan, October and November 2004

7 Correspondence with Bill Cowan, October and November 2004. The Provincial Reconstruction Units were set up as part of the Phoenix pacification programme, which was effectively run by the CIA and which sent out teams to kill Viet Cong suspects and collect intelligence (see John Prados, *President's Secret Wars*, Quill, New York, 1988).

8 Correspondence with Bill Cowan, October and November 2004

9 Information provided to the author in confidence

10 Interview with Bill Cowan for *PBS Frontline: Target America*, available at http://www.pbs.org/wgbh/pages/frontline/shows/target/interviews/cowan.html

11 *ibid*

12 Information provided to the author in confidence

13 Interview with Bill Cowan for *PBS Frontline: Target America*, available as above

14 Tom Clancy with General Carl Stiner, *Shadow Warriors: Inside the Special Forces*, Pan, London, 2002

15 *ibid*

16 Interview with Bill Cowan for *PBS Frontline: Target America*, available as above

17 Information provided to the author in confidence

18 Information provided to the author in confidence

19 Operation Betrayal, *Soldier of Fortune*, October 1989; Land of Hope and Travail, *Sports Illustrated*, 5 September 1983; David C Martin and John Walcott, *Best Laid Plans: The Inside Story of America's War Against Terrorism*, Touchstone, New York, 1988; Hostages clean up mess from bloody rescue, *United Press International*, 9 July 1983; Courage and code helped free hostages aid workers in Kenya, *United Press International*, 16 July 1983; Reagan Hails Sudanese Rescue, *The Associated Press*, 9 July 1983; Five ex-hostages reach Khartoum, *The New York Times*, 13 July 1983

20 David C Martin and John Walcott, *Best Laid Plans: The Inside Story of America's War Against Terrorism*

21 Susan L Marquis, *Unconventional Warfare: Rebuilding US Special Operations Forces*, Brookings Institute Press, Washington DC, 1997

22 Invitation to September 11, *Insight*, 1 June 2004; Tom Clancy with General Carl Stiner, *Shadow Warriors: Inside the Special Forces*

23 A Warm, Sunny, Lazy Sunday Morning of Horror, *Associated Press*, 30 October 1983

24 Tom Clancy with General Carl Stiner, *Shadow Warriors: Inside the Special Forces*

25 Information provided to the author in confidence

26 Susan L Marquis, *Unconventional Warfare: Rebuilding US Special Operations Forces*

27 Reagan Takes Blame for Beirut Security Failure; Military Report Criticizes Commanders and Policy; Reagan Bars Punishment of Officers, *Facts on File World News Digest*, 31 December 1983; Report Hits U.S. Reliance on Force In Lebanon, *The Washington Post*, 29 December 1983; The Politics of Blame, *Newsweek*, 9 January 1984

28 Interview with Bill Cowan for *PBS Frontline: Target America*, available as above; What America hasn't learned from its greatest peacekeeping disaster, *Washington Monthly*, October 1989

29 Invitation to September 11, *Insight*, 1 June 2004

30 Susan L Marquis, *Unconventional Warfare: Rebuilding US Special Operations Forces*; James Adams, *Secret Armies: The Full Story of the SAS, Delta Force and Spetsnatz*, Pan, London, 1988; Lucien S Vandenbroucke, *Perilous Options: Special Operations as an Instrument of US Foreign Policy*, OUP, New York, 1993

31 Information provided to the author in confidence; James Adams, *Secret Armies: The Full Story of the SAS, Delta Force and Spetsnatz*

32 Information provided to the author in confidence

33 Eric L Haney, *Inside Delta Force*

34 Correspondence with Bill Cowan, October 2004–March 2005

35 Colonel John T Carney and Benjamin F Schemmer, *No Room for Error: The Covert Operations of America's Special Tactics Units from Iran to Afghanistan*, Ballantine Books, New York, 2002

Chapter 5

1 Information provided to the author in confidence

2 Information provided to the author in confidence. William V Cowan, Clandestine and Covert Operations in Lt-Col H T Hayden USMC, *Shadow War: Special Operations and Low Intensity Conflict*, Pacific Aero Press, Vista CA, 1992; interview with Bill Cowan for *PBS Frontline: Target America*, available at http://www.pbs.org/wgbh/pages/frontline/shows/target/interviews/cowan.html; Steven Emerson, *Secret Warriors: Inside the Covert Military Operations of the Reagan Era*, Putnams, New York, 1988

3 Information provided to the author in confidence; Steven Emerson, *Secret Warriors: Inside the Covert Military Operations of the Reagan Era*

4 William V Cowan, Clandestine and Covert Operations in Lt-Col H T Hayden USMC, *Shadow War: Special Operations and Low Intensity Conflict*; interview with Bill Cowan for *PBS Frontline: Target America*, available as above

5 US Bombers hit Lebanon, Syrians Down 2, Reagan Issues Warning, 8 Marines Killed, *The New York Times*, 5 December 1983

6 Correspondence with Bill Cowan, May 2005

7 Correspondence with Bill Cowan, May 2005; Steven Emerson, *Secret Warriors: Inside the Covert Military Operations of the Reagan Era*

8 Interview with Bill Cowan for *PBS Frontline: Target America*, available as above

9 Invitation to September 11, *Insight*, 1 June 2004

10 Steven Emerson, *Secret Warriors: Inside the Covert Military Operations of the Reagan Era*

11 Strike Back? Just as Soon as the Paperwork's Ready, *Washington Post*, 23 April 1989

12 *ibid*

13 Eric L Haney, *Inside Delta Force*, Dell, New York, 2002

14 Strike Back? Just as Soon as the Paperwork's Ready, *Washington Post*, 23 April 1989; interview with Bill Cowan for *PBS Frontline: Target America*, available as above

15 Strike Back ? Just as Soon as the Paperwork's Ready, *Washington Post*, 23 April 1989

16 Terrorists kidnap American professor, *United Press International*, 10 February 1984; Abductees Rescued by Militia, *Fact on File World News Digest*, 27 April 1984; US Civilians Evacuated From Beirut, *The Washington Post*, 11 February 1984

17 US envoy Seized in West Beirut, *The New York Times*, 17 March 1984; Tom Clancy with General Carl Stiner, *Shadow Warriors: Inside the Special Forces*, Pan, London, 2002

18 Information provided to the author in confidence

19 Information provided to the author in confidence; Jeffrey T Richelson, 'Truth Conquers All Chains': The US Army Intelligence Support Activity, 1981–1989, in *International Journal of Intelligence and Counterintelligence*, Volume 12, Number 2

20 *ibid*

21 Jeffrey T Richelson, 'Truth Conquers All Chains': The US Army Intelligence Support Activity, 1981–1989, in *International Journal of Intelligence and Counter-intelligence*, Volume 12, Number 2

22 The Island Paradise that's becoming a Communist Stronghold, *Business Week*, 19 November 1984; Rene re-elected president of Seychelles, *United Press International*, 18 June 1984

23 Steven Emerson, *Secret Warriors: Inside the Covert Military Operations of the Reagan Era*

24 William V Cowan, Clandestine and Covert Operations in Lt-Col H T Hayden USMC, *Shadow War: Special Operations and Low Intensity Conflict*

25 Steven Emerson, *Secret Warriors: Inside the Covert Military Operations of the Reagan Era*

26 Information provided to the author in confidence

27 Information provided to the author in confidence

28 Information provided to the author in confidence

29 Tim Weiner, *Blank Check: The Pentagon's Black Budget*, Warner Books, New York, 1990

30 *ibid*

31 Steven Emerson, *Secret Warriors: Inside the Covert Military Operations of the Reagan Era*

32 Tim Weiner, *Blank Check: The Pentagon's Black Budget*; Steven Emerson, *Secret Warriors: Inside the Covert Military Operations of the Reagan Era*

33 Information provided to the author in confidence

34 Information provided to the author in confidence

35 Who's In Charge Here, *The New York Times*, 20 December 1987

36 Information provided to the author in confidence

37 Tim Weiner, *Blank Check: The Pentagon's Black Budget*

38 The Secret Army; Ambitious goals, exotic names – but disappointing results, *Time Magazine*, 31 August 1987; Army Court Overturns Court-Martial of Secret Unit's Chief, *The Washington Post*, 1 July 1988; Army Colonel is Ordered Freed, *The New York Times*, 26 November 1986; Tim Weiner, *Blank Check: The Pentagon's Black Budget*

Chapter Six

1 Operation Betrayal: Delta/SEAL Rescue Force Poised to Snatch American Hostages in Lebanon, *Soldier of Fortune*, October 1989; Hostage Rescue: US Has Done No Detailed Planning Since An Effort Was Abandoned in '86, *Newsday*, 12 August 1989

2 Beirut's Friday Bomber, *Newsweek*, 18 March 1985; Beirut Bombings Trigger Threats Against US, *The New York Times*, 10 March 1985; Car Bomb Kills 62 Outside Beirut Near Home of a Top Shi'ite Cleric, *The New York Times*, 9 March 1985; Bob Woodward, *Veil: The Secret Wars of the CIA, 1981–1987*, Simon and Schuster, New York, 1987; Judith Miller, Faces of Fundamentalism, *Foreign Affairs*, November/December 1994

3 Interview with Bill Cowan for *PBS-Frontline: Target America*, available at http://www.pbs.org/wgbh/pages/frontline/shows/target/interviews/cowan.html

4 The Secret Army; Ambitious Goals, Exotic Names – But Disappointing Results, *Time Magazine*, 31 August 1987

5 Information provided to the author in confidence; Special Operations in Latin America: Overview II – The 'North American Connection', *Defense and Foreign Affairs*, July 1986

6 United States Claims Nicaraguans Running Guns to Honduras, *IPS-Inter Press Service*, 29 April 1985; Nicaraguan President Moscow Visit 'Strengthens Ties With Moscow', *United Press International*, 29 April 1985

7 United States Army Intelligence Support Activity 1986 Historical Report, obtained under FOIA by Jeffrey Richelson; After-Action Report For Operation Canvas Shield, dated 30 July 1985, obtained under FOIA by Jeffrey Richelson; Holly Sklar, *Washington's War on Nicaragua*, South End Press, Cambridge, Mass, 1988; US Military Is Termed Prepared for Any Move Against Nicaragua, *The New York Times*, 4 June 1985; An Invasion is Openly Discussed, *The New York Times*, 5 June 1985; information provided to the author in confidence

8 Susan L Marquis, *Unconventional Warfare: Rebuilding US Special Operations Forces*, Brookings Institute Press, Washington DC, 1997; Steven Emerson, *Secret Warriors: Inside the Covert Military Operations of the Reagan Era*, Putnams, New York, 1988; Tom Clancy with General Carl Stiner, *Shadow Warriors: Inside the Special Forces*, Pan, London, 2002

9 Information provided to the author in confidence; Steven Emerson, *Secret Warriors: Inside the Covert Military Operations of the Reagan Era*; Tom Clancy with General Carl Stiner, *Shadow Warriors: Inside the Special Forces*; Operation Betrayal: Delta/SEAL Rescue Force Poised to Snatch American Hostages in Lebanon, *Soldier of Fortune*, October 1989; Mission Improbable, *Washington Monthly*, June 1990

10 Tom Clancy with General Carl Stiner, *Shadow Warriors: Inside the Special Forces*

11 Strike Back? Just as Soon as the Paperwork's Ready, *Washington Post*, 23 April 1989

12 Steven Emerson, *Secret Warriors: Inside the Covert Military Operations of the Reagan Era*; Jeffrey T Richelson, 'Truth Conquers All Chains': The US Army Intelligence Support Activity, 1981–1989, in *International Journal of Intelligence and Counterintelligence*, Volume 12, Number 2

13 Tom Clancy with General Carl Stiner, *Shadow Warriors: Inside the Special Forces*

14 John Tower, Edmund Muskie, Brent Scowcroft, *The Tower Commission Report*, Bantam/ Times Books, New York, 1987; David C Martin and John Walcott, *Best Laid Plans: The Inside Story of America's War Against Terrorism*, Touchstone, New York, 1989

15 Interview with Bill Cowan for *PBS Frontline: Target America*, available as above

16 National Security Decision Directive Number 207, The National Programme for Combating Terrorism, dated 20 January 1986

17 Operation Betrayal: Delta/SEAL Rescue Force Poised to Snatch American Hostages in Lebanon, *Soldier of Fortune*, October 1989; Hostage Rescue: US Has Done No Detailed Planning Since An Effort Was Abandoned in '86, *Newsday*, 12 August 1989; United States Army Intelligence Support Activity 1986 Historical Report, obtained under FOIA by Jeffrey Richelson

18 Operation Betrayal: Delta/SEAL Rescue Force Poised to Snatch American Hostages in Lebanon, *Soldier of Fortune*, October 1989

19 John Tower, Edmund Muskie, Brent Scowcroft, *The Tower Commission Report*

20 United States Army Intelligence Support Activity 1986 Historical Report, obtained under FOIA by Jeffrey Richelson

21 United States Army Intelligence Support Activity 1986 Historical Report, obtained under FOIA by Jeffrey Richelson; information provided to the author in confidence

22 Operation Betrayal: Delta/SEAL Rescue Force Poised to Snatch American Hostages in Lebanon, *Soldier of Fortune*, October 1989

23 Operation Betrayal: Delta/SEAL Rescue Force Poised to Snatch American Hostages in Lebanon, *Soldier of Fortune*, October 1989; Steven Emerson, *Secret Warriors: Inside the Covert Military Operations of the Reagan Era*; Hostage Rescue: US Has Done No Detailed Planning Since An Effort Was Abandoned in '86, *Newsday*, 12 August 1989

24 Information provided to the author in confidence

25 John Tower, Edmund Muskie, Brent Scowcroft, *The Tower Commission Report*; David C Martin and John Walcott, *Best Laid Plans: The Inside Story of America's War Against Terrorism*

26 Information provided to the author in confidence; United States Army Intelligence Support Activity 1986 Historical Report, obtained under FOIA by Jeffrey Richelson

27 Operation Betrayal: Delta/SEAL Rescue Force Poised to Snatch American Hostages in Lebanon, *Soldier of Fortune*, October 1989

28 *ibid*

29 Hostage Rescue: US Has Done No Detailed Planning Since An Effort Was Abandoned in '86, *Newsday*, 12 August 1989; Mission Improbable, *Washington Monthly*, June 1990; American Abducted At Beirut University; Second Kidnapping This Week Shakes Dwindling School Staff, *The Washington Post*, 13 September 1986; American Kidnapped in Beirut, Islamic Jihad Says School Director was a Spy, *Chicago Tribune*, 10 September 1986

30 United States Army Intelligence Support Activity 1987 Historical Report, obtained under FOIA by Jeffrey Richelson

31 John Tower, Edmund Muskie, Brent Scowcroft, *The Tower Commission Report*; US Sent Iran Arms for Hostage Releases, *Los Angeles Times*, 6 November 1986

32 Interview with Bill Cowan for *PBS Frontline: Target America*, available as above

Chapter Seven

1 Mark Bowden, *Killing Pablo: The Hunt for the Richest Most Powerful Criminal in History*, Atlantic Books, London, 2002; Martinez Extradited, *The Associated Press*, 6 September 1989; Drug Violence Clouds Colombia's Day of Love, *Los Angeles Times*, 17 September 1989; A Hireling in the Footsteps of Pablo Escobar, *The Independent*, 16 September 1989; Terror in the Drug World, *Maclean's*, 11 September 1989; Colombia Rocked by 5 Explosions, *St. Louis Post-Dispatch*, 18 September 1989

2 Reagan Order Defines Drug Trade as Security Threat, Widens Military Role, *Washington Post*, 8 June 1986

3 Ronald Reagan, National Security Strategy of the United States, released by the White House in January 1988, *Department of State Bulletin*, April, 1988; Walter Fischer,

Why More Special Forces Are Needed For Low-Intensity War, *Heritage Foundation Report*, 12 November 1987

4 Mark Bowden, *Killing Pablo: The Hunt for the Richest Most Powerful Criminal in History*

5 Jeffrey T Richelson, 'Truth Conquers All Chains': The US Army Intelligence Support Activity, 1981–1989, in *International Journal of Intelligence and Counterintelligence*, Volume 12, Number 2; information provided to the author in confidence

6 Susan L Marquis, *Unconventional Warfare: Rebuilding US Special Operations Forces*, Brookings Institute Press, Washington DC, 1997

7 Colonel David A McKnight, MI Corps Hall of Fame: 2003 Military Intelligence Corps Hall of Fame inductees, *Military Intelligence Professional Bulletin*, April–June 2003; information provided to the author in confidence; *US Special Operations Command, 10th Anniversary History*, April 1997; US Military Leaders Prepare Plans for Possible Retaliation, *Washington Post*, 17 October 1987; US Destroyers Shell Iranian Military Platform in Gulf; Retaliation for Silkworm Attack Called 'Measured and Appropriate', *Washington Post*, 20 October 1987; Special Army Helicopter Unit Attacked Iranian Ship, *Associated Press*, 24 September 1987; US Plans to Send Elite Units to Gulf; Pentagon Counters New Iranian Threats, *Washington Post*, 5 August 1987

8 Army Officer Charged With Theft of 201 Guns, *Associated Press*, 15 September 1988. [Michael L Smith is no relation to the author.]

9 Jeffrey T Richelson, 'Truth Conquers All Chains': The US Army Intelligence Support Activity, 1981-1989, in *International Journal of Intelligence and Counterintelligence*, Volume 12, Number 2; Signal from CDRUSAISA to various addresses entitled: Termination of USAISA and "Grantor Shadow" and dated 31 March 1989; United States Army Intelligence Support Activity 1986 Historical Report, obtained under FOIA by Jeffrey Richelson; William M Arkin, *Code Names: Deciphering US Military Plans, Programs, and Operations in the 9/11 World*, Steerforth Press, Hanover, NH 2005

10 Information provided to the author in confidence

11 *US Special Operations Command, 10th Anniversary History*, April 1997; Colonel John T Carney and Benjamin F Schemmer, *No Room for Error: The Covert Operations of America's Special Tactics Units from Iran to Afghanistan*, Ballantine Books, New York, 2002; Night Airdrop in Panama Surprises Noriega's Forces, *Aviation Week & Space Technology*, 1 January 1990; The Force of the Future, *Newsweek*, 17 June 1991; Sowing Dragon's Teeth, *Time Magazine*, 1 January 1990; US drug policy on trial, *The Nation*, 2 December 1991; 'Silent option': Navy's elite SEALs, *VFW Magazine*, 1 June 2002; Special, Short, and Stealthy, *The National Journal*, 29 September 2001; Fallen OC warrior's name will carry on, *Orange County Register*, 25 April 1998; Special Forces: Checkered Past and Rambo Image Haunt America's Warrior Elite, *Chicago Tribune*, 26 August 1990; Communications Problems Hindered First Stage of Panama Invasion, *Jane's Defence Weekly*, 30 April 1990; Inside the Invasion, *Newsweek*, 25 June 1990

12 US is Sending Military Specialists to Train the Colombians, *The New York Times*, 1 September 1989; Ken Connor, *Ghost Force: The Secret History of the SAS*, Weidenfeld & Nicolson, London, 1998; UK enters Colombia drug war: Major pledges Royal Navy frigate and military advisers, *The Guardian*, 28 September 1989; British team sets up Colombian aid package, *The Guardian*, 11 September 1989

13 Hearing of the Permanent Investigations Sub-Committee of the Senate Government Affairs Committee on US Anti-Drug Activities in the Andean Region, *Federal News Service*, 26 September 1989; Drug war zone; Army Special Operations Forces reported combat in South America, *The Nation*, 11 December 1989

14 Ken Connor, *Ghost Force: The Secret History of the SAS*

15 Ken Connor, *Ghost Force: The Secret History of the SAS*; Andy McNab, *Immediate Action*, Bantam, London, 1995; Mike Curtis, *CQB: Close Quarter Battle*, Bantam, London, 1997

16 Mark Bowden, *Killing Pablo: The Hunt for the Richest Most Powerful Criminal in History*

17 CECOM's EW/RSTA: Developing a New Generation of Electronic Warfare System, *Defense Electronics*, October 1991; Who's Afraid of Cellular Phones; the Digital Cellular Threat, *Journal of Electronic Defense*, April 1999; COMINT goes to Cell Hell, *Journal of Electronic Defense*, June 1998; Locating Criminals by the Book, *Cellular Business*, June 1996

18 Locating Criminals by the Book, *Cellular Business*, June 1996; Mark Bowden, *Killing Pablo: The Hunt for the Richest Most Powerful Criminal in History*

19 CECOM's EW/RSTA: Developing a New Generation of Electronic Warfare System, *Defense Electronics*, October 1991; Who's Afraid of Cellular Phones; the Digital Cellular Threat, *Journal of Electronic Defense*, April 1999; COMINT goes to Cell Hell, *Journal of Electronic Defense*, June 1998; Locating Criminals by the Book, *Cellular Business*, June 1996; Mark Bowden, *Killing Pablo: The Hunt for the Richest Most Powerful Criminal in History*; Rowan Scarborough, *Rumsfeld's War: The Untold Story of America's Anti-Terrorist Commander*, Regnery Publishing, Washington, 2004

20 Special Forces for Special Times, *Milwaukee Journal Sentinel*, 30 September 2001; Simon Strong, *Whitewash: Pablo Escobar and the Cocaine Wars*, Macmillan, London, 1995

21 Colombia Candidate Slain; Bogotá Blames Drug Lord, *Los Angeles Times*, 23 March 1990; Government Blames Medellín Cartel In Candidate's Killing, *Associated Press*, 23 March 1990; Colombia, DL, *The Canadian Press*, 23 March 1990; Cartel blamed for Jaramillo's murder, *Latin America Regional Reports: Andean Group*, 12 April 1990

22 Mark Bowden, *Killing Pablo: The Hunt for the Richest Most Powerful Criminal in History*; Simon Strong, *Whitewash: Pablo Escobar and the Cocaine Wars*

23 Simon Strong, *Whitewash: Pablo Escobar and the Cocaine Wars*; Clare Hargreaves, *Snowfields: The War on Cocaine in the Andes*, Zed Books, London, 1992

24 Information provided to the author in confidence; General Sir Peter de la Billiere, *Storm Command*, HarperCollins, London, 1993; John Parker, *SBS: The Inside Story of the Special Boat Service*, Headline, London, 2003; Colonel John T Carney and Benjamin F Schemmer, *No Room for Error: The Covert Operations of America's Special Tactics Units from Iran to Afghanistan*

25 Douglas C Waller, *The Commandos: The Inside Story of America's Secret Soldiers*, Dell, New York, 1994; Revealed, *Sunday Times*, 26 August 1990; Tom Clancy with General Carl Stiner, *Shadow Warriors: Inside the Special Forces*, Pan, London, 2002; US bombs pipeline to stem oil flow; Preventive strike was ruled out, *Washington Times*, 28 January 1991; General Sir Peter de la Billiere, *Storm Command*

26 Information provided to the author in confidence; James Bamford, *Body of Secrets*, Century, London, 2001; General Sir Peter de la Billiere, *Storm Command*

27 Mark Bowden, *Killing Pablo: The Hunt for the Richest Most Powerful Criminal in History*

28 Mark Bowden, *Killing Pablo: The Hunt for the Richest Most Powerful Criminal in History*; Simon Strong, *Whitewash: Pablo Escobar: and the Cocaine Wars*; Special Forces for Special Times, *Milwaukee Journal Sentinel*, 30 September 2001

Chapter Eight

1 The Wily Warlord; Obituary: Mohammad Farah Aideed, *The Guardian*, 3 August 1996; Mark Bowden, *Killing Pablo: The Hunt for the Richest Most Powerful Criminal in History*, Atlantic Books, London, 2002

2 Major Clifford E Day, *Critical Analysis on the Defeat of Task Force Ranger*, The Research Department, Air Command and Staff College, March 1997; Colonel David A McKnight, MI Corps Hall of Fame: 2003 Military Intelligence Corps Hall of Fame inductees, *Military Intelligence Professional Bulletin*, April–June 2003; Mark Bowden, *Killing Pablo: The Hunt for the Richest Most Powerful Criminal in History*; Colonel John T Carney and Benjamin F Schemmer, *No Room for Error: The Covert Operations of America's Special Tactics Units from Iran to Afghanistan*, Ballantine Books, New York, 2002; information provided to the author in confidence

3 The Raid That Went Wrong; How an Elite U.S. Force Failed in Somalia, *Washington Post*, 30 January 1994; Senate Armed Services Committee Hearing: US Military Operations in Somalia, *Federal News Service*, 12 May 1994

4 The Raid That Went Wrong; How an Elite U.S. Force Failed in Somalia, *Washington Post*, 30 January 1994; After-Action Report, *Washington Post*, 27 February 2000

5 The Raid That Went Wrong; How an Elite U.S. Force Failed in Somalia, *Washington Post*, 30 January 1994; Mark Bowden, *Black Hawk Down*, Corgi, London, 1999;

After-Action Report, *Washington Post*, 27 February 2000; Aideed's Simplicity Baffles Rangers; Technology Passes Over Warlord, *Washington Times*, 1 September 1993

6 The Raid That Went Wrong; How an Elite U.S. Force Failed in Somalia, *Washington Post*, 30 January 1994; UN Mission in Somalia Seen Beset by Infiltrators, *Washington Post*, 7 September 1993

7 US Faults Intelligence in Failed Somalia Raid, *Los Angeles Times*, 31 August 1993; UN Mission in Somalia Seen Beset by Infiltrators, *Washington Post*, 7 September 1993; The Raid That Went Wrong; How an Elite U.S. Force Failed in Somalia, *Washington Post*, 30 January 1994; Mark Bowden, *Black Hawk Down*; After-Action Report, *Washington Post*, 27 February 2000

8 The Raid That Went Wrong; How an Elite U.S. Force Failed in Somalia, *Washington Post*, 30 January 1994; After-Action Report, *Washington Post*, 27 February 2000

9 UN Mission in Somalia Seen Beset by Infiltrators, *Washington Post*, 7 September 1993; Aideed's simplicity baffles Rangers, Technology passes over warlord, *Washington Times*, 1 September 1993; After-Action Report, *Washington Post*, 27 February 2000; Tracking Aideed Hampered By Intelligence Failures, *Washington Post*, 8 October 1993

10 After-Action Report, *Washington Post*, 27 February 2000; Mark Bowden, *Black Hawk Down*

11 The Raid That Went Wrong; How an Elite U.S. Force Failed in Somalia, *Washington Post*, 30 January 1994; Major Clifford E Day, *Critical Analysis on the Defeat of Task Force Ranger*, The Research Department, Air Command and Staff College, March 1997

12 Major Clifford E Day, *Critical Analysis on the Defeat of Task Force Ranger*; Mark Bowden, *Black Hawk Down*; A History of SF Operations in Somalia: 1992–1995, *Special Warfare*, 1 June 2002

13 Mark Bowden, *Black Hawk Down*; Thomas K Adams, *US Special Operations Forces in Action: The Challenge of Unconventional Warfare*, Frank Cass, London, 1998

14 Special Report, Interview with Timothy G Connolly, *Armed Forces Journal International*, November 1993

15 Details of U.S. Raid in Somalia: Success So Near, a Loss So Deep, *The New York Times*, 25 October 1993

16 Hunting War Criminals: The First Account of Secret US Missions in Bosnia, *US News and World Report*, 6 July 1998; Secret Meetings Foiled Karadžić Capture Plan; US Says French Jeopardized Mission, *The Washington Post*, 23 April 1998

17 US Moves Against Balkan War Criminal Karadžić's Support Network, *Federal Information and News Dispatch*, 7 March 2003; The Hunt For Karadzic, *Time Magazine*, 10 August 1998

18 Envisioning a Future of Casualty-free Pushbutton Wars? Get Over It, *The American Enterprise*, 1 October 2001; Britain Condemns US Plans to Seize Serb Leader, *Sunday Times*, 4 August 1996

19 Covert Unit Alive and Kicking, *Intelligence Newsletter*, 29 June 1995; http://www.asafm.army.mil/secretariat/document/dfas37-100/fy2003/docs/A0-2020D.doc; Prepared Statement of Jacquelyn L. Williams-Bridgers, Inspector-General of US State Department to House Committee on International Relations, *Federal News Service*, 17 July 1997

20 The Hunt For Karadžić, *Time Magazine*, 10 August 1998; When there's no place to hide, *The Herald*, 11 January 1999; Armando J Ramirez, *From Bosnia to Baghdad: The Evolution of US Army Special Forces from 1995–2004*, Naval Postgraduate School, Monterey, California, September 2004; Christian Jennings, *Midnight in Some Burning Town: British Special Forces Operations from Belgrade to Baghdad*, Weidenfeld & Nicolson, London, 2004

21 France Denies Officer Who Met With Karadžić Compromised Plans for Arrest, *Washington Post*, 24 April 1998; Karadžić Capture Foiled by Secret Talks, *Facts on File World News Digest*, 14 May 1998; The Hunt For Karadžić, *Time Magazine*, 10 August 1998

22 Hunting War Criminals: The First Account of Secret US Missions in Bosnia, *US News and World Report*, 6 July 1998; Malcolm Brailey, *Not Many Jobs Take a Whole Army: Special Operations Forces and the Revolution in Military Affairs*, Institute of Defence and Strategic Studies, March 2004

23 Hunted 'Mafia' Pair Ran Omarska Killing Grounds, *The Guardian*, 11 July 1997; Peacekeeping Troops Kill and Arrest War Crimes Suspects, *International Enforcement Law Reporter*, August 1997

24 Information provided to the author in confidence; Nato Troops Kill a Serbian Suspect in War Atrocities, *The New York Times*, 11 July 1997; NATO Moves on War Crimes Suspects; British Troops Kill One Bosnian Serb in Gunfight; Another Apprehended, *Washington Post*, 11 July 1987; Bosnian Serb Pleads Not Guilty to Genocide at Yugoslav Tribunal, *ANP English News Bulletin*, 1 August 1997; Peace-keeping Troops Kill and Arrest War Crimes Suspects, *International Enforcement Law Reporter*, August 1997; Dead or alive, *Sunday Times*, 13 July 1997

25 Alleged Bosnia War Criminals Nabbed, *Associated Press*, 18 December 1997; Dutch Troops Seize Two War Crimes Suspects, Wounding One, *The New York Times*, 19 December 1997; Arrest of Bosnian Croat war crimes suspects just the start: SFOR, *Agence France Presse*, 18 December 1997

26 Hunting War Criminals: The First Account of Secret US Missions in Bosnia, *US News and World Report*, 6 July 1998; Ex-war crimes prosecutor blasts US for inaction in Bosnia, *Agence France Presse*, 17 April 1998; The Reluctant Gendarme, *The Atlantic Monthly*, 1 April, 2000

27 US Troops in Bosnia Seize Genocide Suspect, *Los Angeles Times*, 23 January 1998; Bosnian Serbs plead not guilty to war crimes, *Agence France Presse*, 17 February 1998; Hunting War Criminals: The First Account of Secret US Missions in Bosnia, *US News and World Report*, 6 July 1998; Department of the Army Office of the Deputy Chief of Staff for Intelligence, Annual Historical Review, 1 October 1992 to 30 September 1993

28 Secret Meetings Foiled Karadžić Capture Plan; U.S. Says French Jeopardized Mission, *Washington Post*, 23 April 1998; The Reluctant Gendarme, *The Atlantic Monthly*, 1 April, 2000

29 Information provided to the author in confidence; Bosnian War Crimes Suspects Arrested; Two Are Accused In 1992 Atrocities, *Washington Post*, 9 April 1998; Arrest Refines Task of UN Conference, *Washington Post*, 16 June 1998; Department of the Army Office of the Deputy Chief of Staff for Intelligence, Annual Historical Review, 1 October 1992 to 30 September 1993

30 Information provided to the author in confidence; SAS Carried out Serbia Raid, *The Times*, 11 November 1998

31 Cees Wiebes, *Intelligence and the War in Bosnia 1992-1995*, LIT, Hamburg, 2003; NATO detains Bosnian Serb general charged with genocide, *Associated Press*, 2 December 1998; Bosnian Serb Wanted for Genocide Arrested; War Crimes Tribunal Charges General Led Massacre of Muslims, *Washington Post*, 3 December 1998; Major Bosnian War Crimes Suspect Caught, *Los Angeles Times*, 3 December 1998; Nato Arrests Serb Accused of Bosnia Massacre, *The Scotsman*, 3 December 1998; Special Forces for Special Times, *Milwaukee Journal Sentinel*, 30 September 2001; Bosnia Evidence Secret, *Newsday*, 8 November 1995

32 Statement on Fiscal 2005 Budget, by General James L Jones, Commander EUCOM, to House Armed Services Committee, *Federal Document Clearing House Congressional Testimony*, 24 March 2004

Chapter Nine

1 Lives Spared, Targets Destroyed, *Washington Post*, 23 November 2001; Colonel John T Carney and Benjamin F Schemmer, *No Room for Error: The Covert Operations of America's Special Tactics Units from Iran to Afghanistan*, Ballantine Books, New York, 2002; information provided to the author in confidence

2 Information provided to the author in confidence

3 Richard Clarke testimony, NSC Coordinator of Counterterrorism 1993–2001, to Joint Inquiry Briefing by Staff on US Counterterrorism Organizations (Before 11 September 2001) and on the Evolution of the Terrorist Threat and US Response 1986–2001, United States Senate Select Committee on Intelligence and US House of Representatives Permanent Select Committee on Intelligence, 11 June 2002

4 *ibid*; William M Arkin, *Code Names: Deciphering US Military Plans, Programs, and Operations in the 9/11 World*, Steerforth Press, Hanover NH, 2005; Charles Cogan, Hunters not Gatherers: Intelligence in the Twenty-First Century, in LV Scott and PD Jackson, *Understanding Intelligence in the Twenty-First Century: Journeys in the Shadows*, Routledge, London, 2004; Showstoppers: Nine Reasons Why We Never Sent Our Special Operations Forces After al-Qa'eda Before 9/11, *The Weekly Standard*, 26 January 2004

5 Richard Clarke testimony, as above; Plan to nab bin Laden stymied: Clinton-era memo Failed to Reach Defense Secretary in 1998, *Washington Times*, 19 March 2004; Inside the Ring: Ignored War Plan, *Washington Times*, 26 March 2004

6 Information provided to the author in confidence; Thomas H Kean, Chair, and Lee H Hamilton, Vice Chair, *The 9/11 Report: The National Commission on Terrorist Attacks upon the United States*, St Martin's Paperbacks, New York, 2004

7 Thomas H Kean, Chair, and Lee H Hamilton, Vice Chair, *The 9/11 Report: The National Commission on Terrorist Attacks upon the United States*; Richard Clarke testimony, as above; Bob Woodward, *Bush at War*, Pocket Books, New York, 2003; Bin Laden Attack Plan, *Washington Times*, 14 September 2001

8 Richard Clarke testimony, as above; Bob Woodward, *Bush at War*; Michael Smith, *The Spying Game: The Secret History of British Intelligence*, Politicos, London, 2003

9 Richard Clarke testimony, as above

10 Information provided to the author in confidence; Allies will fight for 'hearts and minds', *The Daily Telegraph*, 1 October 2001; Bob Woodward, *Bush at War*; Michael Smith, *The Spying Game: The Secret History of British Intelligence*

11 Bob Woodward, *Bush at War*; information provided to the author in confidence

12 Bob Woodward, *Bush at War*

13 *ibid*

14 *ibid;* Dead or Alive: Hunting Osama bin Laden, *NPR Morning Edition*, 2 May 2005

15 Information provided to the author in confidence. See also: Michael Smith, *The Spying Game: The Secret History of British Intelligence*

16 Gary C Shroen, *First In: An Insider's Account of how the CIA Spearheaded the War on Terrorism*, Ballantine, New York, 2005; Bob Woodward, *Bush at War*; Michael Smith, *The Spying Game: The Secret History of British Intelligence*; information provided to the author in confidence

17 Gary C Shroen, *First In: An Insider's Account of How the CIA Spearheaded the War on* Terrorism; Bob Woodward, *Bush at War*; Robin Moore, *Task Force Dagger: The Hunt for Bin Laden*, Pan, London, 2004

18 Bob Woodward, *Bush at War*; Dana Priest, *The Mission: Waging War and Keeping Peace with America's Military*, Norton, New York, 2004; Sean Naylor, *Not a Good Day to Die: The Untold Story of Operation Anaconda*, Berkley Caliber, New York, 2005

19 List of Special Forces in Place, *Intelligence Online*, 4 October 2001; Commandos start missions in Afghanistan, *Washington Times*, 29 September 2001; Raid Targeted a Residence of Taliban Leader, *Los Angeles Times*, 21 October 2001; Edward F Bruner, Christopher Bolkum and Ronald O'Rourke, *Special Operations Forces in Operation Enduring Freedom: Background and Issues for Congress*, Congressional Research Service, 15 October 2001

20 Information provided to the author in confidence

21 Gary C Shroen, *First In: An Insider's Account of How the CIA Spearheaded the War on Terrorism*; unidentified US Special Forces officer during a classified briefing, October 2001, quoted in Robin Moore, *Task Force Dagger: The Hunt for Bin Laden*

22 Robin Moore, *Task Force Dagger: The Hunt for Bin Laden*; Bob Woodward, *Bush at War*; Dana Priest, *The Mission: Waging War and Keeping Peace with America's Military*

23 Information provided to the author in confidence; US Special Forces Beat Retreat as Enemy 'Fought Back Like Maniacs', *Daily Telegraph*, 26 October 2001; Escape and Evasion, *New Yorker*, 12 November 2001; Analysis: Repointing Special Ops, *United Press International*, 12 November 2001; US Soldiers Seize Airfield From Taliban, *Washington Times*, 21 October 2001; Raid Targeted a Residence of Taliban Leader, *Los Angeles Times*, 21 October 2001; Omar's Compound Was Raided; Airfield Also Hit In Rangers' Hunt For Intelligence, *Washington Post*, 21 October 2001

24 Christian Jennings, *Midnight in Some Burning Town: British Special Forces Operations from Belgrade to Baghdad*, Weidenfeld & Nicolson, London, 2004; Mark Nicol, *Ultimate Risk: SAS Contact al-Qa'eda*, Pan, London, 2003; A Carrier's Quiet, Key Mission; *Kitty Hawk* Heads Home After Hosting Special Forces, *Washington Post*, 24 December 2001; Rowan Scarborough, *Rumsfeld's War: The Untold Story of America's Anti-Terrorist Commander*, Regnery Publishing, Washington, 2004; Admiral Vernon E. Clarke, USN, Chief of Naval Operations, in speech to the 34th IFPA-Fletcher Conference on National Security Strategy and Policy Security Planning and Military Transformation after Iraqi Freedom, Washington DC, 2/3 December 2003; Elite US unit keeps heat on terrorists; Task Force 11 hunts leaders, *Washington Times*, 12 July 2002

25 Information provided to the author in confidence; Michael Smith, *The Spying Game: The Secret History of British Intelligence*; Bob Woodward, *Bush at War*; Robin Moore, *The Hunt for Bin Laden: Task Force Dagger – On the Ground with Special Forces in Afghanistan*; Bin Laden's voice detected; U.S. troops pick up terrorist on radio in Tora Bora area, *Washington Times*, 15 December 2001; 10-Month Afghan Mystery: Is bin Laden Dead or Alive?, *The New York Times*, 30 September 2002; Elite US unit keeps heat on terrorists; Task Force 11 hunts leaders, *Washington Times*, 12 July 2002; Document: Bin Laden Evaded U.S. Forces, *Associated Press*, 23 March 2005

26 Matthew F Bogdanos, Joint Inter–Agency Cooperation: The First Step, *Joint Force Quarterly*, Issue 37, June 2005; Sean Naylor, *Not a Good Day to Die: The Untold Story of Operation Anaconda*

27 *ibid*; Stephen Biddle, *Afghanistan and the Future of Warfare: Implications for Army and Defense Policy*, US Army War College, November 2002

28 Sean Naylor, *Not a Good Day to Die: The Untold Story of Operation Anaconda*

29 US Mounts Spy Mission in Somalia, *Daily Telegraph*, 12 December 2001; US Special Units 'are already at work in Somalia', *Daily Telegraph*, 12 December 2001; US Prepares Bombings in Somalia, *Washington Times*, 3 January 2002; Allies Step Up Somalia Watch, *Washington Post*, 4 January 2002; Special Forces train for Somalia Duty, *Washington Times*, 19 February 2002; Somalia and al-Qa'eda: Implications for the War on Terrorism, *Heritage Foundation Reports*, 5 April 2002; Operation Endless deployment, *The Nation*, 21 October 2002; Rowan Scarborough, *Rumsfeld's War: The Untold Story of America's Anti-Terrorist Commander*

30 Pentagon cheers CIA shake-up, Sees changes in terror tactics, *Washington Times*, 17 November 2004; Special Operations Forces Take Care of War on Terror, *Jane's Intelligence Review*, 23 December 2002; Inside the Ring, Covert Action Training, *Washington Times*, 13 August 2004

31 Professor Richard Shultz, 'Preempting Terrorists was not an Option: The Non-Use of SOF CT Units in the 1990s', quoted in Rowan Scarborough, *Rumsfeld's War: The Untold Story of America's Anti-Terrorist Commander*

32 *ibid*

33 *ibid*

34 Rowan Scarborough, *Rumsfeld's War: The Untold Story of America's Anti-Terrorist Commander*

35 *ibid*; William M Arkin, *Code Names: Deciphering US Military Plans, Programs, and Operations in the 9/11 World*; Seymour M Hersh, *Chain of Command: The Road from 9/11 to Abu Ghraib*, HarperCollins, New York, 2004; information provided to the author in confidence

36 Rowan Scarborough, *Rumsfeld's War: The Untold Story of America's Anti-Terrorist Commander*; Yemen: US Strike Kills al-Qa'eda Suspects, *Facts on File World News Digest*, 3 November 2002; CIA Missile in Yemen Kills 6 Terror Suspects, *Los Angeles Times*, 5 November 2002; Assassination by remote control; Hunting terrorists, *Economist.Com*, 5 November 2002; The CIA is Reported to Kill a Leader of Qaeda in Yemen, *New York Times*, 5 November 2002; US Strike Kills Six in Al Qaeda; Missile Fired by Predator Drone; Key Figure in Yemen Among Dead, *Washington Post*, 5 November 2002; Al-Qa'eda stalked by the Predator, *Sunday Times*, 10 November 2002

Chapter Ten

1 Information provided to the author in confidence; Christian Jennings, *Midnight in Some Burning Town*, Weidenfeld & Nicolson, London, 2004; Robin Moore, *Hunting Down Saddam: The Inside Story of the Search and Capture*, St Martin's Paperbacks, New York, 2004; Hussein's 2 Sons Dead in Shootout, U.S. Says, *New York Times*, 23 July 2003; A Good Day in Iraq, *Washington Post*, 23 July 2003; Uday and Qusay die in firefight with U.S. troops: Pair cornered in house in northern Iraqi city, *International Herald Tribune*, 23 July 2003; And Then There Was One: An informant's tip leads US forces to the Hussein brothers. Now the focus is on Saddam, *Time*, 4 August 2003; Anatomy of the raid on Hussein's sons, *Christian Science Monitor*, 24 July 2003

2 Bob Woodward, *Bush at War*, Pocket Books, New York, 2003; John Keegan, *The Iraq War*, Hutchinson, London, 2004; Rowan Scarborough, *Rumsfeld's War: The Untold Story of America's Anti-Terrorist Commander*, Regnery Publishing, Washington, 2004

3 The President's State of the Union Address, *Federal Documents Clearing House, Regulatory Intelligence Data*, 29 January 2002; The Radical – What Dick Cheney really believes, *New Republic*, 1 December 2003

4 Cabinet Office Overseas and Defence Secretariat Secret UK Eyes Only document entitled Iraq: Options Paper, dated 8 March 2002, seen by the author

5 'Failure is not an option, but it doesn't mean they will avoid it', *Daily Telegraph*, 18 September 2004

6 William M Arkin, *Code Names: Deciphering US Military Plans, Programs, and Operations in the 9/11 World*, Steerforth Press, Hanover NH, 2005; Secret – Strictly Personal memo from Sir David Manning to Prime Minister entitled 'Your Trip to the US', dated 14 March 2002, seen by the author

7 Confidential and Personal FCO memo from PF Ricketts, Policy Director, to Secretary of State entitled Iraq: Advice for the Prime Minister, dated 22 March 2002, seen by the author

8 *ibid*; Secret and Personal letter from Jack Straw, Foreign Secretary, to Prime Minister, Ref PM/02/019, entitled Crawford/Iraq, dated 25 March 2002; Cabinet Office Overseas and Defence Secretariat Secret UK Eyes Only document entitled Iraq: Options Paper, dated 8 March 2002; all seen by the author

9 Cabinet Office Secret UK Eyes Only Briefing Paper 'Iraq Conditions for Military', dated 21 July 2002, seen by author; Blair Hit by New Leak of Secret War Plan, *Sunday Times*, 1 May 2005; 'Failure is not an option, but it doesn't mean they will avoid it', *Daily Telegraph*, 18 September 2004

10 Bob Woodward, *Plan of Attack*, Pocket Books, New York, 2004

11 Secret and Strictly Personal UK Eyes Only Downing St memorandum from Matthew Rycroft to David Manning recording minutes of meeting of British war

cabinet, 23 July 2002; Foreign Office legal advice, entitled Iraq: Legal Background and dated 8 March 2002; both seen by the author

12 Answers to Parliamentary Written Questions posed by Sir Menzies Campbell, Liberal Democrat Foreign Affairs Spokesman dated 27 November 2002 and 10 March 2003; 100 Jets Join Attack on Iraq, *Daily Telegraph*, 6 September 2002; William M Arkin, *Code Names: Deciphering US Military Plans, Programs, and Operations in the 9/11 World*

13 Blair has 10 Days to Opt for War, *Daily Telegraph*, 14 December 2002; Rowan Scarborough, *Rumsfeld's War: The Untold Story of America's Anti-Terrorist Commander*

14 Study Urges Wider Authority for Covert Troops vs. Terror, *Washington Times*, 15 December 2002; Jennifer Kibbe, The Rise of the Shadow Warriors, *Foreign Affairs*, March/April 2004

15 Rumsfeld Weighs Covert Activities by Military Units, *The New York Times*, 12 August 2002; Panel Wants $7bn Elite Counter-Terrorist Unit, *United Press International*, 26 September 2002

16 Special Operations and Joint Forces in Countering Terrorism, Defense Science Board, Powerpoint briefing dated 16 August 2002, available on the Federation of American Scientists website at http://www.fas.org/irp/agency/dod/dsbbrief.ppt

17 Study Urges Wider Authority for Covert Troops vs. Terror, *Washington Times*, 15 December 2002; Rowan Scarborough, *Rumsfeld's War: The Untold Story of America's Anti-Terrorist Commander*; The Secret War: Frustrated by Intelligence Failures, the Defence Department is Dramatically Expanding its 'Black World' of Covert Operations, *Los Angeles Times*, 27 October 2002

18 General briefs Rumsfeld on new war plan; Commandos vs. terrorists in rapid-response strikes, *Washington Times*, 3 August 2002; Rumsfeld bolsters special forces: Expands powers in war on terror, *Washington Times*, 6 January 2003; 'Special Ops' gets OK to initiate its own missions, *Washington Times*, 8 January 2003; Expanded role for elite commandos; Rumsfeld elevates Special Operations Command to the counter-terrorist catbird seat, *Armed Forces Journal*, 2 February 2003

19 'Black ops' shine in Iraq War: the scope of US special operations in the Iraq War was the largest in American military history, *VFW Magazine*, 1 February 2004; Special Ops steal show as successes mount in Iraq, *Washington Times*, 7 April 2003; Pentagon says US special operations forces play an 'unprecedented' role in Iraq, *Associated Press*, 4 April 2003; Secretary of Defense Donald H Rumsfeld Address, SOCOM change of command, MacDill AFB, Tampa, FL, Tuesday, 2 September 2003; Armando J Ramirez, *From Bosnia to Baghdad: The Evolution of US Army Special Forces from 1995–2004*, Naval Postgraduate School, Monterey, California, September 2004

20 'Black ops' shine in Iraq War: the scope of US special operations in the Iraq War was the largest in American military history, *VFW Magazine*, 1 February 2004; Tim Ripley, *Air War Iraq*, Pen & Sword, Barnsley, 2004

21 'Black ops' shine in Iraq War: the scope of US special operations in the Iraq War was the largest in American military history, *VFW Magazine*, 1 February 2004; Armando J Ramirez, *From Bosnia to Baghdad: The Evolution of US Army Special Forces from 1995-2004*; Linda Robinson, *Masters of Chaos: The Secret History of the Special Forces*, Public Affairs, New York, 2004; How Green Berets Beat the Odds at an Iraq Alamo, *The New York Times*, 22 September 2003

22 Information provided to the author in confidence; Taking a risk by 'playing with Saddam's mind', *Washington Times*, 21 March 2003; Tim Ripley, *Air War Iraq*; Covert Unit Hunted for Iraqi Arms, *Washington Post*, 13 June 2003; Christian Jennings, *Midnight in Some Burning Town: British Special Forces Operations from Belgrade to Baghdad*; Statement of Brigadier-General Donald Wurster, US Air Force, Director Center for Intelligence and Information Operations United States Special Operations Command, before the Strategic Forces Sub-Committee for the Senate Armed Services Committee on the Fiscal Year 2005 Tactical Intelligence and Related Activities (TIARA) and Joint Military Intelligence Program (JMIP) Budget Requests, 7 April 2004

23 Rumsfeld Taps Retired General for Army Chief, *Los Angeles Times*, 11 June 2003; America's Secret Soldiers, *Tampa Tribune*, 16 June 2002

24 Professor Richard Shultz, Preempting Terrorists was not an Option: The Non-Use of SOF CT Units in the 1990s, quoted in Rowan Scarborough, *Rumsfeld's War: The Untold Story of America's Anti-Terrorist Commander*

25 From Buck Private to Chief of SOCOM, *National Defense*, 1 February 2004; Jennifer Kibbe, The Rise of the Shadow Warriors, *Foreign Affairs*, March/April 2004

26 Information provided to the author in confidence; press conference held in Baghdad by L. Paul Bremer, Adnan Pachachi and General Ricardo Sanchez to announce the capture of Saddam Hussein, 14 December 2003; How We Got Saddam: 'Don't shoot,' the bearded, submissive man said to the soldiers. He was Saddam Hussein, hiding in a hole, the man the Pentagon called 'High Value Target Number One.' The story of his capture – and what's next, *Newsweek*, 22 December 2003; Tip led U.S. soldiers to Saddam's hiding place; Ex-dictator, two associates were caught with rifles, $750,000, *Washington Times*, 15 December 2003; Saddam's Capture: 'Ladies and Gentlemen, We Got Him.' Inside the daring night-time raid that nabbed Saddam – and what it means for Bush and Iraq, *Time*, 22 December 2003; Anatomy of Hussein's capture: The cellar floor didn't look quite right, *Christian Science Monitor*, 15 December 2003; Analysis: Timeline of the capture of Saddam Hussein near Tikrit, *Weekend Edition, National Public Radio*, 14 December 2003; US soldiers were about to give up search when they found Saddam, *Knight-Ridder/Tribune News Service*, 14 December 2003; 'Black ops' shine in Iraq War: the scope of U.S. special operations in the Iraq War was the largest in American military history, *VFW (Veterans of Foreign Wars) Magazine*, 1 February 2004; Satellite imagery: helps spot Saddam, *Geospatial Solutions*, 1 January 2004; Secret Teams Were Constantly on the Trail of 'Number One', *Daily Telegraph*, 15 December 2003; Robin Moore, *Hunting Down Saddam: The Inside Story of the Search and Capture*

27 Pentagon Says a Covert Force Hunts Hussein, *The New York Times*, 6 November 2003; The Hunt Heats Up, *Newsweek*, 15 March 2004; Agencies unite to find bin Laden: Task Force 121 tightens 'loop', *Washington Times*, 15 March 2004; Pakistan says it has cornered al-Zawahri, *Washington Times*, 19 March 2004; Pakistani restrictions slow U.S. search for bin Laden, *Washington Times*, 24 June 2004

28 Secret Unit Expands Rumsfeld's Domain: New Espionage Branch Delving Into CIA Territory *The Washington Post*, 23 January 2005; Controversial Pentagon Espionage Unit Loses Its Leader: Rumsfeld Reportedly Moving Ahead With Plans to Expand Team's Intelligence Work Worldwide, *Washington Post*, 13 February 2005; US Prepares for Major Overhaul of Intelligence Apparatus, *Jane's Defence Weekly*, 15 December 2004; Pentagon Increases Its Spying Markedly, *Los Angeles Times*, 24 March 2005; Pentagon to Upgrade Intelligence Structure, *Washington Post*, 24 March 2005; DoD Background Briefing on Strategic Support Teams, the Pentagon, 24 January 2005; Operationalizing Intelligence, *C4ISR, The Journal of Net-Centric Warfare*, Vol 4 No 1, Jan–Feb 2005

29 Boots On Ground, Now Also The Eyes: Special Operations Forces are doing more intelligence gathering in terror war, *Christian Science Monitor*, 11 March 2004

30 US forces get OK to use CIA methods, *Washington Times*, 1 October 2002; Secret Unit Expands Rumsfeld's Domain: New Espionage Branch Delving Into CIA Territory, *Washington Post*, 23 January 2005; Controversial Pentagon Espionage Unit Loses Its Leader: Rumsfeld Reportedly Moving Ahead With Plans to Expand Team's Intelligence Work Worldwide, *Washington Post*, 13 February 2005; Pentagon Increases Its Spying Markedly, *Los Angeles Times*, 24 March 2005; Pentagon to Upgrade Intelligence Structure, *Washington Post*, 24 March 2005; DoD Background Briefing on Strategic Support Teams, the Pentagon, 24 January 2005; Special Forces Enter CIA Territory With a New Weapon, *Los Angeles Times*, 31 October 2004; Law Gives Spending Power to Special Operations Forces, *The New York Times*, 1 February 2005

31 Secret Unit Expands Rumsfeld's Domain: New Espionage Branch Delving Into CIA Territory *The Washington Post*, 23 January 2005; The Coming Wars, *New Yorker*, 24 January 2005; US Uses Drones to Probe Iran For Arms, *Washington Post*, 13 February 2005

32 Bush Wants Plan for Covert Pentagon Role, *The New York Times*, 23 November 2004; Boots On Ground, Now Also The Eyes: Special Operations Forces are doing more intelligence gathering in terror war, *Christian Science Monitor*, 11 March 2004

33 Kathryn Stone, *'All Necessary Means' – Employing CIA Operatives in a Warfighting Role alongside Special Operations Forces*, US Army War College, 7 April 2003; Pentagon Increases Its Spying Markedly, *Los Angeles Times*, 24 March 2005; Pentagon to Upgrade Intelligence Structure, *Washington Post*, 24 March 2005

34 The Coming Wars, *New Yorker*, 24 January 2005; Thomas H Kean and Lee H Hamilton, *The 9/11 Report: The National Commission on Terrorist Attacks upon the United States*, St Martin's Paperbacks, New York, 2004

35 Text of a Letter from the President to the Speaker of the House of Representative, Consolidated War Powers Report to Congress under the terms of the War Powers Resolution, *Global News Wire*, 4 November 2004; Secret Unit Expands Rumsfeld's Domain: New Espionage Branch Delving Into CIA Territory, *Washington Post*, 23 January 2005; Donald Rumsfeld looks to change the role of the US Special Operations Command, *All Things Considered – National Public Radio*, 4 February 2005

36 Two killed in Mirali blast, *Dawn*, 9 May 2005; Surveillance Operation in Pakistan Located and Killed al-Qa'eda Official, *Washington Post*, 15 May 2005; Remotely Controlled Craft Part of U.S.-Pakistan Drive Against al-Qa'eda, Ex-Officials Say, *The New York Times*, 16 May 2005; An extrajudicial execution by the CIA?, *Amnesty International*, 18 May 2005

37 Kerrey SEAL Team Fought Other War, *Associated Press*, 27 April 2001; Congress Is Reviewing Pentagon on Intelligence Activities, *The New York Times*, 4 February 2005; Donald Rumsfeld looks to change the role of the US Special Operations Command, *All Things Considered – National Public Radio*, 4 February 2005

GLOSSARY

7 Sqn RAF UKSF helicopter unit equipped with modified CH47 Chinook helicopters. Based at Odiham, Hampshire.

14 Int British special forces human intelligence unit formed initially for Northern Ireland but expanded to operations in the Balkans and Middle East. It has largely been subsumed into the Special Reconnaissance Regiment. The name is an abbreviation of the original covername 14 Intelligence Company. The codename for its activities was Ajax. Its covername was eventually changed to Joint Communications Unit Northern Ireland. During the Northern Ireland days it was divided into a number of detachments, known as Dets, and as a result became known universally within the UK special forces community as 'the Det'. (*See also* JCUNI *and* SRR)

16th Special Operations Wing US Air Force special operations unit based at Hulbert Field, Florida, flies the AC130 Spectre and Spooky aerial gunships and MC130 Combat Talon aircraft that support special operations missions. It also includes squadrons equipped with the UH1 Iroquois, MH53 Pave Low and MH60 Pave Hawk helicopters.

18 Signal (UKSF) Regiment UK equivalent of the Activity signals intelligence operation, formed in April 2005.

21 SAS The first of two UK Special Air Service reservist units, it is based in southern England and known as 'the Artists' Rifles' after the unit from which the Special Air Service evolved. The SAS was disbanded at the end of the Second World War but former members of the regiment fought a furious rearguard action leading to the formation in 1947 of a reservist unit, 21 SAS Regiment (Artists).

22 SAS The most famous of the British 'Tier 1' special forces units, 22 SAS Regiment was formed during the Malayan Emergency from a merger of one squadron of the reservist 21 SAS Regiment and a locally raised covert reconnaissance unit known as the Malay Scouts. It is known within the UK Special Forces community simply as 'The Regiment' and is based at Credenhill, near Hereford.

23 SAS Second SAS reservist regiment, based in northern England.

24th Special Tactics Squadron US Air Force combat controller unit that works most closely with JSOC and is based alongside both JSOC and Delta at the Pope air force base, Fayetteville, North Carolina (*See CCT*).

47 Sqn RAF UKSF transport unit equipped with modified C130 Hercules aircraft. Based at Lyneham, Wiltshire.

75th Ranger Regiment The US Rangers, based at Fort Benning, Georgia, are the leading US airborne light infantry unit. One of their primary roles is to provide close support for JSOC direct action operations.

108th Special Operations Corps Dutch Army equivalent of SAS/Delta.

160 SOAR 160th Special Operations Aviation Regiment. Army special operations helicopter unit originally set up as Task Force 160 to provide helicopters and aviators capable of flying at night, for Snow Bird, the second attempt to rescue the Tehran hostages. Their night-flying capability earned them the nickname of 'Night Stalkers'. It was officially established as a special operations unit in October 1981 as 160th Aviation Battalion, became 160th Special Operations Aviation Group in 1986 and 160th Special Operations Aviation Regiment in 1990. It is based at Fort Campbell, Kentucky. Motto: 'Night Stalkers Don't Quit'.

264 (SAS) Signal Squadron UK Royal Signals unit that provides communications and cryptographic support to the SAS. Based at Credenhill, near Hereford.

A6E Intruder US Navy twin-seater, carrier-based medium attack bomber used extensively in Vietnam and operational into the early 1990s.

A7E Corsair US Navy single-seater, light attack, carrier-based bomber used extensively in Vietnam and operational into the early 1990s.

A10 Thunderbolt Versatile attack aircraft, also known as the Warthog or Tankbuster. It is designed to provide maximum close air support for ground troops. Its most famous weapon is the 30mm machine-cannon mounted in the nose of the aircraft, which can disable an armoured vehicle at a distance of around four miles, but the A10 is also capable of carrying a full range of other bombs and missiles.

A&S The Activity's Assessment and Selection process.

ABH *Armija Bosna i Hercegovina.* The Bosnian Muslim Army.

AC130H/U Spectre/Spooky Aerial gunship based on the C130 Hercules and specifically designed to provide close air support to special operations troops. The latest variant, codenamed Spooky, possesses an astonishing array of computerised surveillance and weapons systems including a 25mm Gatling gun; a 40mm Bofors cannon and a 105mm howitzer. There are eight Spectres and thirteen Spookies available to US Special Operations Command and alongside close air support they also carry out interdiction, armed reconnaissance, surveillance and combat search and rescue.

AFO Advance Force Operations. A team of around forty-five special operators attached to the Task Force Bowie intelligence fusion cell at Bagram in Afghanistan to provide operational preparation of the battlefield for Task Force 11. The AFO included half a dozen recce teams, each custom-made for the mission it was to perform, using a combination of Delta or DevGru shooters, Activity intelligence experts and Air Force Special Tactics combat controllers.

AGM-114 Hellfire Air-to-ground laser-guided anti-armour missile originally designed for use from attack helicopters but more recently fired from Predator UAVs to take out al-Qa'eda terrorists.

AH6 Little Bird Light attack helicopter gunship based on the OH6 Cayuse reconnaissance helicopter.

AH64 Apache Helicopter gunship designed to operate as an aerial cavalry, destroying enemy armour. Its main armament is the Hellfire air-to-ground missile.

AK47 Kalashnikov assault rifle The most common military rifle in the world is also among the easiest to use and most reliable. Designed for use by Soviet motorised infantry, the 7.62 'AK' was first produced in 1949.

Amal Shi'ite Muslim militia group in Lebanon, which represented the majority of Muslims during the 1980s civil war. Led by Nabih Berri, lawyer and politician.

Amber Star Joint allied operation launched in the summer of 1997 to capture war criminals in the former Yugoslavia and deliver them to the international criminal tribunal at the Hague.

Anaconda Battle during the 2001–2 war in Afghanistan which involved allied special operations forces, two US infantry battalions and local Afghan forces and was designed to end large-scale Taliban and al-Qa'eda resistance for good.

AQT al-Qa'eda terrorist(s).

Aquacade Codename given to the US geostationary signals intelligence satellites after the previous codename Rhyolite was compromised.

Army of South Lebanon Lebanese Christian militia based on the border with Israel and allied to it.

ASD SO/LIC Assistant Secretary of Defense for Special Operations and Low-Intensity Conflict, the senior Pentagon official responsible for the Activity and other US special operations forces.

A-team Shorthand term for smallest operational team of US Special Forces, more correctly termed Operational Detachment Alpha.

ATV All-Terrain Vehicle. Special operations vehicle which is a cross between a motorbike and a four-wheel-drive golf buggy and as the name suggests is capable of operating in all terrains.

Black List One US military code for Saddam Hussein.

BMMAT Briefcase Multi-Mission Advanced Tactical Terminal. Special operations man-portable three-channel communications terminal and laptop computer, contained in a briefcase and weighing only 40lbs, which allows access to near real-time operational intelligence from both national agencies (ie CIA/NSA/DIA) and tactical sources.

BMP Standard tracked Soviet armoured infantry combat vehicle introduced in the mid-1960s and capable of carrying eleven personnel including the three-man crew.

Brand X One of the earliest codenames given to the US Air Force special tactics teams.

Brigade Patrol Troop The elite pathfinding element of the UK's 3 Commando Brigade.

BTR60 Standard Soviet Army wheeled armoured personnel carrier from the 1950s up until the late 1980s, when it was gradually replaced by the BTR80.

Buckeye Large-scale US-led intelligence operation involving the Activity, the CIA, the NSA, Delta and Britain's secretive 14 Int, collecting covert intelligence for snatch operations against indicted war criminals in Bosnia during the late 1990s.

C5 Galaxy Extraordinarily large cargo aircraft, 247 feet long and capable of carrying 430,000lb of cargo, the Galaxy was first introduced into service with the US Air Force in 1969. Its cargo hold opens up at both the rear and front of the aircraft providing an easy drive-on, drive-off facility.

C17 Globemaster Most modern cargo aircraft in service with the US Air Force and the RAF, first introduced in 1995. There are fourteen of these aircraft dedicated to US Special Operations Command. At 174 feet long, it is not as big as the Galaxy but is still capable of carrying 170,900lb of cargo and 102 troops.

C130 Hercules The workhorse of both the US Air Force and RAF transport fleets, the Hercules, first introduced in 1956, is nearly 98 feet long and capable of carrying

36,000lb of cargo plus 92 troops. It also forms the basis for a number of special operations aircraft, most notably the MC130E/H Combat Talon, the AC130H Spectre and the AC130U Spooky.

C141 Starlifter Long-range US Air Force troop and cargo transport aircraft, 168 feet long and capable of carrying more than 90,000lbs of cargo.

Canvas Shield Operational security assessment of Grazing Lawn, a 1985 Activity signals intelligence mission in Honduras.

Capacity Gear Special access programme codename for the Activity, initiated in March 1989 and subsequently replaced by Titrant Ranger.

CBRN Chemical, Biological, Radiological, Nuclear. Military term replacing the Cold War NBC (Nuclear, Biological and Chemical) and taking into account the potential of radiological 'dirty bombs', ie radioactive material wrapped around high explosive.

CBT Combating terrorism.

CCT US Air Force Special Tactics Combat Control Team, which provides specialist ground-to-air liaison to bring down close air support for special operations teams.

CD Counter-drugs operations.

Centcom US Armed Forces Central Command covers an area extending from eastern Africa in the west to Pakistan in the east and Kazakhstan in the north. Strangely it covers Egypt and Jordan but not Israel, Syria or Lebanon, and Pakistan but not India.

Centra Spike Codename used by the Activity during counter-drugs operations in Colombia which led to the 1993 assassination of drugs baron Pablo Escobar.

CH47 Chinook Highly distinctive twin-rotored transport helicopter first used in Vietnam in 1966 and since used extensively for infiltration, exfiltration and resupply of US and UK special operations forces.

CIA US Central Intelligence Agency.

C/JSOTF Combined Joint Special Operations Task Force. The combined indicates that the force is made up of multinational forces, usually but not exclusively US, UK and Australian.

CNN Cable News Network. US-owned international satellite television 24-hour news network.

COIN Counter-insurgency.

COMINT Communications Intelligence, information derived from intercepting the communications of the enemy.

CSAR Combat Search and Rescue. Recovery of friendly personnel trapped behind enemy lines.

CSO Center for Special Operations. The nerve centre for hunting terrorists and other 'high-value targets' worldwide. It continually draws up contingency plans and monitors the whereabouts and readiness of special mission units for special operations.

CT Counter-Terrorist/Counter-Terrorism.

CTC CIA's Counter-Terrorism Center.

CTJTF Counter-Terrorist Joint Task Force An organisation directly subordinate to the Joint Chiefs of Staff which plans counter-terrorist operations to prevent attacks on US interests, citizens and/or property outside the United States.

DA Direct Action. Any offensive action designed to attack or damage enemy positions or to snatch or kill enemy personnel.

Dayton Accord Peace deal signed in December 1995 to end four years of internecine fighting in the former Yugoslavia. The governments of Bosnia, Croatia and Yugoslavia agreed to respect each other's territory. It split Bosnia into areas controlled by the Bosnian government and the Bosnian Serbs. The end to the fighting was to be overseen by the Nato Implementation Force I-For.

DCI Director Central Intelligence. Title given to the Director of the CIA signifying that he was, in theory if not in practice, in charge of all the US intelligence agencies. This role ended in February 2005 when President George W Bush named John Negroponte as the first Director of National Intelligence, a direct response to the intelligence failures that preceded the 11 September attacks.

DCSINT Deputy Chief of Staff for Intelligence.

DEA US Drugs Enforcement Agency.

Delenda Codename for National Security Council plan that would combine diplomatic and financial persuasion with covert action and special operations missions aimed at preventing countries from giving al-Qa'eda sanctuary.

Delta The US Army's 'Tier 1' counter-terrorist special operations unit. Set up in 1988 by Colonel Chargin' Charlie A Beckwith on the model of the UK SAS, with which he had served on attachment. The name Delta, often extended to Delta Force, derives from the unit's original title, 1st Special Forces Operational Detachment – Delta. It was renamed Combat Applications Group, but Delta stuck. The unit is based in a compound that straggles Fort Bragg and the Pope air force base at Fayetteville, North Carolina.

Desert One Forward operations base for the Eagle Claw mission and scene of the mission's disastrous demise. It was in the Dasht-e-Kavir desert, about 250 miles south-east of the Iranian capital Tehran.

Det Common term for 14 Int within the UK special forces community (*See 14 Int*).

DevGru Abbreviated form of Naval Special Warfare Development Group, the correct title for the US Navy's 'Tier 1' counter-terrorist and special operations unit commonly known as SEAL Team Six.

DGSE *Direction Générale de la Sécurité Extérieure*. French foreign intelligence service, subordinate to the Ministry of Defence.

DHS Defense Humint Service. Pentagon's own human intelligence service.

DIA US Defense Intelligence Agency.

Diana US Army one-time pad code system.

DNI Director of National Intelligence. US cabinet level official in charge of all US intelligence organisations, a post created in 2005 as a direct response to the intelligence failures that preceded the 9/11 attacks.

DOD US Department of Defense, more commonly known as the Pentagon.

Druze Islamic sect with around a million members, centred on Lebanon, Syria, Jordan, Israel and Turkey. The Lebanese Druze militia of the Progressive Socialist Party, led by Walid Jumblatt, were major players in the fighting in Lebanon during the 1980s.

Eagle Claw The failed 1980 operation to rescue the US hostages held in Tehran.

ELINT Electronic intelligence derived from the monitoring and assessment of electronic signals, eg radar pulses.

Enduring Freedom Allied invasion of Afghanistan in the wake of the 11 September attacks.

EUCOM US Armed Forces European Command, covering Europe, the whole of Russia, Israel, Syria and Lebanon.

Exile Pirate Joint Activity/SEAL Team Six exercise in October and November 1986.

F117A Nighthawk The world's first stealth strike aircraft, introduced into the US Air Force in 1982.

Falcon Aviation Covername for Activity aerial signals intelligence operation in Colombia.

FARC *Fuerzas Armadas Revolucionarios de Colombia* – Revolutionary Armed Forces of Colombia. Colombian Marxist rebel group set up in 1964 by the Colombian Communist Party as its military wing. Its initial role was to defend Communist-controlled areas but it swiftly moved to mounting terrorist acts designed to bring about a Communist regime. It is one of the most effective rebel groups in the world, controlling a third of Colombia, mostly in the south-east, and running active cells in Bogotá and other main cities.

Farm The Farm is the CIA Operations Directorate training base at Camp Perry, near Williamsburg, Virginia.

FBI Federal Bureau of Investigation. Its roles include domestic counter-espionage and counter-terrorist operations.

Felix Network Christian Lebanese Forces militia spy network in Lebanon run by the Activity in the mid-1980s.

FID Foreign Internal Defense is the official title for US counter-insurgency operations in support of allied governments.

Field Operations Group The original special operations intelligence unit put together by Jerry King for the second Iran rescue mission and forerunner of the Activity.

First Rotary Wing Test Activity The official name for a top secret air force unit codenamed Sea Spray, originally due to provide air support for the ISA, using aircraft with civilian markings, but which was taken over by the US Army Special Operations Division.

FMLN The left-wing Faribundo Marti Liberation Front fought a long guerrilla campaign against the Salvadoran government during the 1980s, but by 1989 was involved in peace talks that led to the FMLN abandoning the military struggle and becoming a political party.

FUBAR (US military slang) F***ed up beyond all recognition.

GCHQ Government Communications Headquarters, the British signals intelligence and cryptology agency, the equivalent of the US National Security Agency.

GE/Seniors Codename given to former mujahideen employed by the CIA to carry out covert action against the Taliban and/or al-Qa'eda in Afghanistan.

Glass Man Activity signals intelligence operation initiated in December 1986.

Gothic Snake The Task Force Ranger operation to take down Somali warlord Mohammed Farah Aideed.

Grand Eagle False Activity operation to rescue MIAs from south-east Asia created in order to find out what Colonel James 'Bo' Gritz was doing in his one-man search for US POWs.

Grantor Shadow ISA special access programme terminated in March 1989 and replaced by Capacity Gear.

Graphic Book Activity signals intelligence operation in Latin America in 1982.

Grazing Lawn Codename for 1985 Activity signals intelligence operation gathering intelligence on the Sandinista government in Nicaragua ahead of a possible invasion.

Great Falcon Activity operation in 1981 to try to obtain a T72 tank and a Soviet-made Hind D helicopter gunship from Iraq in exchange for US artillery in a deal negotiated with Uday Hussein, Saddam Hussein's eldest son.

Green Light Anglo–US operation to snatch Radovan Karadžić, the former Bosnian Serb leader, and his military commander, General Ratko Mladić, set up after Amber Light was deemed to have been deliberately compromised by the French.

Grey Fox Codename used by the Activity during the war in Afghanistan.

GSA *Groupement Spécial Autonome* French special operations command of which the main unit is *1er RPIMa,* the 1st Parachute Regiment, Marine Infantry, which despite its name is not simply an airborne infantry regiment but a direct descendant of the French wartime Special Air Service and the French Army 'Tier 1' counter-terrorist special operations unit.

H1, H2 and H3 Airfields in western Iraq alongside pumping stations on the old oil pipeline from Iraq to Jordan, which were designated H1, H2 and H3. The airfields were taken by allied special operations forces in early 2003 as forward operating bases in the Iraq War.

HAHO High altitude, high opening. Parachute method designed to allow covert infiltration from distance, enabling the parachutist to jump from an aircraft some distance from the landing zone over friendly or neutral territory and then glide into the target area.

HALO High altitude, low opening. Covert parachuting method requiring aircraft to pass directly over the drop zone in which special operators freefall before opening their chutes at low altitude.

Hezbollah Quite literally 'Party of God'. Prominent Iranian-backed Shi'ite militant organisation that originated in Lebanon and spread to the Occupied Territories.

Honey Badger Air planning side of Snow Bird, the second mission to rescue the hostages held in Tehran.

Humint Human intelligence, the gathering of information using human sources.

HVO *Hrvatsko Vijece Obrane.* Literally 'Croatian Defence Council', actually the Croatian Army during the war in the former Yugoslavia during the first half of the 1990s.

HVT High Value Target. Senior member of enemy government/forces or terrorist organisation.

ICTFY International Criminal Tribunal for the Former Yugoslavia in the Hague.

IDA Institute for Defense Analyses. Pentagon-funded research organisation set up in 1954 to carry out research on defence issues. Based in Alexandria, Virginia.

IDF Israel Defence Force. Israeli armed forces.

I-For Nato Implementation Force in Bosnia (*See Joint Endeavour*).

Infiltration Act of covertly entering hostile territory or introducing agents or operators from one's own side into hostile territory.

INSCOM US Intelligence and Security Command based at Fort Belvoir, Virginia.

Iraqi Freedom Allied codename for 2003 invasion of Iraq.

ISA Intelligence Support Activity.

ISI Pakistan's Inter-Service Intelligence service which backed the Taliban regime heavily and was therefore seriously compromised in the wake of the 11 September attacks.

Islamic Amal Extremist breakaway group once part of Lebanon's Shi'ite Amal militia and backed by the Iranian Revolutionary Guard Corps. It was led by Hussein Musawi under whose command it evolved into the Hezbollah terrorist group.

Islamic Jihad Terrorist group based in Damascus. Name used by several groups to claim responsibility for terrorist attacks mainly in Israel and Lebanon.

J2 Nato term for intelligence staff, also refers to military commander's intelligence adviser. J1 is Personnel; J3 Operations; J4 Logistics; J5 Planning; and J6 Communications.

Jamiat-i-Islami Afghan mujahideen group led by Ahmed Shah Masood until his assassination by al-Qa'eda in September 2001. The most powerful of the various factions in the north and the main force within the Northern Alliance.

Jawbreaker The CIA team sent into Afghanistan to coordinate opposition forces as part of the war against the Taliban and al-Qa'eda.

JCS US Armed Forces Joint Chiefs of Staff.

JCUNI Joint Communications Unit Northern Ireland. Covername for British Army's secret surveillance unit in Northern Ireland previously known as 14 Int and colloquially known as the Det. Still current mid-2005 but subsequently changed. (*See 14 Int*)

Jedburgh teams Small joint French/British/US teams of special operators who parachuted into northern France during the 1944 D-Day landings to gather intelligence and organise attacks behind enemy lines.

JIACG Joint Inter-Agency Coordination Group. Organisation set up by US Central Command in October 2001 to coordinate counter-terrorist actions of all national agencies in the Centcom area of operations.

JIATF-CT Joint Inter-Agency Task Force – Counter-Terrorism, codenamed Task Force Bowie. JIACG team deployed to Bagram air base in November 2001 to provide an intelligence fusion cell, included UK and US special operations personnel, plus representatives of the NSA, CIA, DIA, FBI and State Department.

Joint Endeavour Nato operation by Implementation Force (I-For) sent into Bosnia to monitor compliance with the 1995 Dayton Accord.

Joint Guard Nato follow-up operation to Joint Endeavour under which a Stabilisation Force, S-For, sought to create a situation in which allied troops could eventually withdraw from Bosnia.

JSFSG Joint Special Forces Support Group. New UK special forces unit based on a battalion from the British Army's Parachute Regiment and roughly equivalent to the US Rangers. Its role is to provide close support to SAS and SBS operations. It is based at the St Athlan air base in south Wales.

JSOC Joint Special Operations Command. Set up in 1980 to try to solve some of the inter-service coordination problems experienced during the failed Eagle Claw mission, JSOC's public role is 'to study the special operations requirements of all US military services to ensure standardization'. But its real mission is to command and coordinate operations by all US 'Tier' 1 special operations units, the so-called special mission units which include Delta, DevGru, 160 SOAR, and the Activity. It is based at Fort Bragg, Fayetteville, North Carolina.

JTF Joint Task Force. Any group of forces from different military units brought together for a particular operation.

Just Cause 1989 operation to remove General Manuel Noriega from power in Panama.

Katyusha Literally 'Little Katie'. Soviet medium-range rocket system, normally multi-barrelled but can be fired individually, first introduced during the Second World War when it acquired the nickname 'Stalin's Organ'.

KH11 Crystal satellite US 'Keyhole' imagery intelligence satellite.

KIA Killed in action.

KISS Keep it simple, stupid! Standard special operations dictum.

Lebanese Forces Lebanese Phalangist (Christian) militia set up by Bashir Gemayel in 1976. Worked with the Activity during the 1980s to track the US hostages, most notably via the Felix Network.

Lebanese Front Umbrella grouping of the various Phalangist militia and other political groupings keen to keep the Christian domination of Lebanon as institution-alised in the 1943 constitution.

LIC Low-Intensity Conflict. Military conflict short of war, normally involving the use of a combination of terrorist violence and political pressure to achieve political aims, and attempts by governments to counter such methods.

MACV Military Assistance Command, Vietnam. US command structure in Vietnam, originally providing military aid and advice to the South Vietnam government, but eventually under the same name becoming fully involved in combat operations.

MC130E/H Combat Talon Based on the C130 Hercules aircraft, the Combat Talon's primary role is infiltration, exfiltration and resupply of special operations forces.

Meaconing Process whereby control of a mobile telephone is taken over by a fake base station in order to allow interception of all conversations made on it.

MH53 Pave Low Modification of the HH-53 Super Jolly Green Giant helicopter which was used for special operations in Vietnam. The Pave Low's technology allows it to fly in virtually any conditions day or night. Its primary role is covert infiltration, exfiltration and resupply of special operations forces.

MH60 Pave Hawk Special operations helicopter based on the UH60 Black Hawk. Its role is infiltration, exfiltration and resupply of special operations troops in all conditions.

MI6 British foreign intelligence service more correctly designated the Secret Intelligence Service, SIS.

Mi17 Hip Russian multi-purpose helicopter capable of carrying troops or cargo or acting as a gunship.

Mi24 Hind D Russian helicopter gunship used to great effect during the Soviet war in Afghanistan.

MIA Missing in action, most often used in reference to US soldiers whose bodies were never recovered during the Vietnam War.

MiG25 Foxbat Soviet fighter aircraft designed to intercept enemy strike aircraft armed with four Acrid air-to-air missiles and capable of speeds up to Mach 3. First entered service in 1972.

Mossad Israeli foreign intelligence service.

MQ1/MQ9 Predator USAF and CIA operated Hunter/Killer UAV used to assassinate al-Qa'eda terrorists and on operations in the Balkans. The MQ9 can carry fourteen Hellfire missiles and has also successfully dropped a 500lb Paveway II laser-guided bomb. It has an operational ceiling of 50,000 feet.

MTSO Mobile telephone switching office. The station that controls the network of base stations that make up a mobile telephone network.

NA Northern Alliance, the main opposition grouping in northern Afghanistan during Taliban rule was used as a proxy force by the allies to defeat the Taliban in the north with coordination from the CIA, MI6 and coalition special operations forces.

NALT Northern Afghanistan Liaison Team. The CIA team, codenamed Jawbreaker, that coordinated Northern Alliance operations with those of the allies during the 2001–2 war in Afghanistan.

National Reconnaisance Office The US intelligence agency that runs the country's spy satellites.

Naval Special Warfare Development Group The US Navy officially describes this unit as responsible for 'overseeing development of Naval Special Warfare tactics, equipment and techniques'. In fact it is the correct title for the Navy's 'Tier 1' counter-terrorist and special operations unit commonly known as SEAL Team Six and was adopted in 1987 after a series of scandals affecting the unit. The name has, however, never really stuck and SEAL Team Six remains in common use.

NBC Nuclear, Biological, Chemical. Outmoded military term for weapons of mass destruction (See CBRN).

Night Stalkers Nickname for members of the 160th Special Operations Aviation Regiment deriving from their ability to operate as well by night as by day.

NISTs National Intelligence Support Teams. Run by the CIA Office of Military Affairs to work alongside commanders on the ground, providing them with CIA, DIA and NSA intelligence. They were created following widespread criticism from military commanders during the 1991 Gulf War that they never saw intelligence collected by the CIA and NSA in time to make use of it.

NOCS *Nucleo Operativo Centrale di Sicurezza*. Crack Italian police counter-terrorist unit set up in the wake of the Red Brigades' 1978 kidnapping and murder of former Prime Minister Aldo Moro. It was the NOCS that rescued General James Lee Dozier from the Red Brigades in January 1982. Members of the unit are nicknamed the Leatherheads after the all-leather balaclava-style helmets they wear.

NSA National Security Agency, the US signals intelligence organisation, equivalent of the British GCHQ.

NSC National Security Council. The body that advises the US President on all defence, security and foreign policy issues.

ODA Operational Detachment Alpha. The smallest US Special Forces team, made up of twelve men and more popularly known as an A-team.

OH6 Cayuse Light observation helicopter first introduced in 1968. It formed the basis for the AH6 Little Bird.

OH58 Kiowa Reconnaissance and intelligence-gathering helicopter with two-man crew, capable of feeding real-time video back to commanders.

OPAT Operations, Plans, and Training Advisors. US Special Forces officers placed inside the Salvadoran Army command structure during the early 1980s to advise on counter-insurgency tactics (*See FMLN*).

OPB Operational Preparation of the Battlefield. The role of the Activity.

OPS-35 The Studies and Observations Group (SOG) cross-border surveillance element which carried out interdiction operations along the Ho Chi Minh Trail across the border in Laos.

Optimize Talent Programme to legalise ISA existence putting in place safeguards against illegality and ensuring oversight.

OSS Office of Strategic Services. US Second World War intelligence and special operations organisation.

P2OG Proactive Pre-emptive Operations Group. Activity-style unit proposed by Defense Science Board in August 2002 in response to Rumsfeld insistence on special operations forces' dominance of War on Terror.

P3 Orion US Navy Cold War anti-submarine warfare aircraft first introduced into service in 1962 but more recently extended in use to general surveillance. Capable of feeding real-time video of what is happening on the ground back to military commanders.

Pasdaran Iranian Revolutionary Guard Corps (IRGC). Iranian paramilitary force entrusted with guarding the revolution both at home and abroad. The IRGC operates abroad in support of groups like Hezbollah and Islamic Jihad that are backed by Iran.

Pathfinding Reconnaissance operation designed to prepare the battlefield for troops that will follow.

Phalangist General term for Lebanon's Maronite Christian militia from the *Phalanges Libanaises* founded in 1936 by Pierre Gemayel, based on the Nazi party, and designed to protect the Maronites' dominant position in Lebanon.

Phoenix Controversial programme in Vietnam in which teams were tasked to collect intelligence and 'neutralize' Viet Cong suspects.

PIFWC Person indicted for war crimes. Term used in Bosnia with regard to the hunt for those indicted for war crimes by the International Criminal Tribunal for the Former Yugoslavia in the Hague.

PLO Palestine Liberation Organisation. Set up in 1964 by a number of Arab states with the intention of returning Israel to a Palestinian state. In the wake of the Israeli victory in the 1967 Six Day War, it turned to terrorism, acting as an umbrella group for a number of fedayeen groups carrying out a number of 'spectacular' hijackings and bombings designed to attract attention to its cause. It was dominated by the Fatah organization of Yasser Arafat, whose 1990 renunciation of violence led eventually to the takeover of the so-called occupied territories by the PLO. Arafat died in 2004 and was replaced as PLO chairman and Palestinian President by Mahmoud Abbas.

Popular Forest Special Operations counter-terrorist exercise held in Savannah, Georgia, in September 1986 in which the Activity trained for a hostage rescue in a semi-permissive environment, infiltrating and exfiltrating the hostage rescue team and collecting both human and signals intelligence.

POW Prisoner of war.

Powerful Gaze Counter-terrorist operation held in the Jacksonville/New Bern area of North Carolina in March 1986 to which the Activity provided human and signals intelligence support.

Presidential Finding Declaration by the president required in order to allow special operations teams like the Activity to operate in countries where America is not at war as with Iran during the 1987 operation Prime Chance 1.

Project Otto Operation to smuggle Bashir Gemayel back into Lebanon after secret talks in Washington.

PSP Lebanon's Druze-dominated Progressive Socialist Party (*see Druze*).

Quasar Talent Codename given to the Sea Spray air operations after they were transferred to the Activity.

Queen's Hunter Activity signals intelligence operation in El Salvador in 1983.

Quiet Falcon Codename given to the 'take' from the Activity's Grazing Lawn signals intelligence operation in Honduras.

Quincy Acid Joint counter-terrorist exercise with Delta in March 1986.

Quiz Icing Special operations counter-terrorist exercise in June 1986 in which the Activity trained for a hostage rescue in a non-permissive environment, infiltrating and exfiltrating the hostage rescue team and collecting both human and signals intelligence.

RAF UK Royal Air Force.

Rangers Primary US airborne light infantry unit whose role includes providing close support for JSOC direct action operations.

RC135 Rivet Joint US Air Force reconnaissance aircraft capable of gathering all types of signals intelligence.

Red Brigades Left-wing Italian terrorist group formed in 1969 with the aim of turning Italy into a Marxist-Leninist state and pulling it out of both Nato and the then European Community, now known as the European Union. Its two major successes were the 1978 kidnapping and murder of former Prime Minister Aldo Moro and the 1981 kidnapping of US General James Lee Dozier. Virtually destroyed by a series of arrests in 1989 and now largely dormant.

RG1 Predator US Air Force medium-altitude unmanned aircraft vehicle providing real-time video of the battlefield to front-line commanders. It has a range of 400 nautical miles and operates at a height of 25,000ft. Capable of staying in the air for more than forty hours.

RG4A Global Hawk US Air Force high-altitude UAV provides near real-time high-resolution imagery intelligence to military commanders. Has a range of 12,000 nautical miles and flies at altitudes up to 65,000 feet at speeds of more than 400 mph. When Revolutionary Guard armoured units stationed around Baghdad tried to use the cover of a major sandstorm to redeploy during the 2003 Iraq War, one Global Hawk circling above the Iraqi capital was able to see through the sandstorm, providing imagery intelligence that led to the destruction of the bulk of the Revolutionary Guards units.

RH53 Sea Stallion US Navy helicopter normally used for mine-clearing and reconnaissance but deemed most suitable for the Eagle Claw operation because of its size, range and the fact that the helicopters had to be carrier-based.

Rooster Court Unidentified 1987 Activity operation in Latin America.

Root Pain Unidentified 1987 Activity operation in Latin America.

Round Bottle Activity operation in 1986 to rescue US citizens held hostage by pro-Iranian terror groups in Lebanon, cancelled to allow Colonel Ollie North to seek the hostages' release in return for providing Iran with missiles.

Royal Cape Codename for first official Activity special access programme, continued in use as a reference to the Activity into the 1990s.

RPG Soviet rocket-propelled grenade launcher developed in the early 1950s and based on the German Second World War Panzerfaust. Normally RPG7, but there are a number of variants. Shoulder-held, it fires a fin-stabilised, rocket-assisted HEAT (High-Explosive Anti-Tank) grenade. Very cheap and easy to obtain in the Middle East, East Africa and Central Asia and a very effective weapon against both vehicles and helicopters.

SAS Special Air Service. The British Army's main 'Tier 1' special forces unit. Originally set up during the Second World War, it was disbanded at the end of the war and then reformed initially in 1947 as a reservist unit 21 SAS Regiment (Artists). It returned as a regular army unit in 1951 during the Malayan Emergency with 22 SAS Regiment created from a merger of one squadron of 21 SAS and a locally raised unit known as the Malay Scouts. Based at Credenhill near Hereford, close to the Welsh border.

SBS Special Boat Service. The Royal Navy's 'Tier 1' special forces unit. Evolved from a number of wartime units including the Special Boat Sections, which merged to become the Special Boat Squadron, and the Small Operations Group (SOG), which was formed in south-east Asia. The units merged at the end of the war as the Small Raids Wing and reclaimed the name Special Boat Squadron in the early 1950s. It was renamed the Special Boat Service after the 1982 Falklands conflict. Trained in counter-terrorist operations both at sea and on land and specialises in maritime insertion but is increasingly interchangeable with the SAS. Based at Poole in southern England.

SEALs Sea-Air-Land teams. US Navy special operations force set up in the early 1960s on the orders of President John F Kennedy. There are six SEAL teams organised into two Naval Special Warfare Groups (NSWG). NSWG One is based at Coronado, California and includes SEAL Team One, which covers south-east Asia, SEAL Team Three, responsible for south-west Asia, and SEAL Team Five, covering the north Pacific. NSWG Two is based at Little Creek, Virginia, and includes SEAL Team Two, which covers Europe; SEAL Team Four, responsible for Central and South America; and SEAL Team Eight, covering the Caribbean, Africa and the Mediterranean.

SEAL Team Six Set up in the wake of Eagle Claw as the US Navy's 'Tier 1' counter-terrorist and special operations unit, it was renamed the Naval Special Warfare Development Group in 1987 in the wake of a series of financial scandals that saw its legendary founder Richard Marcinko jailed; but the old title still sticks and is widely used. Like Delta and the Activity, SEAL Team Six is subordinate to JSOC. It is based at Dam Neck, Virginia.

S-For Allied Stabilisation Force in Bosnia (See Joint Guard).

Shi'ite One of the two main branches of Islam. The Shi'ites split from the Sunni over the succession to the Prophet. Shi'ite Muslims believe that Ali ibn Abu Talib, Mohammed's cousin and father of the Prophet's only descendants should have succeeded him. The Sunni believe the actual succession, by Abu Bakr, was correct.

Shooters Special operations teams designed to carry out 'direct action'. In the case of the Activity, members of the Operations Squadron who provide support to the intelligence teams.

Sigint Signals Intelligence. Collection of intelligence from any electronic signal.

SIS UK Secret Intelligence Service better known as MI6.

SMU Special Mission Unit. US 'Tier 1' special operations unit, eg Delta or DevGru.

SNAFU (UK military slang) Situation normal, all f***ed up!

Snow Bird Codename for second operation to free the US hostages in Tehran.

SOCOM Special Operations Command, based at Tampa, Florida.

SOF Special Operations Forces.

SOFLAM Special Operations Forces Laser Marker. Laser target designator used by special operations troops to mark targets for aircraft providing close air support.

SOG Studies and Observations Group. Despite the academic sounding name this was a special operations command formed in Vietnam in 1965. It specialised in reconnaissance and surveillance missions aimed at collecting tactical intelligence about Viet Cong bases and supply dumps; infiltrating secret agents across the border into North Vietnam, carrying out psychological warfare, including so-called 'dirty tricks'; mounting hit-and-run raids on the North Vietnamese coast from the sea; and interdicting enemy traffic on the Ho Chi Minh Trail. It mounted several thousand highly successful cross-border reconnaissance missions into Laos, Cambodia and North Vietnam.

Somali National Alliance Somali military and political grouping led in the early 1990s by General Mohammed Farah Aideed.

Southern Sudan Liberation Front Libyan-backed rebels in southern Sudan who kidnapped a number of Western hostages, including seven US citizens, in 1983. The organisation was destroyed by Sudanese forces who rescued the hostages with the assistance of a combined Activity and Delta team.

Special Activities Deniable operations by special operations forces, usually special reconnaissance operations but occasionally direct action missions conducted in places where the existence of US troops would be embarrassing or unwelcome.

Special Activities Division CIA special operations team, largely recruited from former members of US special operations forces.

Special Boat Units US Navy maritime special operations teams. They are organised into two Special Boat Squadrons. Special Boat Squadron One is based at Coronado, California, and Special Boat Squadron Two at Little Creek, Virginia.

Special Forces This term has a different meaning in America than in other English-speaking countries, where it is a general term equivalent to the US special operations forces. In the US, it refers to one specific force – the US Army's Special Forces, sometimes referred to as the Green Berets. The US Special Forces are divided into five active service Special Forces Groups, each comprising three separate battalions. They normally operate in twelve-man teams known as Operational Detachments Alpha, or simply A-Teams. There are eighteen A-Teams per battalion.

Special Forces Mobile Training Teams US Special Forces teams set up to advise the armed forces of friendly countries, as with Lebanon in the mid-1980s.

Special Operations Division Small US Army planning staff special operations cell created in the wake of the Eagle Claw operation under the command of Lt-Col James Longhofer.

Special Operations Review Group The inquiry panel that investigated the failure of the Eagle Claw mission. Chaired by former Chief of Naval Operations Admiral James L Holloway III and as a result more commonly known as the Holloway Commission.

Special Reconnaissance Covert reconnaissance behind enemy lines, one of the main specialities of special operations forces.

Sqn Squadron.

SR71 Blackbird Long-range strategic reconnaissance aircraft capable of collecting both signals and imagery intelligence. It can fly at speeds of well over Mach 3 and at heights of up to 85,000 feet.

SRR Special Reconnaissance Regiment. British equivalent of the Activity based on two human intelligence units formed for operations in Northern Ireland – the Joint Support Group, a team of specialist agent-runners formerly known as the Force Reconnaissance Unit (FRU), and Joint Communications Unit Northern Ireland, a military surveillance unit formerly known as 14 Intelligence Company. The SRR was set up in 2005. (*See* 14 Int *and* JCUNI)

SSB Strategic Support Branch. Pentagon human intelligence unit which puts together small teams of interrogators, intelligence analysts and agent-runners to provide Activity-style support for non-special operations units.

SSMS Special Operations Forces Signals Intelligence Manpack System. Lightweight signals intelligence broadband scanner, intercept and direction-finding system capable of being carried on the operator's back.

Sunni One of the two main branches of Islam (*See Shi'ite*).

Sussex teams MI6/OSS teams parachuted into northern France during the 1944 D-Day landings to gather intelligence and organise local resistance groups.

T55 Soviet main battle tank introduced in 1958 and exported to all Warsaw Pact states and a number of Soviet client states such as Iraq. It has a 100mm rifled gun and is probably the most widely used tank since the Second World War.

T72 Soviet main battle tank introduced in the early 1970s. It has a 125mm smooth bore gun and was capable of disabling a US M1 Abrams tank at a distance of 1,000 metres. Not as impressive as it sounds since the Abrams could pick off a T72 at 2,000 metres.

Tactical Concept Detachment Original covername for the Activity.

Tactical Coordination Detachment New covername given to the Activity after it was supposedly terminated in March 1989.

Task Force 5 Designation of 'Tier 1' Combined Joint Special Operations Task Force in Afghanistan during early summer 2003.

Task Force 11 Designation given to 'Tier 1' Combined Joint Special Operations Task Force in southern Afghanistan (Task Force Sword) at the end of 2001.

Task Force 20 Designation of 'Tier 1' Combined Joint Special Operations Task Force set up in Iraq at the end of the 2003 Iraq War to capture the leading members of Saddam's regime who were designated as 'High Value Targets'.

Task Force 121 Designation of 'Tier 1' Combined Joint Special Operations Task Force, an amalgamation of Task Force 5 and Task Force 20, set up in July 2003 to track down Saddam Hussein, Osama bin Laden and their leading cohorts.

Task Force 160 Helicopter unit set up as part of Honey Badger, the air planning side of the second attempt to rescue the US hostages in Tehran. It eventually became 160th Special Operations Aviation Regiment.

Task Force Bayonet Generic title for the US special operations forces, largely Army Special Forces but also Delta, SEAL and ISA operators, deployed as 'military advisers' across Central America in the 1980s.

Task Force Blue Code used to refer to any DevGru/SEAL Team Six personnel during joint operations.

Task Force Bowie Intelligence 'fusion cell' set up at Bagram air base in November 2001 to coordinate all special operations intelligence. (*See JIATF-CT*)

Task Force Dagger (1) Codename for Joint Special Operations Task Force - West during the 2003 Iraq War. It was based at the Shaheed Muwaffaq airfield near Azraq in eastern Jordan and made up of US Rangers, US Army Special Forces, and British and Australian SAS. (2) Codename for Joint Special Operations Task Force – North during the 2001 war in Afghanistan, which was largely built around Central Command's 5th Special Forces Group (Airborne).

Task Force Gecko Delta team which attacked a compound just outside Kandahar known to be used by Mullah Omar in an operation that was given maximum publicity by the Pentagon. The mission turned into what one participant called 'a total goat-fuck' when it met more resistance than expected but it did lead to the capture of useful intelligence.

Task Force Green Code used to refer to any Delta personnel during joint operations.

Task Force K-Bar Codename for Combined Joint Special Operations Task Force – South, a Tier 2 special operations 'Direct Action' team operating in southern Afghanistan in late 2001. It was led by US Navy SEALs but also included special forces from Denmark, Germany, Australia, Norway, Canada and New Zealand. Its role was to attack locations while Task Force Sword targeted 'high value targets' like Osama bin Laden and Mullah Omar.

Task Force Orange Code used to refer to any Activity personnel during joint operations.

Task Force Ranger Covername for the Joint Special Operations Task Force sent into Somalia to capture Mohammed Farah Aideed and withdrawn as a result of the losses incurred in the 'Black Hawk Down' incident.

Task Force Sword 'Tier 1' Combined Joint Special Operations Task Force in southern Afghanistan tasked to carry out the more difficult operations. It was made up of Delta, DevGru (the old SEAL Team Six), and the Activity, augmented by A and G squadrons of Britain's 22 SAS Regiment and C Squadron of the SBS. It operated from bases in Pakistan, the Omani island of Masirah, and from the US aircraft carrier *Kitty Hawk* in the Persian Gulf. The main role of Task Force Sword was to pursue 'high value targets' and to cut off the Taliban and al-Qa'eda troops as they attempted to flee into Pakistan's Tribal Areas.

Task Force Viking Codename for Combined Joint Special Operations Task Force – North during the 2003 Iraq War. This task force, made up of members of allied special operations forces, including Delta, Special Forces, the SAS and the SBS, organised the Peshmerga forces to seize the key cities of Kirkuk and Mosul and directed air support for their attacks in an operation designed to mirror the successful use of the Northern Alliance in Afghanistan.

Titrant Ranger Codename for the Activity special access programme during the 2003 Iraq War.

Torn Victor Codename used by the Activity during operations to snatch indicted war criminals in the former Yugoslavia.

TOW Tube-launched, optically tracked, wire-guided anti-tank missile introduced into service with the US armed forces in 1970 and given to Iran in exchange for proffered assistance in releasing the US hostages held in Lebanon in the mid-1980s.

U2 Dragon Lady US Air Force single-seater surveillance aircraft capable of carrying both signals and imagery intelligence payloads and flying at heights of up to 90,000 feet. The first U2 was introduced into service in 1956. The aircraft achieved notoriety in May 1960 when a U2 piloted by Gary Powers was shot down over the Soviet Union.

UAS Unmanned Aerial System. Increasingly used instead of UAV (see below) to emphasise that the aerial vehicle is only the front end of a complete surveillance system.

UAV Unmanned Aerial Vehicle.

UH1 Iroquois Multi-purpose helicopter known as the 'Huey' introduced into service with the US Army in 1958. It was made famous by the Vietnam War.

UH60 Black Hawk Multi-purpose US Army helicopter capable of carrying eleven infantrymen or acting as an aerial gunship.

UKSF UK Special Forces units.

UNOSOM United Nations Operation in Somalia. UN peacekeeping force sent into Somalia in 1992 to monitor ceasefire between warring factions.

USAF United States Air Force.

USAISA United States Army Intelligence Support Activity.

US Office of Military Cooperation Beirut-based organisation that ran US military operations on the ground in Lebanon in the 1980s.

USSOCOM United States Special Operations Command (*See SOCOM*).

UW Unconventional Warfare. Any guerrilla operations or special operations, including covert sabotage, reconnaissance or intelligence operations.

Velvet Hammer Operation planned by former US Marine Colonel James 'Bo' Gritz to rescue MIAs allegedly held captive in Laos.

West Wing Codename given to Shaheed Muwaffaq airfield near Azraq in eastern Jordan used as a base by allied special operations forces for the 2003 Iraq War.

Winter Harvest Activity operation in 1981–2 to rescue General James Lee Dozier from the Italian Red Brigades terrorist group.

WMD Weapons of Mass Destruction. Generally taken to mean any chemical, biological, radiological, or nuclear weapon regardless of likely level of destruction.

Wolverine 1 and 2 Codenames given to farm buildings in the Iraqi village of al-Dawr, ten miles south of Tikrit where Saddam was captured.

Yellow Fruit 'Black' counter-espionage and security team set up in June 1982 to provide 'operational security and counter-intelligence support to classified, sensitive special operations and intelligence elements', including the Activity.

ZSU-23 *Zenitnaya Samokhodnaya Ustanovka*, literally 'anti-aircraft self-propelled system'. Highly effective Soviet anti-aircraft gun introduced in the early 1960s. The 23mm guns are normally mounted in fours on an armoured vehicle known as the ZSU-23-4. Nato codename Awl.

BIBLIOGRAPHY

Adams, James, *Secret Armies: The Full Story of the SAS, Delta Force, and Spetsnaz*, Pan, London, 1988

Adams, Thomas K, *US Special Operations Forces in Action: The Challenge of Unconventional Warfare*, Frank Cass, London, 1998

Anderson, Terry, *Den of Lions: Memoirs of Seven Years in Captivity*, Hodder and Stoughton, London, 1994

Arkin, William M, *Code Names: Deciphering US Military Plans, Programs, and Operations in the 9/11 World*, Steerforth Press, Hanover NH, 2005

Bamford, James, *Body of Secrets*, Century, London, 2001

Barker, Geoffrey T, *A Concise History of US Army Special Operations Forces*, Anglo-American, Fayatteville, 1988

Beckwith, Colonel Charlie A (Ret) and Knox, Donald, *Delta Force: The Inside Story of America's Super-secret Counterterrorist Unit*, Fontana/Collins, Glasgow, 1985

Biddle, Stephen, *Afghanistan and the Future of Warfare: Implications for Army and Defense Policy*, US Army War College, November 2002

Bowden, Mark, *Black Hawk Down*, Corgi, London, 1999

Bowden, Mark, *Killing Pablo: The Hunt for the Richest Most Powerful Criminal in History*, Atlantic Books, London, 2002

Brailey, Malcolm, *Not Many Jobs Take a Whole Army: Special Operations Forces and the Revolution in Military Affairs*, Institute of Defence and Strategic Studies, March 2004

Bruner, Edward F; Bolkum, Christopher; and O'Rourke, Ronald, *Special Operations Forces in Operation Enduring Freedom: Background and Issues for Congress*, Congressional Research Service, 15 October 2001

Carney, Colonel John T and Schemmer, Benjamin F, *No Room for Error: The Covert Operations of America's Special Tactics Units from Iran to Afghanistan*, Ballantine Books, New York, 2002

Clancy, Tom, with Stiner, General Carl, *Shadow Warriors: Inside the Special Forces*, Pan, London, 2002

Collins, John M, *Special Operations Forces: An Assessment*, National Defense University Press, Washington DC, 1994

Connor, Ken, *Ghost Force: The Secret History of the SAS*, Weidenfeld & Nicolson, London, 1998

Cordesman, Anthony H, *The Intelligence Lessons of the Iraq War*, Center for Strategic and International Studies, Washington, 2004

Corum, Dr James S, The Air War in El Salvador, *Aerospace Power Journal*, Summer 1998

Curtis, Mike, *CQB: Close Quarter Battle*, Bantam, London, 1997

Day, Major Clifford E, *Critical Analysis on the Defeat of Task Force Ranger*, The Research Department, Air Command and Staff College, March 1997

de la Billiere, General Sir Peter, *Storm Command*, HarperCollins, London, 1993

Department of the Army, *Counterinsurgency Operations*, FMI 3-07.22, October 2004

Emerson, Steven, *Secret Warriors: Inside the Covert Military Operations of the Reagan Era*, Putnams, New York, 1988

Fischer, Walter, Why More Special Forces Are Needed For Low-Intensity War, *Heritage Foundation Report*, 12 November 1987

Franks, General Tommy (with McConnell, Malcolm), *American Soldier*, Regan Books, New York, 2004

Gritz, James 'Bo', *A Nation Betrayed*, Lazarus, Boulder City, 1988

Hammond, Lieutenant-Colonel Jamie, Special Operations Forces: Relevant, Ready and Precise, *Canadian Military Journal*, Autumn 2004

Haney, Eric L, *Inside Delta Force*, Dell, New York, 2002

Hargreaves, Clare, *Snowfields: The War on Cocaine in the Andes*, Zed Books, London, 1992

Hayden, Lt-Col H T, USMC, *Shadow War: Special Operations and Low Intensity Conflict*, Pacific Aero Press, Vista CA, 1992

Hersh, Seymour M, *Chain of Command: The Road from 9/11 to Abu Ghraib*, Harper-Collins, New York, 2004

Jennings, Christian, *Midnight in Some Burning Town: British Special Forces Operations from Belgrade to Baghdad*, Weidenfeld & Nicolson, London, 2004

Joint Doctrine Division, Joint Staff, Pentagon, *Joint Special Operations Operational Procedures*, Joint Pub 3-05.3, 1 October 2004

Kean, Thomas H and Hamilton, Lee H, *The 9/11 Report: The National Commission on Terrorist Attacks upon the United States*, St Martin's Paperbacks, New York, 2004

Keegan, John, *The Iraq War*, Hutchinson, London, 2004

Kelly, Ross, Special Operations in Latin America: Overview II – The 'North American Connection', *Defense and Foreign Affairs*, July 1986

Kelly, Ross, Special Operations In El Salvador, *Defense and Foreign Affairs*, August/September 1986

Kelly, Ross, Special Operations in Honduras, *Defense and Foreign Affairs*, October 1986

Kibbe, Jennifer, The Rise of the Shadow Warriors, *Foreign Affairs*, March/April 2004

Kyle, Colonel James H, with Eidson, John Robert, *The Guts to Try*, Ballantine, New York, 1995

Livingstone, Neil and Halevy, David, Operation Betrayal: Delta/SEAL Rescue Force Poised to Snatch American Hostages in Lebanon, *Soldier of Fortune*, October 1989

Marquis, Susan L, *Unconventional Warfare: Rebuilding US Special Operations Forces*, Brookings Institute Press, Washington DC, 1997

Martin, David C, and Walcott, John, *Best Laid Plans: The Inside Story of America's War Against Terrorism*, Touchstone, New York, 1988

McNab, Andy, *Immediate Action*, Bantam, London, 1995

Miller, Judith, Faces of Fundamentalism, *Foreign Affairs*, November/December 1994

Moore, Robin, *Hunting Down Saddam: The Inside Story of the Search and Capture*, St Martin's Paperbacks, New York, 2004

Moore, Robin, *Task Force Dagger: The Hunt for Bin Laden*, Pan, London, 2004

Naylor, Sean, *Not a Good Day to Die: The Untold Story of Operation Anaconda*, Berkley Caliber, New York, 2005

Nicol, Mark, *Ultimate Risk: SAS Contact al-Qa'eda*, Pan, London, 2003

Parker, John, *SBS: The Inside Story of the Special Boat Service*, Headline, London, 2003

Phillips, James A, Standing Firm in Lebanon, *Heritage Foundation Reports*, 24 October 1983

Phillips, James A, Somalia and al-Qa'eda: Implications for the War on Terrorism, *Heritage Foundation Reports*, 5 April 2002

Prados, John, *President's Secret Wars*, Quill, New York, 1988

Priest, Dana, *The Mission: Waging War and Keeping Peace with America's Military*, Norton, New York, 2004

Ramirez, Armando J, *From Bosnia to Baghdad: The Evolution of US Army Special Forces from 1995–2004*, Naval Postgraduate School, Monterey, California, September 2004

Richelson, Jeffrey T, 'Truth Conquers All Chains': The US Army Intelligence Support Activity, 1981-1989, *International Journal of Intelligence and Counterintelligence*, Volume 12, Number 2

Ripley, Tim, *Air War Iraq*, Pen & Sword, Barnsley, 2004

Robinson, Linda, *Masters of Chaos: The Secret History of the Special Forces*, Public Affairs, New York, 2004

Rudner, Martin, Hunters and Gatherers: The International Coalition Against Islamic Terrorism, *International Journal of Intelligence and Counterintelligence*, Volume 17, Number 2, Summer 2004

Scarborough, Rowan, *Rumsfeld's War: The Untold Story of America's Anti-Terrorist Commander*, Regnery Publishing, Washington, 2004

Schemmer, Benjamin F and Carney Jr, Col John T, *US Special Operations Forces*, Special Operations Warrior Foundation, Tampa, 2003

Scott, LV and Jackson, PD, *Understanding Intelligence in the Twenty-First Century: Journeys in the Shadows*, Routledge, London, 2004

Shroen, Gary C, *First In: An Insider's Account of How the CIA Spearheaded the War on Terrorism*, Ballantine, New York, 2005

Shuger, Scott, What America hasn't learned from its greatest peacekeeping disaster, *Washington Monthly*, October 1989

Shultz, Richard, Showstoppers: Nine Reasons Why We Never Sent Our Special Operations Forces After al-Qa'eda Before 9/11, *The Weekly Standard*, 26 January 2004

Simpson, Charles N, *Inside the Green Berets*, Presidio Press, Navato, California, 1983

Sklar, Holly, *Washington's War on Nicaragua*, South End Press, Cambridge, 1988

Smith, Michael, *The Spying Game: The Secret History of British Intelligence*, Politicos, London, 2003

Special Operations Review Group, *Rescue Mission Report*, Washington DC, August 23, 1980

Stone, Kathryn, *'All Necessary Means' – Employing CIA Operatives in a Warfighting Role alongside Special Operations Forces*, US Army War College, 7 April 2003

Strong, Simon, *Whitewash: Pablo Escobar and the Cocaine Wars*, Macmillan, London, 1995

Thompson, Loren B, *Low-Intensity Conflict: The Pattern of Warfare in the Modern World*, Lexington Books, Lexington, 1989

Tower, John, Muskie, Edmund and Scowcroft, Brent, *The Tower Commission Report*, Bantam/Times Books, New York, 1987

Turner, Stansfield, Intelligence for a New World Order, *Foreign Affairs*, Fall 1991

US Congress, Senate Select Committee on POW/MIA Affairs, *POWs/MIA*, Washington DC, US Government Printing Office, 1993

US Special Operations Command, 10th Anniversary History, USSOCOM, Tampa, 1997

Vandenbroucke, Lucien S, *Perilous Options: Special Operations as an Instrument of US Foreign Policy*, OUP, New York, 1993

Waller, Douglas C, *The Commandos: The Inside Story of America's Secret Soldiers*, Dell, New York, 1994

Weiner, Tim, *Blank Check: The Pentagon's Black Budget*, Warner, New York, 1990

Westmoreland, William C, *A Soldier Reports*, New York, Doubleday, 1976

Wiebes, Cees, *Intelligence and the War in Bosnia 1992–1995*, LIT, Hamburg, 2003

Woerner, Fred, The Strategic Imperatives for the US in Latin America, *Military Review*, February 1989

Woodward, Bob, *Veil: The Secret Wars of the CIA, 1981–1987*, Simon and Schuster, New York, 1987

Woodward, Bob, *Bush at War*, Pocket Books, New York, 2003

Woodward, Bob, *Plan of Attack*, Pocket Books, New York, 2003

INDEX